World Famous in New Zealand

World Famous in New Zealand

How New Zealand's Leading Firms Became World-Class Competitors

COLIN CAMPBELL-HUNT

John Brocklesby

Sylvie Chetty

Lawrence Corbett

Sally Davenport

Deborah Jones

Pat Walsh

AUCKLAND UNIVERSITY PRESS

This project was funded by the Public Good Science Fund under contract VIC806, and by grants from the New Zealand Trade Development Board and Victoria University of Wellington.

First published 2001

Auckland University Press
University of Auckland
Private Bag 92019
Auckland
New Zealand
http://www.auckland.ac.nz/aup

© CANZ, 2001

ISBN 1 86940 249 9

Cover design by Sarah Maxey

Printed by Astra Print Ltd, Wellington

Contents

Appendix: Brief Company Histories

Acknowledgements

This study relied wholly on the goodwill of the very busy people who devoted many hours of their time to share with the research team their recollected wisdom on what it takes to grow world-class businesses from New Zealand's economic soil. We are grateful to them for allowing us to share this project with them, and for everything we learnt from them. It was a great two years. Thank you.

The Criterion Group: Wally Smaill and Brian Smaill, Executive Directors

Formway Furniture: Rick Wells, Managing Director and Colin Campbell, General Manager New Zealand

Gallagher Group: Bill Gallagher, Managing Director and Margaret Comer, Corporate Services Manager

Kiwi Dairies: Shona Glentworth, Strategic Development Manager and Roy Baker, Chief Executive Officer Fencepost

Montana Wines: Peter Hubscher, Managing Director and Peter Anderson, Management Services Manager

Nuplex Industries: Fred Holland, Chairman and Geoff Swailes, Commercial Manager Resins

PEC New Zealand: John Williams, Chief Executive Officer (retired)

Scott Technology: Graham Batts, Director

Svedala Barmac: Andi Lusty, Managing Director and the entire company

Tait Electronics: Sir Angus Tait, Chairman and Warren Rickard, Chief Executive Officer

We are grateful, too, for the guidance we received from the project's advisory panel. They directed us towards the exemplar organisations for our study, commented on our ideas and organised forums in which we could test our ideas with management practitioners.

Ministry of Commerce (Ministry of Economic Development): Graeme Davis, Yvonne Lucas and Stephen Knuckey

New Zealand Institute of Management: David Chapman

New Zealand Manufacturers and Employers Federation: David Moloney

New Zealand Trade Development Board: Michael Hannah

Authorship

This book is the joint product of a large research team. We worked together for two years and during that time shared impressions of the companies we studied, and borrowed and built on each other's ideas. Within that collective enterprise, each of us took responsibility for particular aspects of the enquiry, and for drafting particular chapters as shown below.

John Brocklesby	Chapter 9
Colin Campbell-Hunt	Introduction, Chapters 1, 6, 8
Sylvie Chetty	Chapter 2
Lawrence Corbett	Chapter 4
Sally Davenport	Chapter 3
Deborah Jones	Chapter 7
Pat Walsh	Chapter 5

The book is also based on histories of the participating companies written by the following people.

The Criterion Group	Colin Campbell-Hunt
Formway Furniture	Sherif Millad
Gallagher Group	Dianne Lee
Kiwi Dairies	Jayne Krisjanous
Montana Wines	Pauline Copland
Nuplex Industries	Ken McCarthy and Douglas Mabey
PEC New Zealand	Haiming Guo
Scott Technology	Gavin Ng
Svedala Barmac	Ken McCarthy and Colin Campbell-Hunt
Tait Electronics	Ken McCarthy

Amy Harrison and Clinton Haswell summarised these histories for the appendix. Diane Campbell-Hunt edited the entire manuscript and drafted the final chapter.

Colin Campbell-Hunt read English Language and Literature at Oxford. He also holds an MBA from York University, Canada, and a PhD in economics from Victoria University of Wellington. He is currently Reader in Strategic Management at Victoria University of Wellington and has also been a Visiting Professor of Management at St Andrews in Scotland. He will shortly take up an appointment as a Professor of Management at the University of Otago.

John Brocklesby is Professor of Management at Victoria University of Wellington. Previously he was employed in the steel industry in Britain. He has an undergraduate degree from Coventry University, an MSc from the London School of Economics, and a PhD from Warwick Business School. Recent publications have appeared in the *International Journal of Strategic Management*, the *Australian Journal of Management*, the *Journal of Organisational Change Management*, the *Journal of the Organisational Research Society*, *Systems Practice*, and *Systems Research*. A rather sad aspect of his life is that he has supported Scunthorpe United Football Club since 1962, and Coventry City Football Club since 1973.

Sylvie Chetty is Senior Lecturer in Marketing at the College of Business, Massey University, Albany. She is one of New Zealand's leading researchers in international business and has published widely on the export success of New Zealand firms, and the use of business networks in internationalisation.

Lawrence Corbett is Associate Professor of Operations Management at Victoria University of Wellington. In a long research career, Professor Corbett is perhaps best known for his regular series of studies of the manufacturing sector in New Zealand, as part of the global research network, the Manufacturing Futures Project.

Sally Davenport is a senior lecturer and Director of Graduate Studies in the School of Business and Public Management at Victoria University of Wellington. She has previously worked for a consulting firm in London and as a research chemist at Oxford University. Her teaching is mainly in the areas of technology strategy and policy on the Master of Management Studies (in Technology) course. Her research interests focus on research alliances and joint ventures and the commercialisation of technological research, while her consulting work has mainly been in developing research strategies for industries and evaluation of research for policy agencies.

Deborah Jones is Senior Lecturer in Organisation Behaviour at Victoria University of Wellington. She has published research on communication, culture, gender and ethnicity in New Zealand organisations. She has a special interest in qualitative approaches to organisational research.

Pat Walsh is Professor of Industrial Relations and Human Resource Management at Victoria University of Wellington, where he is also Head of the School of Business and Government Management. He is one of New Zealand's most prolific researchers of labour market flexibility and human resource management.

Introduction

This is the story of how ten of New Zealand's finest companies became world-class competitors. We think the story is important. Whatever regime of economic management is in force — and these companies can remember Robert Muldoon as well as Roger Douglas — we look to business enterprises for our wealth, our jobs and the products and services we need to live and to trade.

These companies have delivered on these expectations in spades — in trailer-loads, in fact. They have also been generous in agreeing to share their experience in the hope that some of what they have learnt might help other New Zealand businesses on their road to world-class success.

The New Zealand economy has passed through a decade or more of dislocative change during which many old habits have been broken. In the process, many organisations — and many careers — have suffered the same fate. All this change has been aimed at just one thing: to improve the capability of New Zealand enterprises to deliver those necessary incomes, jobs and products — but now in the face of international competition.

Our research question is: *how do you grow world-class competitive capability?* There is no available wisdom anywhere on how this is done so we have to answer this question ourselves. As it turns out, the answers we have come up with over the last two years seem to be peculiar to New Zealand's type of economy: very small and on the edge of the world. Even if those great knowledge machines in the Northern Hemisphere had offered answers to our question, we now think they would have been the wrong answers for New Zealand.

'THE EVOLUTION OF COMPETITIVE CAPABILITY' PROJECT

We worked on this question for two years from July 1998. The project was funded by the Public Good Science Fund, with additional grants from the Trade Development Board and Victoria University. The research team was multidisciplinary because we expected that many different aspects of organisational life would contribute to a firm's performance. Specialists in marketing, strategy, human resource management, operations management, organisation behaviour, organisation theory, and the economics of the firm were part of the team from the outset. As the project developed, other researchers in technology management and decision processes joined the team.

The twelve organisations initially involved in the research were selected by an advisory panel of business and policy leaders to represent organisations that have created and sustained strong competitive positions, both within New Zealand and overseas. They were mostly of medium scale, employing between 100 and 1000 people. As conditions changed for our participating firms, the twelve organisations we started with have dropped back to ten: Criterion Group, Formway Furniture, Gallagher Group, Kiwi Dairies, Montana Wines, Nuplex Industries, PEC New Zealand, Scott Technology, Svedala Barmac and Tait Electronics. One, not listed here, suffered a downturn: the CEO was replaced, and the new management was too busy to spend time with us. The story of another, LNet (not its real name), turned out to be too different from that of the other firms to be fully integrated into our analysis.

There are important implications to be drawn from these events. One is that the stories we tell here are not the only stories to be told. LNet beat its own path to success in ways that suited its industry and its time; many other companies will do the same.

Another implication is that success is not guaranteed forever. As we explain in Chapter 1, a capability is an advantage created for a time, and for a particular competitive context. When the world moves on capabilities must be recreated. Our organisations have done this several times in their history, but we do not claim (and neither would they) that they will always get it right.

The Criterion Group, for example, suffered a radical change to its competitive position in its principal American market at the start of the decade and has had to work hard to re-establish a new business model for itself. When John Williams retired as owner and CEO of PEC, his company was sold to the Gallagher Group, which happens to be another of our participating companies.

So our conclusions should not be read as a prescription: 'do these twelve things and your business will thrive forever'. If you are in a position to influence the strategic development of an enterprise, you will be perceptive enough to realise that every company must win its own unique battles for competitive success.

We have set out to describe, in careful detail, the evolutionary paths these particular firms have taken, and how they have created and sustained a successful competitive position for themselves over many years, indeed decades.

In so doing we have arrived at a greater understanding of what has been involved in these evolutions. We believe that these new insights will help other businesses to diagnose their own competitive situation more clearly, and to better shape their response to the distinctive challenges they face.

Finally, we can offer no 'proof' of our answer about how to grow a world-class competitive enterprise in New Zealand. This is an empirical study that has aimed to create a set of hypotheses, well grounded in the experiences of those who have succeeded in this venture. It is unlike other research, where the objective is to test an established theory, or to assess how well a theory might fit the New Zealand experience. In the absence of a theory on our question, we set out to create one. When research tests existing theory, large samples are needed. Our objective, by contrast, requires us to gain a deep understanding of how individual enterprises have grown, and to grasp the context of their growth. Previous research also suggests that competitive capabilities are, to an important degree, path-dependent, i.e. what the firm is today is strongly influenced by its past history.

Our research therefore used case study (Eisenhardt, 1989) and historio-graphic (Goodman and Kruger, 1988) methods to develop rich descriptions of the history of each enterprise. We deliberately chose companies with long histories so we could pick up the full force of evolutionary processes shaping each company's development. In particular, we selected companies that predated the 1984 reforms to see what effect these had on their progress.

Our study involved the full range of enquiry techniques used in research of this kind:

- interviews with senior managers (including the current CEO) who have been involved at the strategic level for a decade or more;
- assembly of all publicly available information on the companies and any internal documents and reports that the firms shared with us;
- writing case histories and asking the companies to comment on these;
- discussions within the research team to share and refine perceptions;
- feedback workshops with the firms to improve and confirm our understanding of each company's experience.

In order to test our ideas, we have conducted a series of seminars with managers around the country in conjunction with the New Zealand Institute of Management, the Export Institute, the New Zealand Strategic Management Society and the Turnaround Management Association. We presented papers on our work to several major global conferences in management studies, which helped us to validate our theories with others working in the same field.

We are confident, therefore, that our theory is relevant to the issues facing New Zealand managers today. But that relevance is less than total. The world is very different from what it was when these companies were growing up. A regime of border protection that sheltered many of them from the full force of international competition has been removed. Information and communication technologies have developed that will radically transform the organisation of economic activity at all levels: countries, regions, industries and organisations. In our seminars with practising managers we were told that the pace of competitive evolution is now very much faster than what we describe here. We are beginning further work that we hope will shed light on these new realities.

AND THE BAD NEWS IS . . .

It is customary to begin analyses of New Zealand business and its economy with the bad news. The companies we had the privilege and the pleasure of working with for two years taught us not to do that. Of course there is always bad news to be found: these firms have faced life-threatening challenges several times in their past and most of them face potentially disastrous challenges. But they make a practice of not selling themselves short. Without being proud — indeed they are very self-critical — they have a confidence in themselves, in their resources and in their ability to apply those resources to advantage. They also avoid fights they cannot win. Perhaps they also take a good look at their global competitors and realise that they are not invincible.

So the bad news is that there is bad news. But these firms are not listening.

Chapter 1

Foundations of Competitive Advantage

The ten enterprises involved in this study have demonstrated their competitive prowess over periods of time spanning several decades. What is it about these firms that gives them advantage over their competitors? In what ways do they differ from the 'average' New Zealand enterprise? And why have they sustained their position of advantage for so long?

RESOURCES, CAPABILITIES, AND ADVANTAGE

In the last ten years our ability to specify and understand the bases of a firm's competitive advantage have been greatly advanced by the resource-based view (RBV) of the firm. Among the first to open up these new perspectives were C. K. Prahalad and Gary Hamel (1990) in their famous paper, 'The Core Competence of the Corporation'.

Resources

The fundamental proposition of the RBV is that all enterprises build up assets, relationships, knowledge and other resources. This portfolio of resources, intangible as well as tangible, will be to some extent peculiar to the firm, and so is capable of producing and sustaining an unusual level of profitability. To give this general proposition more precision, Jay Barney (1997, especially Chapter 5) suggested four criteria that must be met if a resource is to support a sustainable competitive advantage. Collectively, these criteria are known by the acronym VRIO, which stands for value, rare, imitate and organisation. The VRIO criteria have guided our search for the sources of competitive advantage in these leading New Zealand enterprises.

First, the resource must contribute to the creation of market *value*. A firm's portfolio will contain many resources, and not all will contribute equally. As market needs evolve, some resources will lose their former value, or gain a value they formerly lacked.

Second, the resource must be *rare*, or somehow distinctive to the firm. Resources that are widely used by competitors cannot be a source of competitive advantage.

Third, if returns are to be sustained, the resource must be hard to *imitate*, which may well imply that it will be hard to acquire in the first place. There are several reasons why imitation may be difficult:

- resources may need time to accumulate, as do the assets of trust and goodwill that can grow within networks of business relationships;
- leading innovators can lock in an initial advantage by using their experience to learn more about the next generation of technology;[1]
- resources may be brought together in such complex ways that it is hard for a would-be follower to replicate the whole system.

Fourth, the value created by the resource must be uniquely appropriable to the *organisation*. This criterion rules out the skills of key staff. To have unique value, the resource must be useable by the firm to a distinctive degree, for example its network of suppliers, or a reputation for honest trading. A good test is to ask whether the resource can be traded without selling the firm itself. If it can, it is not a basis for uniquely appropriable value. Conversely, any resource the firm can buy on the open market is also available to its competitors and therefore cannot be the basis for a distinctive advantage.

There is a second aspect to the criterion of organisation: is the organisation doing a better job than its competitors in integrating the resource into the firm's overall activities? The RBV approach has been criticised for encouraging people to look for the sources of advantage one resource at a time. Critics assert that it is the organisation as a whole that is the competitive weapon, and that focusing on individual resources takes our attention away from the more important property of organisational *coherence*, i.e. the firm's ability to weave all of its resources and strategies into a mutually-supportive competitive entity.[2] So the organisation criterion is also a test of the extent to which a resource contributes to, and benefits from, this coherence.

Over the 1990s, a number of organisational resources have been singled out for their potential to meet Barney's four VRIO criteria. These are listed in Table

1. 1, together with some brief notes on how each type of resource can be expected to create distinctive value for the firm. These are the resources we looked for to help us understand the sources of sustained competitive success in our firms.

All these resources are intangible in character; this is what makes them distinctive to the firm and hard for competitors to copy. By contrast, tangible assets such as machines can usually be bought on open markets. Much harder to buy are the assets of trust and goodwill that can accumulate in networks of relationships between the firm and its external business partners; or internally with the firm's employees; or with the firm's customers in the form of a reputation for delivering distinctive value.

Also beyond a competitor's grasp are the complex social constructions that are built into the organisation itself and cannot be bought or sold:

- the set of norms that make up the organisation's culture,
- the complex web (or configuration) of interdependent strategies that channels the whole organisation's disparate activities into a coherent value proposition for the customer,
- the firm's ability to master and apply multiple technologies (an example of configuration),
- the set of attitudes, norms of behaviour, and both formal and informal processes that allow the firm to learn from its experiences,
- and to sustain the advantage of some initial innovation.

Later in the chapter we assess the contribution of each of these resources to the competitive advantage of our firms, but first we need to make an important distinction between a resource and a capability.

Capabilities and competitive advantage

As discussed so far, resources are assets: relatively long-lived attributes that an organisation can draw on repeatedly to create distinctive market value. Firms can invest in these assets and nurture them over time to improve their competitive potential. Our companies have done this energetically.

But potential is not the same thing as demonstrated capability. A capability, as the term is used here, is the application of assets to some use[3] — in our study, the creation of a competitive advantage. There are benefits to analysing a firm's competitive advantage at the level of demonstrated market capabilities, rather than of resource potentials. It is much easier to be confident in judgements that a given resource has contributed to a firm's competitive success when it has shown that capability at some time in its history.

In contrast to resources, competitive capabilities can be expected to be valid

TABLE 1.1

Sources of sustainable competitive advantage

	Value?	Rare?	Imitate?	Organisation? appropriability coherence
Relationships — external — internal	mutual cooperation and learning	threat of short-term opportunism	takes time to establish	mutual benefit requires organisation commitment
Reputation	brand value premium for certainty	ditto	ditto	owned brand; requires whole organisation support
Innovation	new consumer functionality appeal	by definition	?lock in advantage in next innovation	shared learning
Learning organisation	ditto	complex social process	complexity; takes time to establish	engage whole organisation
Multiple technologies	ditto	technological difficulty	ditto	Integrate multiple sources of expertise
Organisational configurations	reliably delivers complex value proposition	complexity: social technology knowledge	ditto	requires whole organisation effectiveness
Culture	ditto	alignment by influence only	totally distinctive to organisation	inseparable from organisation itself

only for the specific market conditions, and the time, in which they are applied.[4] As conditions change, the firm will need to re-establish a capability to compete in the new environment. Once again, our firms have shown an ability to do this, several times over.

This approach does not claim that any source of advantage is automatic. The capabilities demonstrated by these firms will not necessarily succeed at other times or in other marketplaces. But these firms have demonstrated competitive capability over a particular range of markets, and over particular periods of time, which used their distinctive resources to their manifest competitive advantage.

THE FOUNDATIONS OF COMPETITIVE ADVANTAGE

This section assesses the importance of each of the above competitive capabilities (Table 1.1) to the success of these exemplar New Zealand firms. But first, some caveats.

The following descriptions present a best estimate of each firm's competitive capabilities when the assessment was made in late 1998 and life has moved on for several firms since then. But unless there is evidence to the contrary, a capability demonstrated in the past is reported as still contributing to the firm's competitive advantage. Former capabilities can be lost as market conditions change, but the loss of capability in these histories is the exception rather than the rule. These assessments have also been shared with the companies themselves and modified in light of their feedback.

The decision to assess demonstrated capabilities rather than resources is likely to lead to the reverse problem of not recognising sources of advantage. This is particularly so for the complex, organisationally embedded capabilities that rarely contributed overtly to a period of competitive success. Organisation culture, configuration and learning processes are particularly affected by this bias. We gained insights into these sources of advantage when we were studying particular aspects of a firm's operations in more detail, or during extended feedback seminars involving the whole management team. These opportunities were not uniform across the companies, however, so judgements in these areas are both patchy and problematic.

More generally, the focus on demonstrated capabilities means that the assessment will sometimes omit sources of advantage that are important to a firm's competitive success. But these assessments are based on unusually extensive contact with these firms. So, although this is probably not the whole story on these companies' success, it is likely to be much of it.

Given these caveats, the assessment of competitive capabilities in these leading enterprises is given in Table 1.2. The following sections describe firms that illustrate

TABLE 1.2
Competitive capabilities

	External relationships	Internal relationships	Reputation	Innovation	Organisation learning and decision processes	Multiple technologies	Production capability	Culture	Market Scope
Gallagher	√	√	√	√	√	√	√	√	G
Montana	√	√	√	√		√	√	√	G
Nuplex	√	√	√	√			√		R
Kiwi	√	√	√	√		√	√		G
PEC	√	√	√	√	√	√	√		R
Formway			√						G
Scott	√	√	√	√	√	√	√	√	G
Tait	√	√	√	√		√	√	√	G
Svedala	√	√	√	√			√		G
Criterion	√	√	√	√	√	√	√	√	R

Key: G = Global, predominantly beyond Australia and New Zealand
R = Regional, predominantly within Australia and New Zealand
N = National, predominantly within New Zealand
√ = Capability demonstrated

each competitive capability to an unusual degree. Since capabilities are demonstrated only for the market to which they are applied, we note where possible what that market scope is, using three deliberately broad categories:

- national: predominantly within New Zealand;
- regional: predominantly within New Zealand and Australia;
- global: predominantly beyond New Zealand and Australia.

Networks of business relationships — Gallagher, Formway and Nuplex[5]

These firms have made extensive use of networks with other businesses to create value in ways that competitors cannot easily copy.

Long-standing relationships of trust, goodwill and reciprocity will encourage both parties to invest in cooperative strategies of mutual benefit for which less-trusted, short-term partners would not be considered (Kay, 1993). These networks can also be an important source of learning (McEvily and Zaheer, 1999). Firms brought together in clusters of supplier relationships find it easier to specialise (Lorenzoni and Lipparini, 1999), to their own competitive advantage and that of other members of the cluster (Porter, 1998).

Bill Gallagher's creation of a network of dealers across Europe in the late 1970s, and in other global markets later, is an excellent example of this competitive capability. The network allowed Gallagher to quickly achieve global reach for his world-leading mains-powered electric fence systems before local competitors could get established. A Danish competitor who was chasing Gallagher hard on the technical side failed to build marketing capability and now has only a minor share of the European market in which Gallagher is the leader. The dealer network remains an important competitive differentiator.

Managing the company's relationships with these independent businesses is among the most important uses of Bill Gallagher's time. They are selected carefully, with a preference for firms that match his own business: family run and entrepreneurial. The relationship is designed to give the dealer a considerable stake in the success of Gallagher products in their area. Gallagher requires his dealers to devote 70–80 per cent of their business to Gallagher products and dealers typically have majority ownership of their business. Each party therefore prospers only to the extent that the other does, and the relationship is one of mutual dependency. Gallagher needs local dealers for on-site customisation, system design and after-sale backup; dealers need Gallagher's leading product performance and product support.

Gallagher recruits his dealers in the expectation of a long-term relationship, and many of his original recruits are still working with him two decades later.

Years of experience in selling the product have been shown to improve dealer performance; countries where dealers are turned over frequently do not do as well. On the other hand, no one takes Gallagher's commitment for granted. He has learnt to balance his dealers' motivation between a degree of security and what he calls 'heat'. Heat is applied by changing the size of a dealer's territory, promising new territory for good performers and reducing territory for desultory performers. To keep these relationships fresh and honest, Gallagher spends up to 120 days annually travelling the world, visiting each dealer between one and three times every year.

Networks are also a crucial strategy for linking suppliers to the firm. Again, the preference is for long-term suppliers who are expected to produce superior quality and reliability in exchange for (and as a result of) a degree of security in their preferred status. Formway's supplier network, which was originally developed to support the firm's Zaf chair innovation in the late 1980s, now stretches to nearly 250 separate suppliers located all over New Zealand, with some key components sourced from Germany. Although the company prefers to make in-house any component in which it can develop distinctive expertise, about half of the total number of components in the Zaf chair are sourced externally. Formway continues to benefit from its distinctive ability to configure complex patterns of supply from its many sources.

There are also instances of more specialised networks. Nuplex Industries has built up over many years a network of about 25 key relationships with other medium-scale, regionally focused resins manufacturers in Continental Europe, Asia, Africa, and Britain. Fred Holland visits these associates every two years personally, and there is more frequent contact at the technical level, as the need arises. The companies share proprietary technology and marketing opportunities where they lack the capability to take direct advantage of them. In this way these smaller regional firms are more able to compete with global industry giants such as DuPont and Monsanto.

As can be seen, business relationships play an integral role in the competitive capability of these three firms. Similar evidence of this capability can be seen in eight of the ten firms (Table 1.2). Chapters 2 and 3, on international growth and technology strategy, will return to the contribution these networks have made to the evolution of competitive capability in those areas.

Networks of internal relationships — Svedala Barmac[6]

The high quality of workplace relations is a salient feature of many of these organisations. Jeffrey Pfeffer (1994) has identified a number of practices that create and support these high-quality relationships. The strategies are based on the expectation that the employment relationship will be long-term. Considerable attention is paid to recruiting quality people and to sustaining training throughout a career.

- There is an expectation of high levels of performance, which is reflected in higher-than-normal rates of pay. A variety of schemes is used to share the firm's prosperity with the people who help create it.
- Work is a collective effort: people work in teams and share information, decisions and skills. To sustain the ethos of collective enterprise, wage differentials are kept within limits and symbols of privilege are removed.
- Finally, all these practices stem from deeply held beliefs about how the firm will do business with its employees, indeed with any person it comes in contact with.

Although several other companies would also serve as exemplars of these practices, Svedala Barmac richly illustrates the competitive benefits of high-quality workplace relations. The chief competitive advantage of the Barmac VSI rock crusher is that it is easy to build (a backyard workshop will do) but not easy to tune to meet the specific characteristics of moisture and rock-size mix each machine must cope with. This capability is what separates Svedala Barmac from the many licence-breaking pirates who spring up to attack the company's market position in local markets around the world. It is a capability that is created entirely by people.

Assembling high-quality staff begins with careful selection. In Svedala Barmac's team-based structure, the teams themselves select the people who will work with them. As managing director Andi Lusty explains:

> I don't get involved at all beyond approving the extra member of staff. They're responsible for hiring their own staff and they live and die with the staff they hire. I don't get involved . . . usually until they want to lay somebody off. Maybe one in five, or one in ten doesn't work out.

Anyone joining the sales team must have a mining qualification, which requires working underground for six months. This means that Barmac sales people relate comfortably to the no-nonsense savvy of their quarry-owning customers. It takes a further two years to train a Barmac operator to use the machine effectively. The pursuit of product knowledge continues in the company's service schools around the world where customers, Barmac service engineers and product support and development staff from Matamata gather to improve their mastery of the technology.[7]

All employees share in the company's financial success. A profit-sharing scheme, based on the company's annual return on investment, can add three weeks' pay as an end-of-year bonus when budgets are beaten. In addition, the company provides life insurance and superannuation benefits. In Andi Lusty's assessment:

> We have a good long-term relationship with our staff. I think we're pretty good in terms of the extras we add on. I think the benefits are probably worth 21 per cent per annum to people including average bonuses. The bonuses have generally been well above average in the 1990s.

The 90 plus staff at Matamata work in self-managing teams. Some ten team leaders report directly to Andi Lusty. As we have seen, a team's authority to run its own work is extensive, including the selection of team members. A culture of honest, direct communication, combined with open-door informality, means that information is widely available and accumulating knowledge is shared. The egalitarian ethos of a Waikato farming town pervades the Matamata facility: everybody, including Andi Lusty, wears an identical Svedala-Barmac T-shirt, and they don't get changed for visitors.

The closeness of the employer–employee relationship spills over into the local community, especially when that community is small. Svedala Barmac is a major employer in Matamata and both Paul Tidmarsh, the company's founder, and Andi Lusty are local residents and strongly committed to the town — a commitment that receives prominent appreciation in letters from local community leaders, proudly displayed in the company's entrance lobby.

These human resource practices flow naturally from some deeply held beliefs among the firm's leadership on how employees should be treated. This deep commitment almost cost Paul Tidmarsh the company, then known as Tidco, when a recession in the late 1980s produced a 35 per cent slump in sales. In the end, it was the company's new owner, Svedala Barmac, which recognised the inevitability of job losses. In two rounds of downsizing, more than half of the workforce had to leave. The redundancies had a major impact on the town, leading to business closures in Matamata and the surrounding area. The memory of these impacts on staff and the town remains painful. A major driving force for the company is to ensure that this experience is not repeated. Andi Lusty recalls:

> The second time we pretty much took out all the dead wood that was in the organisation. The guys that were left were not only busy, but they were comfortable working with each other. The change in morale and productivity I think happened within two or three weeks after that.

Eight of the ten firms show similar evidence of people-based competitive capabilities (Table 1.2). This capability is not always evident in the competitive experience of these firms, and these judgments may be conservative. Chapter 5 returns to the role of human resource capabilities in the competitive evolution of these firms.

Quality reputation — Montana[8]

High-quality companies are known by their high-quality products and services. For many of these firms, the quality of their product cannot be assessed easily at the time of purchase but only in the process of use, and when that product is a durable good, the period of use can stretch to years. In these circumstances, a product's or a firm's reputation for consistently delivering a known quality of performance (Frank, 1988) becomes a valuable asset that distinguishes the firm from its competitors (Kay, 1993). Firms may be able to enhance their reputation by establishing a strong brand for the product (Fombrun, 1996).

Montana Wines has devoted nearly 30 years to building a leading reputation for high-quality wines. Not only does the duration of this commitment mark the company out from its competitors, but the complexity of viticultural and winemaking crafts, and the scope of reputation-enhancing strategies pursued by the firm, have created for Montana a proprietary position in local and offshore markets. Montana is New Zealand's leading wine maker both in domestic and export sales, exporting 40 per cent of its production.

Montana's pursuit of quality spans the entire value chain, from the distinctive terroir and climatic conditions of its extensive Marlborough vineyards, right through to establishing its product in consumers' consciousness.

The unique characteristics of Marlborough's Wairau Plain were first pointed out to Frank Yukich, Montana's founder, by Lincoln College viticulturalist Wayne Thomas in 1973. Montana was the first to open a vineyard in the region, and also the first to plant high-quality *Vitis vinifera* varieties at a time when the local industry was concentrating on hybrids. Among these was a strain of sauvignon blanc that was to win international acclaim for New Zealand wines and for Montana in the 1980s. Viticultural practice at Montana's vineyards continues to be developed. A visiting wine writer described the ethos as 'an unceasing quest for quality'. With 70 per cent of wine quality created in the vineyard, Montana's policy is to employ top viticulturalists. Their mastery of canopy management techniques in the 1980s created the fruit-dominant styles for which New Zealand wines are now famous.

At the winemaking stage, Montana has used partnerships with international winemakers to lift its standards to world class. Its Deutz sparkling wine has helped Montana reach international standards in methode traditionelle, and a partnership with Domaine Cordier has brought a bordelais influence to the cabernet sauvignon/merlot wines at Montana's McDonald winery in Taradale. Quality control systems were introduced to assure the consistency of wines. Montana was the first winery in Australasia to gain ISO accreditation.

Another aspect of Montana's consistent value proposition is keeping its prices stable within a given market price point. In the key British market the company has changed its price only once in six years. The company also works for a reputation of consistency in its supply of wines. Contracts are made only when the company is sure of its ability to supply: the policy is to underpromise and overdeliver.

The end product of all this effort: wines that regularly win international awards for quality. To quote some recent examples from a long history:

- International white wine of the year, and white winemaker of the year, International Wine Challenge, London, 1997.
- Gold medal, World Wine Championships, Chicago, 1997.
- Drinks International Design Trophy for best wine presentation, International Wine and Spirit Competition, London, 1998.
- International sparkling wine of the year, International Wine Challenge, London, 1998.
- White wine of the year, and white winemaker of the year, International Wine Challenge, London, 1999.

Top quality in the wine itself is matched by premium positioning in marketing strategy. Montana aims its premium wines at the top 15 per cent of the market. The company also wins awards for bottle design, labelling and presentation. An extensive programme of arts sponsorship positions the wine as the natural accompaniment to fine experiences of all kinds: the New Zealand Symphony Orchestra, *Montana Sunday Theatre*, the Montana New Zealand Book Awards, the Wearable Arts Awards, and numerous theatres, galleries and sporting events. The company's hugely successful Lindauer is also the official bubbly of the All Blacks. These sponsorships are among the most powerful contributors to the strength of the Montana brand, and the company spends $2 million each year supporting the brand through its advertising agency Saatchi & Saatchi.

Commitment to quality across such a broad scope has linked the entire organisation into creating a reputation that is one of Montana's leading competitive differentiators. In Peter Hubscher's words:

Montana has grown significantly because it has built up internal skills across the business. In a company this size no one individual dominates the evolution of wine — the quality of the grape is the determining factor. Without superior grapes the winemaker has nothing to work with.

Similar reputation-based capabilities are a feature in nine of our ten firms (Table 1.2).

Innovation — Tait Electronics[9]

When a company releases some innovative product or service, or improves its production or administrative processes, it has achieved a position of rarity. But how easily might competitors imitate the innovation? Indeed, we should expect huge pressures to come on competitors to do exactly that (Kay, 1993).

So, for that innovation to be a long-term competitive capability, the innovating firm has to have established some lasting advantage. This could arise for a number of reasons:

- The innovation may produce a leading share of market that makes the company's product distinctively attractive to consumers. This may occur via good reputation, or if the product achieves the status of an industry standard (e.g. the advantage captured by Microsoft's MS-DOS PC operating system in the 1980s).
- This 'winner take all' effect will be easier to achieve if the firm is very early in a wave of technical change with great potential to revolutionise the industry, or in the case of knowledge-intensive industries generally (Arthur, 1996).
- Experience with the initial innovation may give the firm a head start in the race to produce the next generation of technology, or may require the assembly of large-scale specialist teams which competitors cannot quickly copy.

More than any other capability, innovation has been responsible for the competitive success of Tait Electronics. On several occasions, Tait has been early to jump onto a wave of technical change and has then 'paddled like hell' to get in front of competitors.

In the late 1940s Angus Tait, newly returned from wartime work on radar in Britain, was among a small group of New Zealand firms to open up the new industry of mobile radio, made possible by recent military advances in technology (and by the foresight of the New Zealand Post Office in erecting a national network of transmitter stations). Twenty years later, he repeated the feat by once again leading the local industry into the application of transistor technologies to mobile radio. Tait was not the only contestant in New Zealand: there was another Christchurch-based manufacturer, and two or three more in the North Island. Furthermore, some imported equipment was allowed past the system of import controls then in place. Tait admits that some of these contestants were building better radios, but his company went after the new market with vigour and within a year or so had 70 per cent of the New Zealand market, taking a leading position that it still holds. 'We were quick off the mark. . . . They were a bit slower and needed to work 23 hours a day.' With nowhere to grow in the New Zealand market, Tait's innovative radio designs were introduced to Britain in 1976, once again quickly establishing a strong market share of 20 per cent, which Tait retains to this day.

Each national government requires distinctive technical standards to be met before a company can sell mobile radios in its territory. By operating across several of these jurisdictions, Tait has built the further capability of designing radios that fit multiple standards. In the late 1970s Tait also played a leading role in the industry-led development of the MPT 1327 (MPT is an acronym for Ministry of Post and Telecoms) standard for trunked radio systems. [10] True to its traditions, Tait was the first company to deliver an MPT 1327 system. It has become the de facto world standard and Tait has sold over 200 systems worldwide, including full national networks.

Thirty years' experience in transistorised mobile radio has left Tait with a prominent reputation in major markets around the world. Tait radios sell in 80 countries and young system design engineers from all over the world come to work with Tait in Christchurch: a third of the recruits to Tait's 200-strong design team, the largest in the field in Australasia, are from overseas. Research and development (R&D) spending has been sustained at between 10 and 15 per cent of sales.

As the technology has developed, fixed costs of system design have ballooned to radically transform the economics of the industry: manufacturers must be able to defray costs over large numbers of units sold in a global market fractionated by national standards. Tait is one of a handful of companies in the world that can still meet these exacting demands. Its own energetic development of this technology has played a significant part in creating the conditions in which only a few companies can now compete.

There is similar evidence of innovation leading to a locked-in competitive advantage in eight of the ten firms (Table 1.2). A decade ago, this assessment would also have included Criterion, but their loss of a leading American market position in stereo system cabinets in the late 1980s shows how transitory innovative capabilities can be when markets and technologies move on. Chapter

3 returns to the contribution of innovation and technology to the development of these firms.

Organisational learning and decision processes — Formway[11]
Earlier in this chapter we made a distinction between resources and capabilities. Organisational learning and decision processes (OLDP) do the job of converting resource potentials into market capabilities. Intense interest in organisations as knowledge-producing systems is producing a growing body of ideas on the importance of various OLDP systems. These encourage us to look for organisational routines (Nelson and Winter, 1982; Teece and Pisano, 1994) and norms and practices of social exchange (Nahapiet and Ghoshal, 1998) which:

- tap into and engage the accumulated learning of all members of the organisation (Crossan et al., 1999);
- share and distribute these around the organisation (Nonaka and Takeuchi, 1995);
- apply the learning effectively to the organisation's business (McGrath et al., 1995).

And these processes will be more effective when the organisation:

- enjoys high levels of social capital, fostering free exchange of ideas (Nahapiet and Goshal, 1998);
- has already accumulated a body of shared understandings (a distinctive language) with which to communicate (Crossan et al., 1999);
- is challenged by its leaders, its norms or its situation to want to do better (Senge, 1990).

Although the contribution of OLDP to past competitive successes is difficult to observe, and hence difficult for this study to assess, at Formway Furniture they are among the organisation's salient attributes. Co-founder and managing director, Rick Wells, believes that accumulated knowledge is *the* basis for the company's competitive differentiation and success.

The company has been able to cycle learning about its technologies, its markets and its organisation through successive waves of product and market development, from the ErgoStation workstation of the early 1980s, to the Zaf chair of the mid-1980s, to the systems furniture of the 1990s. These innovations are derived from capability:

- to be among the first to understand emerging market trends and act on them, for example the development of the ErgoStation to coincide with the PC explosion of the mid-1980s;

- to bring new products to market quickly, with attendant innovations in production and supply management, for example the development of the Zaf chair, and the associated development of a network of 250 suppliers throughout New Zealand;
- to bring down the time between order and delivery, for example the company's Fast Cycle Manufacturing Programme, and its 'delivery windows' strategy.

Formway managers have some simple ways of building speed into the organisation. One manager applies a 'speed down the corridor' test when selecting new staff: quick walkers display energy and enthusiasm, which will fit well with the Formway way of doing business.

The capacity to learn quickly stems from energetic and widespread communication. The company's designers keep in close contact with important influencers of work environments such as architects, ergonomists and health and safety professionals.[12] The organisation's team-based structure fosters involvement and the sharing of decisions and information.

Formway's ability to foster communication across the full scope of its activities enhances opportunities to learn. As *Prodesign* put it in a 1996 article, 'the separate disciplines of research, design, engineering, marketing and product development are in permanent communication mode'. These extended discussions have had a material effect on the direction of the business. As Rick Wells notes, 'We tried to have a path but we have had a lot of debates about those paths. I think that's very helpful and I think we have had quite a few changes along the line.' The company is always open to new ideas. Dominating one wall of the company's meeting room is the homily:

The mind is like a parachute
It works best when it is open.

The company has trained its staff in techniques such as brainstorming and problem-solving and has its own word for a process of thinking outside the current box: 'imagineering'. It seeks to sustain an environment 'where unusual, odd or previously unrecognised ideas can be aired and developed'.

These high levels of energy and involvement stem from a management style that empowers people to find their own way of making a contribution. In Rick Wells's words: 'You can only go at speed with a lot of people pulling it. You'll never get there with one or two people pushing.' Wells speaks of 'creating a space' around his people into which they can grow. He also speaks of striking a balance between chaos and order: enough chaos to stimulate change, but not so much as to close down people's capacity to change.

Formway is also a company where people constantly challenge themselves to do better. When we met Formway's management team, we asked several times whether they felt the company had demonstrated capabilities in various areas. They were inclined to be doubtful until we added 'relative to your competitors'. The real competition appears to be the limits of their own, and the organisation's, creativity.

The elements of OLDP are not as strong in many organisations as they are at Formway: clear examples of OLDP contributing to competitive capability were identifiable in just four of the ten companies (Table 1.2). However, it is likely that even closer familiarity with these firms would add to that number.

Multiple technologies — Nuplex Industries[13]

One of the first suggestions for how companies can develop capabilities distinctive from their competitors is Prahalad and Hamel's notion of core competencies (Prahalad and Hamel, 1990). This traced the origin of success at companies like Canon to their mastery of multiple technologies and their ability to integrate these across many products and markets, making active use of alliances and business partners.

With over 1000 products in its portfolio — more than any other resins maker in the world — Nuplex Industries has learnt how to apply its mastery of several chemical process technologies to a huge range of market applications. Its polymer compounds are used in the paint, printing ink, adhesives and fibreglass-reinforced plastics industries; its resins are used in flooring, coatings, waterproofing, roofing and adhesives products. It has recently applied its skills in handling these diverse chemicals to an entirely new business division based on the collection, processing, recycling and disposal of liquid, hazardous and other wastes.

Over its nearly 50-year history, the company has progressed by continuing to ask two simple questions:

- Is there anything else the company can profitably make for the customers it already serves?
- Are there other uses for the products and the technology the company already possesses or can access?

The company began, in the 1950s, with polymer-based flooring coatings, which were enhanced in the 1960s with an extensive programme of overseas licensing technology. Its competitors meanwhile, typically subsidiaries of overseas firms, stayed focused on their parents' more limited product range. These licensing relationships have matured to the point where many are now two-way channels for product and technology sharing, with Nuplex contributing to the relationship as an equal partner (see p.52). Meanwhile, the original floor-coating product has been extended to new uses: for walls, ceilings and external coatings.

Acquiring licences and building a reactor to manufacture high-temperature resins allowed Nuplex to make alkyds for the paint industry, and the same technology allowed the company to extend its product-market scope again by making the unsaturated polyester resins used in the fibreglass industry. As Fred Holland recalls, 'Every expansion of existing business gave us a touch into a new area and we have branched from that.'

The unusual variety of products and technology Nuplex supports has given it a competitive edge in its gradual expansion into overseas markets. Paradoxically, large global resins manufacturers have tended to specialise in a smaller range of applications. Although it cannot compete with the specialist refinements of these large competitors, Nuplex has found that its familiarity with a range of applications is attractive in niche markets. With their broad experience, Nuplex sales engineers are willing to approach any given problem in a variety of ways. They begin by seeking to understand the customer's need, whereas larger and more specialised competitors often begin and end with their one and only solution.

Nuplex's Fred Holland explained the connection between New Zealand's history of market isolation and the unusual breadth of experience that has accumulated in firms like Nuplex. The result is a resourcefulness that is one of the salient attributes claimed for our national culture. More than one of the CEOs participating in our study wondered whether this trait would survive the globalisation of New Zealand's economy and society. Chapter 7 returns to these issues by focusing on the influence of national culture on the competitive capabilities of these firms.

Similar capabilities in multiple technologies are identifiable in the competitive success of four of the ten companies (Table 1.2).

Production capability — Criterion, Kiwi[14]
Students of RBV theory have so far ignored a firm's manufacturing operations as a source of sustainable competitive advantage; instead they have tended to focus on individual resources and organisational attributes. Yet manufacturing capability has played an important role in every one of our firms at various times in their history, and it did not seem possible to ignore them. With one

probably temporary exception, manufacturing capability remains a competitive differentiator for all ten companies (Table 1.2).

Several of the capabilities already discussed are evident in the firms' manufacturing operations:

- an emphasis on *reputation*-enhancing quality;
- created by high-quality *workplace relationships*;
- and by networks of *supplier relationships* which sustain high standards of quality and delivery;
- and by effective organisational learning and decision processes (*OLDP*);
- and supported also at times by *innovative* machinery and process management technologies;
- the whole coming together in a complex and coherent *configuration* which competitors would struggle to replicate.

These attributes have close similarities to the elements of world-class manufacturing as summarised recently by Flynn et al. (1999).

The Criterion Group's chief competitive capability has, for much of its history, been its East Tamaki manufacturing facility. It has the largest capacity in Australasia for manufacturing high-volume ready-to-assemble (RTA) furniture for home and office use. Over 30 years the company has purchased and developed world-class machinery that enables it to manipulate and process, very cost-effectively, high tensile thermoplastic materials. As a result, the company can engineer design and functionality features into its furniture which no other RTA maker in Australasia can copy. Since 1983 the company has extended its technological scope by operating its own laminating plant, opening up design and production strategies its regional competitors cannot match.

Criterion has succeeded because it captures many of the economies of scale that its large plant was designed for, but on a product mix characterised by high levels of product and volume variety. This is done through careful design of product families around shared components, using computer-aided design (CAD) systems, and complex computer-controlled scheduling of workflows through the plant. A manufacturing resource planning (MRP) system was installed in 1989 with the help of the manufacturing systems research group at the University of Auckland's Department of Mechanical Engineering, and extended to a full enterprise resource planning (ERP) system in 1998.

The flexibility of Criterion's manufacturing systems is also found in its logistics capabilities. As Wally Smaill puts it:

We have a great deal of flexibility, and conceptually if you wanted it in ones, you could have it in ones. If you wanted it in pallet loads, you could have it in pallet loads. If you wanted it in thousands, you could have it in thousands. However, in reality we are not required to manufacture in such small quantities.

The company has learnt to operate with this high level of variety while still improving standard efficiency measures:

- overall factory lead time has been reduced from five to three weeks since 1995;
- productivity per person has increased 30 per cent;
- reworks have fallen by 50 per cent.

Criterion's mastery of high-variety, high-volume manufacturing is in turn built on distinctive capabilities in information systems. The company's linked local area network (LAN) systems in Melbourne and Auckland allow all staff access to an integrated system of accounting, manufacturing and control information.

Criterion embarked on this reconfiguration of its manufacturing strategies in 1989 following the collapse of its mass-production stereo cabinet business in the United States. A key feature of the new strategy has been the pursuit of the high-quality workplace relations described earlier (see pp.11–15). The company has invested heavily in training for its workforce and uses profit-sharing and performance incentives to give staff a share in the company's success. A company-sponsored social club features prominently at the firm's manufacturing site; the main entrance opens directly onto the club's swimming pool.

A long tradition of reliable quality has been a prerequisite to success in Criterion's business. Mass-produced RTA furniture requires components to be manufactured to low error tolerances so that they fit together every time and can be readily assembled by the customer. Criterion's quality reputation, earned first in Australia with consumer electronics manufacturers there, was important in gaining access to the much bigger American market in the 1980s. There, Criterion's stereo cabinets went on to be ranked first, third and fourth in one consumer product test. The tradition of quality is maintained and the company has been certified ISO9001 since 1995.

Kiwi Dairies is another firm whose success is based on distinctive manufacturing capability. The company's facility at Whareroa, just outside Hawera, is the largest dairy factory in the world, processing milk from all over the lower half of the North Island, across to Hawke's Bay. It exports 95 per cent of its production. These world-leading economies of scale in production and milk-supply logistics have been built up steadily over a period of nearly 40 years since the initial merger that created Kiwi Dairies in 1963. The company grew through dozens of successive mergers with smaller dairy companies, guided since 1968 by a vision to consolidate production onto the Hawera site.

Like other companies pursuing world-class manufacturing status, Kiwi has learnt the importance of involving its workforce. Since the early 1990s, when he was appointed CEO, Craig Norgate has led a shift in style towards high-quality workplace relationships, to replace a former culture of 'command and control'.

Chapter 4 returns to the role of production capabilities in the competitive evolution of these firms.

Organisation culture — Svedala Barmac[15]

Some of these organisations were particularly open to our study. In these cases, several members of our research team met a number of the firm's managers and we were able to talk over our assessments with the whole management team. At Svedala Barmac a member of the research team spent several weeks working alongside the company's training manager and met most of the workforce.

In these cases we were able to gain some insight into the deeper organisational attributes that distinguish any enterprise utterly from its competitors, and to see, to some extent, how elements of an organisation's culture contributed to its other competitive capabilities.[16] This was certainly the case at Gallagher, Formway and Svedala Barmac (Table 1.2) and it is very likely that even closer familiarity with the other firms would have added to this number.

At Svedala Barmac, the norms embedded in the organisation's culture include:

- huge pride in and enthusiasm for their world-beating, revolutionary Barmac machines — they describe themselves as 'Barmac nuts';
- an associated determination to show the world that a tiny company from Matamata in the Waikato can be as professional in its products and services as any firm on the planet;
- a 'can do' approach to engineering and technical expertise, derived from a tradition of agricultural engineering in the local community;
- a direct, low-key, non-hierarchical style in interpersonal relationships;
- open and honest communication in which no grudges are held;
- a sense that everybody is there to back each other up; and that knowledge and expertise are shared;
- pride that the company is a good place to work, and is seen in the local community as a firm that cares for its people and its township.

These cultural norms have remained vigorously independent despite nearly a decade of overseas ownership, a tribute both to the distance and autonomous management style of its Swedish parent, and to the fierce pride and independence of the 'Barmac nuts'.

In this study's assessment, the foundations of the company's competitive advantage are (see Table 1.2):

- its reputation for high-quality customisation and service,
- delivered through an extensive network of dealers and Svedala sales organisations around the world,
- and made possible by a highly trained and highly motivated workforce,
- who continue to add to the company's original advantages in world-leading innovation.

It is easy to see how the company's cultural norms support each of these competitive capabilities:

- Its pride and professionalism underpin the company's leading quality reputation.
- The feeling of personal commitment to a shared enterprise produces the high levels of cooperation and mutual support required to install a complex product effectively at customer sites anywhere in the world (including points north of the Arctic Circle).
- Open, honest and direct communication throughout the organisation keeps workplace relationships healthy ('no grudges') and creates opportunities for mutual learning and development.
- Barmac people don't get diverted into big-company politics, and this attribute also serves the company well in its dealings with offshore dealers and sales companies.

PORTFOLIOS, CONFIGURATIONS, AND COHERENCE

This section looks at the overall portfolios of competitive capabilities in these exemplar firms, as summarised in Table 1.2. We ask two questions:

- In what ways are these portfolios different from the profiles of competitive capability in the 'average' New Zealand enterprise?
- Are there attributes of the overall portfolios that further enhance the competitive capability of these firms?

The answers to these questions involve three attributes of these portfolios that have become clear during the study:

- Their scope — the sheer number of competitive capabilities evident in each enterprise;
- Their balance —each capability is strong enough to meet the demands made on it by others, and by the organisation as a whole;
- Their coherence —all capabilities come together in a mutually supportive whole, which several firms see as the ultimate differentiator of the organisation's competitive appeal.

The scope of leading capability portfolios

A striking feature of the capability portfolios portrayed in Table 1.2 is the broad scope of competitive advantage in these leading New Zealand enterprises. No company displays the entire set, and a couple of firms show only two, but these companies demonstrate capability in most of the known sources of sustainable advantage.

Another feature of these capabilities is their broad geographic scope. Six of the ten firms are global leaders (selling predominantly beyond Australasia), and four are regional in scope (selling predominantly within Australasia). Ability to compete on an international scale was one of the criteria we used to select companies for this study, so their exceptional geographic scope is no surprise, but the scope of their competitive capabilities was in no way a product of our selection process. It is a feature which distinguishes these firms strongly from the average New Zealand enterprise.

The typical New Zealand firm bases its competitive appeal on just one or two of these sources of advantage.[17] Since the reforms of the mid-1980s, its predominant focus has been on the quality strategies. Fifteen per cent or less of New Zealand firms use innovation as a competitive differentiator, an attribute they share with overseas samples of competitive strategy.[18] By contrast, eight of these ten leading firms are innovators.

The incidence of world-class manufacturing capabilities in New Zealand stands between one and two firms per 100.[19]

With one (probably temporary) exception, every one of these leading firms demonstrated this capability.

Finally, only one in four New Zealand employers shows evidence of even attempting to establish the kind of high-quality workplace relationships that are contributing to competitive success in eight of these firms.[20]

The breadth of these portfolios is one product of the distinctive evolution of these leading firms. Following chapters shed light on why these portfolios have developed in this way.

In this study's assessment, Kiwi Dairies displays a narrower portfolio of capabilities, compared to the other exemplars. We suggest this is the result of the distinctive ownership structure in the industry. If the Dairy Board and the Dairy Research Institute were included in the assessment, we would expect to see the full scope of capabilities being applied to Kiwi's flow of milk-based products.

Balanced capability portfolios

Several company leaders drew our attention to the need to keep the whole organisation's capability portfolio in some degree of balance. To use Brian Smaill's words, describing Criterion's experience:

> I think the thing is . . . a package. We were doing lots of things simultaneously. The way I describe it, it's a little bit like the hull of a boat. The theory of being good at marketing and not being good at manufacturing is like having the front end of the boat solid but the back having no stern on it, or whatever. So everything has got to be relatively the same strength otherwise it can't withhold. . . . Everything's got to be linked. [When we improve our processes it] is almost like the tide coming in. As the level rises then we've got to make sure that everything's in sync and everything's moving together.

Gavin Ng, in a masters thesis completed before this study, also concluded that a balanced portfolio of capabilities was a key attribute in explaining the differing performance of the two matched pairs of companies in his study.[21] When balance was lost, the firm's competitive success suffered.

A good example of this in Ng's study was the experience of Bendon Industries in the late 1980s. The company had correctly foreseen a need to become Australasian in scope as deregulation altered the economics of producing solely for the local market. The company acquired manufacturing capacity across the Tasman and came up with one of the most inspired marketing innovations of all time by joining with Australia's favourite daughter, Elle Macpherson, to create the Elle brand of women's underwear.

The innovation was a stunning success but Bendon struggled to capitalise on it. The huge growth in volumes stretched the company's manufacturing capabilities beyond their reach. Skilled machinists could not be found or trained in time, and quality suffered. The firm's limited logistics capability also buckled under the strain and Australian department stores were confronted with hordes of unsatisfied customers and empty shelves awaiting delivery. Under the new

CEO, the company has had to radically reconfigure its strategy to recover from the debacle. Logistics were outsourced and the company eventually closed all its manufacturing facilities in New Zealand. The company is now focused on managing its outstandingly valuable brands.

Coherent configurations of capability

As mentioned at the start of this chapter, a criticism of RBV theory is that it has led to a focus on individual resources as potential sources of advantage. The underlying assumption is that each of these resources makes an independent contribution to the success of the firm.

A focus on individual capabilities has, we believe, produced valuable insight into the sources of competitive success in these leading New Zealand firms. But where they had the opportunity (e.g. during feedback seminars), the companies' managers told us very clearly that a simple list of apparently distinct capabilities does not get to the heart of the competitive advantage of their enterprise.

Rather, it is the firm's ability to bring together all its diverse activities and capabilities together into a coherent whole, delivering an integrated bundle of value to the ultimate consumer, that is the most powerful competitive differentiator. Students of these processes describe this whole as a configuration (Miller, 1996), or an activity system (Porter, 1996), and the glue that holds it together as its coherence (Meyer et al., 1993).

Within a configuration, the power of an individual capability is really the product of the power of the whole system, and it is dangerous to think of each making its own independent contribution. To try to unravel one strand of capability from its configuration would be to weaken the whole fabric, and probably strip much of the value from the strand. In this view, we should think (and speak) of one coherent organisational capability, rather than a portfolio of separable capabilities. To quote one executive from our study: 'It's like a bundle of wood, together you can't break it; but each individual piece you can'. The role played by a portfolio's balance and coherence, and what happens when these are disturbed, is central to the theory of competitive evolution that has emerged from this study.

A central question of this study has been to ask how these configurations come about.[22] Are individual components attracted to each other in the way that high-quality workplace relations appear to be important to maintaining a quality reputation, or to world-class production capabilities? Is there a natural order to the development of individual capabilities, as Baden-Fuller and Stopford (1994) suggest? Or are these configurations produced by forces broader than mutual attraction? Is a firm's capability configuration a product of its history, of the strategic choices it has made in the past and the distinctive contexts of its competitive experience? These questions lie beneath the following chapters.

Chapter 2

Internationalisation

This chapter focuses on the internationalisation processes of firms participating in the study, why they internationalise, how they internationalise and what type of international marketing strategies they use. It describes how these firms use their relationships and networks with suppliers, customers, competitors, government agencies and other such bodies to learn about international markets and to develop their capabilities. It shows how New Zealand firms develop such collaboration to overcome the resource constraints of small size. The term 'business network' is used to describe these patterns of collaboration (Ford et al., 1998; Hakansson and Snehota, 1995).

INTRODUCTION

Montana produces wine, which is sold internationally. Through its international relationships it has successfully acquired knowledge in areas such as technology, packaging, labels, distribution and markets. It has also formed relationships to acquire financial resources for international expansion. New manufacturing technology has been acquired through the company's relationships with two French wineries, Champagne Deutz and Cordier. This new technology has improved product quality and provided the product differentiation essential for Montana's international expansion. Montana has also been allowed to use the Deutz brand name on its wine label, which has helped greatly to increase international sales.

To develop packaging, labels and a strong brand for its product internationally, Montana worked with an Italian design house, Robilant and Associates in Milan. This design house was chosen because of its small size and willingness to invest time in becoming familiar with Montana's business. Through this long-term relationship Montana acquired knowledge that it would not have done working alone or with a New Zealand firm. Specialised knowledge on packaging and branding of wines for the international market was not available domestically. The introduction of the new labels improved the product image of Montana in Europe, enabling it to capture a significant portion of that market.

This case illustrates how, by collaborating with other firms, a small to medium-sized firm can accelerate its internationalisation process and achieve success beyond what it could achieve alone. Companies can no longer be competitive in a global market without, to some extent at least, collaborating with other businesses (Madhok, 1997). This is particularly true in a small, open, isolated economy such as New Zealand. The average New Zealand firm is small compared with its international counterparts, and it is increasingly difficult for such small companies to work independently in the complex global business environment. Also, firms with a small domestic market have less chance of achieving economies of scale in research and development, manufacturing or marketing.[1]

THE ROLE OF INTERNATIONALISATION IN COMPETITIVE EVOLUTION

Going global

Ironically, success is one of the greatest threats to a company's balanced config-uration of capabilities. Several of the companies studied have confronted the challenge of suddenly discovering they had a world-beating product on their hands. Scaling up to global markets from a base as small as the New Zealand market is particularly challenging.

Scott Technology's first contract from a major American client involved a project 20 times larger than anything it had done before, and change on this scale throws a company into an entirely new context. Trying to reproduce existing capabilities in a new market involves heroic effort. Scott Technology's first attempt was at once a disaster and a triumph. The project was completed a full year behind schedule, during which the client lost sales because its capacity planning had assumed completion to time. Fortunately the client was prepared to be patient, and this patience was rewarded by transformation of the client's competitive position. The project also made Scott Technology's reputation in the vast American market, although it could just as easily have left it with an indelible black mark.

At Gallagher, the realisation that the company had a world-beating product catapulted Bill Gallagher into an intense six-year battle to secure market access in a standards-ridden industry, and to create a network of distributors before his competitors captured pole position in the rapidly growing new market. He succeeded, but the company had to create entirely new capabilities in the way it structured its relationships with the distribution channel. The change coincided with a shift in control from one generation of family management to the next, and the old regime would probably have been far less open to this change.

Part of the going global challenge is testing the adequacy of the company's accumulated wisdom. When Formway made its first move offshore, Rick Wells methodically investigated every aspect of the venture. He interviewed customers, influencers, potential distributors and suppliers, disciplining himself to rate potential partners against the attributes his experience told him were important, and also asking himself whether each partner 'felt right' for his business.

So world-beating innovations put a strain on their owner's reputation, business networks and knowledge assets. Internal relationships and culture are also destabilised, in ways described below when we consider the gusher.

In all these cases, when one capability suddenly shifts gear to a higher level, the organisation's other capabilities are put under tremendous pressure. If they fail, the organisation's configuration of capabilities may become unbalanced and the company's competitive advantage destroyed.

In Formway's case, the move to Australia was impelled by the potential of the Zaf chair. In the words of Rick Wells, 'we had something of value we wanted to exploit'. Following such potentials has involved all of these managers in intense periods of effort as they try to extend and adapt their configurations of capabilities to the new context.

Another approach is illustrated by PEC. John Williams, aware of the 'national to global' trend from John Naisbitt's *Megatrends*, chose to introduce an intermediate step. His strategy was to go from Australasia to multiregional to global. For the Retail Systems Business Unit at PEC the multiregional step encompassed the Southern Hemisphere, and for its CARDAX Access Control Business Unit selected regional markets.

The gusher

A gusher is a period of dramatically increasing sales following market success; it reflects a company's successful configuration of competitive capabilities. Brian Smaill of Criterion described the experience as follows:

> The way we explained it, it's like being in the middle of the Pacific Ocean and you're out there on a surfboard and what's coming behind you is a great big tidal wave. We've caught this tidal wave on our surfboard and we can't even see the shore. But we're going to surf this wave for as long as we can. There's only one

thing about a wave: every wave reaches the shore at some point in time. What we've got to do is to be smart enough to know that as we get closer to that shoreline we're actually smart enough to kick off the surfboard and kick off that wave and wait for another wave or make another one ourselves or find another opportunity. The other thing we said was this wave's so big, we've got to be realistic that the next one's not likely to be. It could be a while, we could be in a trough and it could be a while to catch another wave.

At Gallagher, PEC and Formway, the gusher came in the shape of three successive years when sales doubled every year. Formway, which now differentiates itself competitively by delivering orders within tightly defined limits, found itself asking clients to wait eighteen weeks for what is now a four-week delivery item! One element of their quality reputation was clearly dented by this episode. Yet, by being scrupulously honest about what it could and could not deliver, the firm emerged with its client relationships intact.

Gushers catapult their victims to success, providing the firms can keep their configuration of capabilities intact. Very rapid growth typically involves very rapid expansion of the workforce. A firm's ability to retain high-quality relationships based on an internal architecture of mutual knowledge and trust is severely challenged by the rapid ingestion of outsiders. Training also comes under pressure and quality problems can steal into the company's operations, damaging its reputation. These problems hit all three of these firms.

Growth beyond a certain size, regardless of the time scale, has put pressure on the network of staff relationships in other companies too. Kiwi Dairies and Nuplex both experienced a change in the nature of their workforce relationships as they grew in scale. At PEC John Williams used outsourcing for several years as a means of keeping the company size at around 100: 'We believed that innovation, quality employee relationships and efficiency all begin to decrease when numbers grow beyond this figure. We had seen so many factories lose innovation as their size grew.' John Williams realised, however, that to expand sales to include PEC's multiregional markets, staff numbers had to increase, and in 1999 these had reached 250 in New Zealand and 50 overseas.

Another challenge inherent in a gusher is that a long-developed and distinctive culture can be overwhelmed by the arrival of large numbers of people who are insensitive to the established norms and know nothing of their value to the rest of the resource configuration. John Williams reported that he had to work hard at retaining the culture he valued so highly when a gusher hit his sales in the early 1990s.

As with going global, the destabilising force of the gusher is created entirely by the evolution of the firm's own configuration of capabilities. Product innovation was the source of this instability in the cases of Gallagher, PEC and Formway. Our exploratory study uncovered a further dramatic example of what can happen to a configuration when a stunningly successful marketing innovation is let loose. And, as mentioned in Chapter 1, Bendon's decision to enter the Australian market was brilliantly executed by creating the Elle brand of women's underwear. Its huge success in the Australian market overwhelmed Bendon's manufacturing and distribution capabilities, and led to the company losing the support of major Australian retail chains.[2]

Sow and reap + focus and grow

International market entry and expansion is challenging for firms with a small domestic market and limited resources. To meet this challenge these firms have adopted the strategy of trying several markets and products simultaneously, waiting to see which provide opportunities and then focusing their efforts on the most promising. They do not follow the textbook strategy of first entering a single market, usually culturally and/or geographically close, and then moving on to more distant markets. The terms we use to describe their preferred strategy are sow and reap and focus and grow.

Sow and reap patterns appear when a firm is exploring how far its capabilities can be stretched. Rather than commit large resources to untried products or markets, companies like Gallagher and Scott Technology initially spread their initiatives across a range of businesses and geographic markets, and later moved in aggressively when the seed showed signs of taking root. In terms of market development, the sow and reap strategy was described succinctly by Gallagher's managing director, Bill Gallagher: 'Any market in the world is on the way from here to Europe'; sales people were expected to stop off en route to the company's major overseas markets.

For Svedala Barmac (which was called Tidco before 1990), market development did not follow a set pattern, but rather evolved as opportunities emerged. Tidco began internationalisation as a small company without the resources to conduct costly market feasibility studies. The company trialled new markets and followed up only where potential customers emerged. This was a more cost-efficient way to fund their market research. Quite frequently the first contact with a new market was through a local agent wanting to sell a Barmac rock crusher to one of his customers.

Svedala Barmac entered the American market by advertising in industry magazines and sending direct mail to quarries. Areas that responded well received a follow-up sales effort. Andi Lusty, who developed the American market for Tidco, concentrated at first on the West Coast of the United States. From these initial interests, the reputation of the Barmac rock crusher spread by word of mouth and competitive success: 'If one bloke bought it and it did him good, and [he] suddenly started producing quality aggregate all the cement companies or concrete companies came to him to buy the stuff. So all the others took notice . . . all his competition.'

During the first three to four years of the North American venture, Andi Lusty spent six months each year following sales leads and appointing dealers, both in the United States and Canada. A dozen dealers were signed up in the United States, and a few more in Canada. Dealers had to pay in advance for machines, thus providing the cash flow for growth and getting dealers' commitment to creating sales. As the number of dealers increased, so did Svedala Barmac's American sales, which rose dramatically from 1982 onwards.

Focus and grow is the converse of sow and reap. When a promising product or market is identified, the firm narrows its focus and devotes increasing resources to the new venture. This strategy is effectively imposed on the firm when it hits a gusher. In a matter of a few years Gallagher discarded the product portfolio it had built up over decades, as the firm focused its capabilities on its star performer, the electric fence. Scott Technology stopped manufacturing washing machines and dryers, and narrowed its focus to the design and manufacture of production machinery for the domestic appliance industry.

Market segments that were the foundation of the business are left behind as a firm discovers new segments to which its emerging capabilities are strongly suited. When Montana started planting better quality vines it marked a milestone in the wine industry, and New Zealand's entry into modern wine production. Montana's sauvignon blanc won international approval in the 1980s, thus placing New Zealand wine on the international market. In this way Montana moved into the premium wine segment of the market and left behind its early 1980s image of being a supplier of high-volume/low-quality wines.

GLOBAL AND REGIONAL LEADERS

We found two strategic groups of companies, global and regional leaders, which have certain features in common.

Global leaders

Six of the firms have clearly achieved strong — in some cases leading — competitive positions on a global scale. They are Kiwi Dairies, Gallagher, Montana, Tait, Svedala Barmac and Scott Technology. Typically, their products are to be found in 50 to 60 countries worldwide. They have a strong market share in key markets (Scott Technology production lines make 80 per cent of the rangehoods sold in the huge American market) and a significant or leading share of the global market (in some cases up to a third of the total). For companies growing from the tiny New Zealand home market, these globalisation levels are remarkable.

The development paths of these global leaders have many features in common. Typically, the origin of globalisation can be traced to a world-leading proprietary innovation. In most cases, technology grants administered through the former Development Finance Corporation (DFC) were used to support these innovations. The global potential of the innovative product confronts the firm with an intense period of growth (the gusher).

To meet the very rapid growth in demand, global leaders had little option but to focus the company's energies, abandoning a broader range of businesses that characterised their New Zealand operations. Some firms focused on the globalising product, abandoning other product lines (Gallagher). Others focused on the needs of particular market segments and served their needs wherever they could be found in the world (Montana). Yet others focused on a particular stage in the value chain where the firm had developed distinctive advantage (Scott Technology).

Over a very few years, the gusher transforms the firm from a small company with local focus and a broad range of businesses into an international competitor. The scale of this internationalisation, when done from a New Zealand base, is exceptionally challenging. For example, when Scott Technology received an offshore order 20 times greater than anything the firm had yet completed, this represented several years' worth of revenue and clearly took the firm well beyond its current capabilities.

The scale of expansion required, and the risks involved, make the financing of internationalisation challenging for domestic capital markets. Seven of the ten exemplar firms are privately owned. At various stages, several of these firms considered bringing in outside equity, but equity markets and institutions were not able to meet their needs. For several, DFC export suspensory loans administered by the former DFC were important in financing this phase of their development. When the needs of controlling owners diverged from the capital needs of the business, competitive development was impeded (see Chapter 6).

These New Zealand firms have gone global in ways quite different from the 'stages' model of internationalisation developed from European and American experience (Johanson and Vahlne, 1977). That model predicts that companies will progress from selling through agents to using their own sales force; from licensing technology to local partners to setting up their own offshore manufacturing plants; and ultimately to globalising even core functions such as R&D. The commitment of resources on this scale is beyond New Zealand's global leaders. Even firms that have been globalised for several decades prefer to keep production concentrated in New Zealand. Several global leaders prefer to keep using independent dealers and distributors to service offshore markets. In this way, the small-scale New Zealand firm is able to engage the local knowledge of local partners, and achieve global reach quickly despite its limited resources.

Similarly, the sow and reap process used to search for international markets is quite different from the elaborate market research followed by large overseas firms.

Regional leaders

Three of the exemplar firms (Formway, Nuplex and PEC) followed another quite different path: focusing on just one offshore market (Australia) and, unlike global leaders, preferring direct involvement in marketing and manufacturing offshore. (Once again, the New Zealand experience is at variance with the stages model — here it is the less globalised firms who choose direct methods.) To defray the higher burden of these overheads, regional leaders are active in a broader range of products than the focused global leaders. Typically, profit margins are somewhat less. Although regional leaders are all active in innovating products and processes, they have not typically come up with a world-beating innovation; or if they have, they have been barred from taking it global for other reasons. For example, mindful of the dangers of a gusher transition, John Williams deliberately kept the growth of PEC within regional bounds, despite the world-leading status of his firm's innovative product.

Are regional leaders global leaders at an earlier stage of development, waiting for the big innovative breakthrough? This may be so in some cases. Two of these four firms (Formway and PEC) have developed, or are developing, products they hope will reach a global market. But the radical differences in strategy between the two groups suggest that regional leaders will be transformed as they go global. Global leadership is not an extension of regional leadership, nor is it automatic.

John Williams's global growth strategy for PEC included a multiregional phase, during which his company would be able to convince potential global strategic partners of the innovation and quality of PEC's products. He was convinced that potential global partners would not regard market leadership in Australasia alone as sufficient 'proof' of PEC's world leadership.

Instead, there is a distinct logic to the regional leadership strategy. Typically, regional leaders believe it is important for them to represent the benefits of their product directly in the marketplace. Some have tried indirect representation and been dissatisfied with results. Their competitors also use direct methods. Nuplex's Fred Holland expresses a typical view:

[We establish direct sales relationships] because we believe that we tailor our products for the customers' needs and nobody but ourselves can establish that relationship. We've tried agents but they really get in between you and the customer. They don't add value, they add cost rather than value.

So it seems that the nature of the product requires the more direct marketing strategy. Similarly, the comparatively low value-to-space ratio of several of these products encourages offshore manufacture.

Regional leaders are also distinctive in the way they have created competitive advantage from the breadth of their product lines. Over several decades of operation in Australia and New Zealand Nuplex has built up a product portfolio of hundreds of variants. By mastering several technologies, and learning the needs of many market applications, this firm can approach its customers with a wide range of potential solutions. Much larger global competitors have tended to specialise and are less flexible in their diagnosis of customers' problems.

Summary on global and regional leaders
Each of our firms has developed its own unique configuration of strategy and capability, but the pattern of similarities and differences discussed above suggests they can be described as either global or regional leaders. The differences between the two groups are summarised in Table 2. 1.

TABLE 2. I
Configurations of global and regional leadership

	GLOBAL LEADERSHIP	REGIONAL LEADERSHIP
Innovation	**World-leading Strong differentiator**	Region-leading or global-constrained
Product, market or value scope	Focus	Broader
Reputation	Global	Regional
External relationships	Mixed: direct + dealers	Direct representation
Production capability	In New Zealand only	**In New Zealand and Australia Strong differentiator**
Internal relationships	high-quality	high-quality

INTERNATIONALISATION OF THE GLOBAL FIRMS

Four of the six global firms displaying continued international success were chosen for further study: Gallagher, Montana, Tait and Svedala Barmac. All four have international sales in a wide range of countries but use a variety of methods to enter and expand markets. Sometimes they export from New Zealand, while simultaneously using agents, sales subsidiaries and foreign direct investment in their international markets. In some cases they leap-frog into more advanced methods such as foreign direct investment to enter a market; in other cases they take a more gradual approach by starting with an agent then using sales subsidiaries and eventually foreign direct investment.

These companies have chosen their first market on the basis of either existing networks or a close psychic distance (culture and language similarity to New Zealand). Tait entered Australia and Britain simultaneously, but when the latter market proved to be highly successful it focused on that rather than on Australia. Tait's entry to the British market in 1976 was made easier because Angus Tait had spent a few years there during the Second World War and had some knowledge of the country. Montana also entered the British market first because the language and culture were similar to New Zealand's and consumers there were interested in New Zealand wine. Montana used both knowledge gained domestically and information from international networks.

Developing collaborative know-how within domestic business networks

All four firms had a strong domestic market base before they started internationalising. They had formed relationships with their suppliers, customers, distributors, universities, competitors and government. For example, Tait was involved in a local industry network and relied on subcontractors for part of its manufacturing. So within the New Zealand market these firms developed, over many decades, their capability to collaborate in a business network. This stood them in good stead when moving offshore, enabling them, among other things, to identify the value of new information and new partners. For instance, Montana and Gallagher used their experience in establishing extensive domestic distribution networks to guide their later launch into international markets.

In some cases the international network and the domestic network have complemented each other. For example, Montana's relationship with the Italian design house complements that with a local printing agency (a relationship that spans 30 years). As Montana has grown so has the printing agency, becoming bigger and more sophisticated to meet the demands of high-quality process and design standards. The same thing happened with Tait; as it expanded internationally, so did its domestic suppliers and subcontractors. In other words, there is a co-dependency between the internationalised firm and its domestic business networks.

Distribution networks

Firms have selected their business partners carefully to gain access to worldwide distribution networks. Chapter 1 described how Gallagher developed a network of dealers across Europe and in other global markets. The company chose those dealers carefully to build a long-term relationship and insisted they be fully committed to Gallagher's products. In the case of Svedala Barmac these business relationships have created both opportunities and constraints. Tidco was bought out in 1990 by a major competitor, Svedala Industri of Sweden. Since then Svedala Barmac has increased its turnover sixfold. Being in such a highly specialised industry, the company had to develop a close relationship with its dealers to acquire market knowledge and information on customer requirements. Before the takeover, it used to deal directly with the dealers, but now has to deal with the parent's sales subsidiaries in each country. On the one hand, Svedala Barmac is now able to enter new markets, such as South America and China, that it would possibly not have entered on its own, or at least not so quickly. On the other hand, it has come up against several constraints:

- The sales subsidiaries also sell a wide range (2500) of the European firm's other products and some local managers promote the other products of Svedala Industri of Sweden more than Svedala Barmac's products.
- In several countries Svedala Barmac's long-term relationships with its dealers were destroyed because established dealers were replaced with Svedala Industri of Sweden's sales subsidiaries.
- Svedala Barmac's own dealers often had more knowledge about the market and the Barmac machine than the parent company's sales subsidiaries.
- In the South African, American and Australian markets Svedala Barmac lost a large market share when the local dealer saw the opportunity to pirate Barmac products and become a competitor.

Svedala Barmac has had to maintain a critical balance between competition and co-operation with its European parent.

Montana is in partnership with a large firm, Seagram, which provides the distribution outlets and market knowledge for the whole of the North American market. Montana's screening process took about two years, during which it carefully examined Seagram's retail and distribution networks. Montana wanted a partner that fitted its cultural and philosophical stance, and Seagram has alliances with other top international companies producing a similar product. Seagram also has good distribution networks, and this relationship has enabled Montana to enter the North American market.

Market knowledge

For the firms in this study, dealers provide crucial knowledge about customers' requirements, and play a key role in the companies' success within particular markets. Astute choice of dealers and regular visits are therefore essential. Both Tait and Gallagher emphasise their attendance at trade fairs to find out about competition, market requirements and to meet potential distributors for their products. 'You can see who is the competition, who's awake and who's developing and who's sound asleep and not developing anything' (Bill Gallagher). Tait's internationalisation approach is to use distributors first to acquire knowledge about the local market and then to set up its own subsidiary. The care that the company takes in choosing those distributors is indicated by the Warren Rickard's comment:

> We examine the market in the country concerned and we have a good idea of where our products would fit. We're able to analyse what share of that market we should be getting given reasonable activity and we look for a company that can produce those sort of results. It has to be a company that is technically competent; they're responsible for servicing equipment after sales obviously and we support them. They have to be financially stable.

For example, Tait has an exclusive distributor for the Southern African region, through which it acquires its knowledge about the local market. Tait has an excellent relationship with this dealer and treats it as part of the firm. Despite careful choice, however, problems can still arise. When Tait entered the Australian market it used a buyers' consortium as its distributor. This effectively gave the company access to the whole of Australia. But, after a while, Tait became dissatisfied with its market share and set up a sales subsidiary in Australia to expand its position. The consortium eventually lost sales and disbanded.

In the early development of its dealer network Tidco had to choose dealers carefully and sometimes made mistakes, especially when dealers later became its competitors. This experience has had an impact on the firm when choosing new dealers: in Andi Lusty's words, 'it makes you nervous to appoint dealers'. Svedala Barmac tries to have a close relationship with its dealers:

I think there's a huge danger for us being remote from the customer. If you use a local dealer you have still got to be there all the time. You've still got to be visiting alongside. There's no replacement for having a local knowledge and a local representative; he can let you know what's going on but at the same time you've still got to be there.

Indeed Andi Lusty and Svedala Barmac's international business manager, Ian Rodger, have spent more than 100 days each year for the past fifteen years visiting their international dealers and keeping in touch with what is going on in the market. During these visits Svedala Barmac works closely with its dealers and sales subsidiaries to keep in touch with customer needs. It runs workshops and seminars internationally to educate its customers about the product and the servicing available, obtaining feedback about the product and ideas to improve its technology and performance.

Market expansion

When these firms expand their markets within a region they use the business network knowledge and experience acquired within one country to expand into neighbouring countries. Tait's internationalisation process illustrates this well. To enter the Chinese market Tait used its dealer network in Hong Kong. To enter the South American market it used its dealer networks in Miami together with contacts from South America established at an international trade fair. To enter other countries in Southern Africa it used its distributor there. Success for Tait with distributors in one market has meant expansion into the whole region.

But some countries' business networks are much more difficult to break into than others and this can constrain market expansion. Tait has been very successful in Britain and now has a large share of that market, aided by its good distribution network. But Tait's expansion within the American market has been constrained, initially because of lack of market knowledge, and latterly because Tait has not managed to break into the local network to gain this knowledge. The distribution system is different, the product specifications are different, and Tait's major competitor (Motorola) is based in the United States.

Fontes and Coombs (1997), in their study of new technology-based Portu-guese firms, found that it was easier for these firms to enter the South American market than the European market. Within Europe Portugal is seen as a comparatively low-technology, less advanced country, and Portuguese firms are disadvantaged by this stereotype. Our global New Zealand firms have had to overcome similar biases in their evolution.

Product development

Tait, Gallagher and Svedala Barmac customise their products to differentiate themselves from the global players who manufacture standardised products. Consequently these firms work closely with customers in product development. For Gallagher, product development was also shaped by the company's direct involvement in setting international product standards. The various international meetings for setting these standards enabled the company to gain:

- a network of contacts,
- the realisation that it had a product superior to its competitors, and
- the knowledge to expand into the European market.

Thus Gallagher was able to seize the opportunity of first mover advantage to expand internationally before its competitors 'woke up and improved their product'.

Chapter 3

Innovation and Technology Strategy

Knowledge was key, passion wasn't enough. (Peter Anderson, Montana)
[We] were the best in the world but didn't know it. (John Williams, PEC)
Only geniuses can develop things by themselves. (Peter Hubscher, Montana)

The competitive capabilities of many of the firms in the study were built partly on their leading edge technological products, superior design and the management of their innovation process. What is it about these firms, tucked away in New Zealand, that has allowed them to build regionally successful or, in many cases, globally successful products? They show attributes that are common to many New Zealand firms, such as being founded by a technological enthusiast with little market knowledge, yet they have managed to build upon their initial successes and embed their first-to-market strategy over several generations of products and managers.

BACKGROUND

To begin with, a useful description of technology:

> A good starting point to understanding Technology Strategy is to affirm that the core of the company is what it *knows* and what it can *do*, rather than the products that it has or the market it serves. Technology Strategy centres on this knowledge and these abilities. It consists of policies, plans and procedures for *acquiring* knowledge and ability, *managing* that knowledge and ability and *exploiting* them for profit. (Ford, 1988:85)

Technology strategy therefore is not just about the tangible aspects of product, process or service hardware, but about the knowledge that is embodied in the firm's output, together with the processes of learning and implementation associated with that knowledge. For a firm to acquire and use knowledge, it must contain prepared ground, or 'absorptive capacity' (Cohen and Levinthal, 1990), which is built up through prior experience and having related knowledge. In other words, a firm must have a certain level of existing technological knowledge in order to recognise the potential of new information or technology.

In recent years, the importance of collaboration to the generation of knowledge has been recognised. The network of an organisation's relationships, its 'social capital' (Nahapiet and Ghoshal, 1998), is often vital to its ability to learn and to exploit its capabilities. Thus a technology strategy also becomes a strategy of managing knowledge through collaboration, alliances and networks (Ford and Thomas, 1997). And networks need constant effort to maintain the trusting relationships upon which they are based.

Not all relationships are useful: it is not the quantity but the quality of the relationships in a firm's network that is critical (Walker, Kogut and Shan, 1997). The deepest and most productive relationships between firms take time to evolve. The term 'co-evolution' has been borrowed from biology to capture this gradual intertwining of firms' strategic trajectories (Eisenhardt and Galunic, 2000).

As described in Chapter 2, global leaders have based their transition into global markets on their world-leading innovation. Of this group, we selected Gallagher, Montana and Tait Electronics for in-depth study of their innovation and technology strategy. Regional leaders also used innovation in a supporting role. Here, Nuplex, Formway and PEC were selected for further analysis.

INNOVATION GENERATIONS: 'LEARNING FROM EACH VINTAGE'

So what do our firms reveal about technology strategy and innovation theory? Each has a unique and complex innovation process that has evolved from very simple beginnings, but there are some common themes. These firms have almost single-mindedly driven themselves through several 'vintages' of technology and product, rising to the challenge of exploring and learning through innovation.

The first vintage of products for many of the firms usually marked an exploratory phase. The products were not always particularly innovative but did satisfy a local demand and allowed the firm to establish itself. This period of product exploration can be viewed as equivalent to the sow and reap strategy seen in the firms' later global marketing efforts (see Chapter 2).[1] The choice of technology in the first generation of products often reflected the passion and experience of the original entrepreneur (see Chapter 6). Angus Tait, for example, had experience of radar technology during the war and brought this interest to his fledgling firm. Montana began with grape plantings by the immigrant Yukich family who had a 300-year-old winemaking tradition.

Initial products were often produced under licence or, when the firm was unable to obtain a licence, were copies of those available overseas. The firms learnt from the experience of producing this first vintage of products and particularly from adapting them to New Zealand conditions. Fred Holland describes Nuplex's experiences with licences:

> We started off [thinking that] anything that was invented overseas was much better than we had here obviously, but every now and again there seemed to be little things that weren't quite right with the technology so we've gradually learnt some expertise in slightly modifying it to suit New Zealand conditions. . . . So we take the basic [product] and adapt it and we got better and better at that.

This first period of development was often shrouded in the protected environment of New Zealand's 'Cold Duck' days, when importing technology was very expensive and the domestic market made do with little choice. Many firms ingeniously developed import substitutes to exploit the market opportunities provided by this protected environment. Angus Tait explains his version of Kiwi ingenuity and how his firm reacted as market conditions changed:

> We started in a protected market at home. We were dominant in the home market [but] all of a sudden everybody buying this equipment in New Zealand was going to be able to buy it from [elsewhere]. So we said to ourselves, we've got to put in place equipment which is world class, which is designed to world class standards. . . . [Now] we say we will produce a product which is comparable with what is being made elsewhere. . . . There is a better phrase than Kiwi ingenuity and that is simply that we are able to do more with less. . . . In another generation or so we won't be very much smarter than the rest of the world because the isolation that gave us the advantage of doing more with less is going away.

In some cases, a government department or large firm played the role of a demanding lead customer by commissioning the first generation product on a scale that far outstripped the firm's production capacity. Examples of organisations that played this role include the Post Office for Tait Electronics, Shell and Caltex for PEC, Telecom and several banks for Formway.

Satisfying this order stretched the capacity of the organisation but enabled it to learn and grow to a stage where it could consider developing the next vintage of products. High demand for the first products generated the cash flow that allowed the firms to experiment with new ideas and technologies. For example, the success of Formway's Ergo Workstation underpinned the effort invested in the creation of the Zaf chair. This sometimes risky but creative phase of dabbling with new ideas is regarded with satisfied irreverence as a fun, playful time in the evolution of the firms' products. Angus Tait described his firm's efforts to tame the transistor: 'I had guys playing with a few transistors and we were getting a feel for the technology and it was actually a terribly difficult technology'.

In developing their second vintage of products the firms displayed several different strategies. In some cases they recognised that the modifications made to a licensed product for the New Zealand environment had generated sufficient added value to warrant separation into a new product or the development of new proprietary products. From its first licence Nuplex took 20 years to develop the confidence to export its own product. Now, after a further 20 years, 50 per cent of its products are based on Nuplex's own technology. Fred Holland explains the transition:

> We got to the stage where we would chase around for the technology and we just couldn't get anywhere. Some people might have it and but weren't prepared to license it, so let's have a go at doing it ourselves. . . . So where we couldn't license technology we started to develop it.

A second approach to product development involved gaining experience with the new technologies by choosing an application that was seen as relatively low risk. PEC, for example, decided that introducing microprocessors into petrol pumps dedicated to taxi drivers would provide a lower risk trial market than extending to all petrol pump installations from the outset. The learning acquired from the trial technology application often led to a radically new product. PEC for example, chose access control as a medium for learning about reading magnetic swipe cards. Combined with their knowledge of microprocessors, PEC were able to develop their CARDAX commander system, launching a whole new business for them.

In early product vintages, particularly in New Zealand's protected days, being first to market allowed some of the firms to rely solely on good technology, particularly if it was available to the customer at lower cost. As Angus Tait puts it: 'We built a rather utilitarian little box, which . . . didn't look as pretty as their radio. It worked well and cost a little less. By and large we were [selling] them as fast as we could make them.'

But many of the firms quickly found that good technology was not enough. Low product cost did not sit well with the desired image of high-quality technology and performance. Nor was product quality assessed on the basis of performance alone, but also on good product design and packaging. The product needed to look at least as good as rival products to indicate that its functionality was also of the highest standard. For the customer, exceptional product design probably counter-balanced the perceived risk of buying from a small producer in a far-off country. John Williams of PEC recalled how he found out about the importance of industrial design in the 1970s: 'I learnt once and for all . . . if you've got a world-class product inside you've got to package it in a world-class box'.

KNOWLEDGE: ACQUIRING AND SHARING

As part of the learning from each vintage product development strategy, customer feedback was naturally very important but, as Bill Gallagher explains, care was taken in searching out the most valuable customer from which to learn:

> My definition of the customer is the end user. Of course my staff's definition of a customer is the person we sell to who is not the end user and you've got to be very careful. I know we're getting our product information through a pretty heavy filter. Filter being the dealer and the distributor. . . . We do get our R&D guys in and usually they are there a few days afterwards and they get out to dealers and get out on the farms.

In searching for learning opportunities firms were not self-conscious about how they learnt or from whom. For example, when assessing its petrol pump trials PEC was equally as interested in talking to petrol pump attendants as distribution managers. For these firms, this lack of status consciousness embodies New Zealand culture; New Zealanders are comfortable with most people, irrespective of rank and status.

For high-technology products, the key to market success often lies in sharing some of the firm's knowledge with customers. In the Netherlands, for example, Gallagher runs a very well subscribed hotline on New Zealand's unique practices in low-cost controlled grazing. The company is, in effect, selling its grazing knowledge as part of the fencing package. This knowledge is taken for granted in New Zealand, but the willingness to share it helps to differentiate the product in the marketplace. In the United States, Montana's strategy is to educate about New Zealand as much as it is to sell wine, as Peter Anderson explains:

> We must never assume that people will buy our wine just because we think it is good wine. . . . Our first task in selling wine into the USA was to inform our

potential customers about New Zealand. . . . We had to sell what New Zealand is and what the attributes and values of New Zealand are.

Thus another core part of the firms' product development strategies has been to educate the customer about the product and, in some cases, educate the customer's customer. Montana, for example, runs wine education courses for many of its distributors and also supports a wine college for the general public. This knowledge sharing has the added benefits of contributing to the development of strong, trusting relationships with distributors, and encouraging customer loyalty to the product and company.

There is no doubt that, for many of these firms, substantial investment in R&D is their major source of new knowledge and innovations. At first R&D investments were fairly small, and often in time rather than cost. Government funding of technology projects helped several of the firms lift both the quantity and quality of their performance. Bill Gallagher describes his father's early R&D efforts:

At that time R&D was really knife and fork on the kitchen table kind of stuff. . . . We never measured the amount of money. It was sort of every night and weekends. . . . What really took us from the kitchen table knife and fork was an R&D grant when we got paid 50 per cent of the increased expenditure on R&D. . . . That made sure you were doing it properly, not doing it on a shoestring, and that really made quite a difference.

Over several decades, these firms have built substantial R&D capabilities in a range of disciplines that represent a priceless reservoir of historical learning and tacit know-how. Ploughing profits back into the firm, at a rate of up to 10 per cent of revenue, was a given for many firms. The importance of investing in R&D was taken for granted; it was part of each firm's ethos.

The firms were very aware that to carry out effective R&D they must recruit and retain technically skilled people. This became even more important as the complexity of their product technology increased and as production methods were streamlined. Warren Rickard of Tait Electronics, a company that now employs over 160 engineers and software designers in the largest electronic R&D facility in Australasia, explains the transition:

In those days [30 years ago], a radio was designed by one person and it took hundreds of people to manufacture it. Nowadays, you almost need no one to manufacture it, but it takes hundreds of people to design it. . . . So right now we are looking at what we have to do to give highly creative engineering people and software people an environment . . . which enables them to be creative. . . . We have done a lot of work on a career path for technical people.

Whether the technical skills were obtained through education or experience, they were highly valued by the firms' managers. The self-confidence of these firms is evidenced by their willingness to recognise when and where they had skill deficiencies, and to rectify their knowledge gaps. In turn this emphasis on skills and learning is attractive and some firms found that potential recruits from all parts of the globe were targeting them.

> A simple philosophy, if you don't know, get somebody who does, or if you don't want to do it, get somebody who will do it for you. (Angus Tait)

> We are quite prepared to admit that we don't have all the answers, and we are even more prepared to go out and ask the questions of those that do have the answers. (Peter Anderson, Montana)

The skill base was not necessarily brought in-house. Skills were also accessed through specialists as contractors. Rick Wells explains how Formway approached the firm's skill needs:

> We've always worked on the premise that you don't want to be constrained in design and therefore the more technical knowledge you have the better and some of that knowledge can be built by what you do internally and other development is dependent on working with expert contractors.

In many cases, these experts became significant mentors for the organisations, providing guidance and vision about future technological directions. PEC's critical early move into solid-state electronics arose because of strong relationships developed with electronic engineering and strategy consultant Rob Wilkinson, and technical manager Kevin Low,[2] who predicted the potential of the microprocessor. Montana recognised its need to move into new techniques and developed technological partnerships with Champagne Deutz and Cordier, enabling the company to learn more about producing high-quality sparkling wine and bordeaux-style red wines respectively. As Montana's Peter Hubscher says, 'They are as much people relationships as they are technology relationships'.

Over time, knowledge sharing has become more evenly balanced as the New Zealand partners have discovered they have much highly desirable knowledge to offer. Peter Hubscher: 'We have technical discussion and it's not all the information flowing into New Zealand but a lot flowing out'.

By developing a range of these types of alliances, the firms find themselves part of a large knowledge-sharing network, usually global in scope. For many of the firms, these international networks are at the core of their efforts to maintain regional or global leadership (see Chapter 2). Often these networks have evolved as natural extensions of the professional contacts maintained by their specialist staff so that networks of 'peer' firms have been established. Nuplex has one of the most extensive examples of a peer network: the company has specialist knowledge-sharing alliances with its 'technology associates', resin companies around the world. And, as Fred Holland explains, this network has some added benefits:

> Our technology relationships are now really a networking set-up where we exchange ideas; we might even agree to work on a joint project together with somebody overseas. It's fairly broad reaching, because there are a lot of medium-size resin manufacturers around the world like us who feel a little exposed in today's economy, and they are appreciating the opportunity to be able to globalise without the investment.

Nuplex is very conscious of the value of its position in the network and how precarious such trusting knowledge-sharing relationships can be. This was evident during a phase in Nuplex's history when Monsanto had ownership interests in the company (see Chapter 6). Fred Holland explains: 'Monsanto [is] a multinational chemical company and we had a little bit of a problem with technology sources saying "but we haven't struck any [deal] with them".... and we had a bit of explaining to do'.

The international knowledge-sharing peer networks of these firms is usually a substitute for capable local partners.[3]

Peter Hubscher describes Montana's need for such relationships:

> Most people are only as good as the peer group that they work with.... To be successful you really need good peers. And in New Zealand Montana is more advanced than any of the other local companies.... So it really needed to look for peers who are more international to approach.

CO-EVOLUTION: GROWING THE LOCAL

Although these firms look offshore for their knowledge networks, their growth and success have often had a profound effect on local capability. Many of the firms have used local suppliers where they could, or where there was a tradition of doing so, and often these suppliers have lifted their game to deliver at the required capacity and quality. Several of the core firms intentionally guided the supplier to the level required, so that both firms grew in tandem. Montana, for example, has a 30-year supply relationship with Panprint, which has grown and become more sophisticated to meet Montana's demands for high-quality process and design standards.

> We consider our key suppliers as business partners in every sense. We share a lot of information with them and we expect them to do likewise. Sharing knowledge and expectations enhances the value of the partnership for we seek innovation and quality improvement in everything we do. (Peter Anderson, Montana)

Angus Tait is very aware of his firm's role in co-evolution in Christchurch:

> We don't build anything mechanically, it's all done outside. But when we first went out to the local tinsmith, he wasn't accustomed to building things to the type of tolerances that we were wanting. We had to grow his ability. We didn't have to persuade him but he bought the better machinery because he saw industry growing around it. . . . The growing of support services is something that you do both consciously and it happens subconsciously because other people are seeing the company grow and you're placing increasing demands, tighter and tighter demands, in terms of quality, time, availability, back-up and resources. We've got enough now to say, that's good, this guy is great, we'll buy another bit of plant to support them.

As the firms co-evolve, a clustering effect begins to occur. The core firms are likely to initiate this effect by supporting the co-evolution of several suppliers, who in turn will influence their own suppliers. When this is also extended to other related industry sectors, such as educational suppliers, an embryo cluster begins to develop. Angus Tait again:

> [Christchurch] has a lot of infrastructural people who produce plastic bits, people who cut and fold metal and they make metal shapes and they paint it and plate it. There's this infrastructure that has grown and this is all part of the business covering about 45 years.

PRODUCT BRANCHING: KNOWING THE LOCAL

Product modifications for the local market also produced another trait in these firms that later stood them in good stead on the internationalisation road. In order to fill the gaps left by other suppliers, many of the firms either supplied a greater breadth of products to the same customer or developed a large number of product variants for different customers. In some cases they used both strategies; this is discussed in more detail in Chapter 4. Thus products were customised for many different situations, which gave the companies a very wide product range. In tandem, the firms licensed or developed a range of related products in order to make optimum use of plant capacity that was employed mainly for small runs.

> We will make anything that is required for the markets we service and we will try to sell anything which can be made in the units we've got. . . . Every expansion of an existing business gave us a touch into a new area and we have branched from that. (Fred Holland, Nuplex)

It was the early competitive environment that supported this product branching. During the formative years of these firms' development, New Zealand's natural isolation from the global economy was made even more distant by an extensive regime of border tariffs and licensing. The result was an economy characterised by many small, isolated niche markets — a 'rugged landscape'.[4] The firms were supplying only small local markets that were hidden in the 'valleys' of the rugged landscape. Close and frequent contact with these few customers enabled the firms to develop expertise in a wide range of products (Gallagher, Nuplex, Montana) and in multiple technologies (PEC). Unrecognised by most at the time, this particular expertise profile stood the firms in good stead as they embarked on their global quests.

GOING GLOBAL: KNOWING WE WERE GOOD

For some of the firms, the fact that they had regional or world-leading technology was not immediately obvious. A few felt that their products, designed to be the best in New Zealand, might also be successful further afield, but others needed to be persuaded by international experts that their products were indeed highly valuable. Finding out the market value of their technology and products lifted the self-confidence of these firms, enabling them to take the going global leap.[5]

> We always believed that we could produce some outstanding wine and it has been an evolutionary process. The time came for us to believe what other people were telling us, which was that our wine was unique. It had a much stronger bouquet, was more flavoursome, fruity and aromatic, with fresh acidity. We came to appreciate that we really did have something different to overseas equivalents. (Peter Anderson, Montana)

In the early 1970s you wouldn't expect something you designed in New Zealand to be the best in the world. We were told by people who travelled around the world that it was far ahead of anything and we were lucky to learn at an early stage of our development. (John Williams, PEC)

[The Zaf chair was] well resolved and we were really fussy. But when we finally got there . . . it was a great product and as soon as one or two of our retailers saw this product they said this is a great product. Within a year we knew it was a great product. (Rick Wells, Formway)

What has often made these firms distinctive in their chosen international markets has been their ability to differentiate their products from their global competitors. Where the large players provided a standard product, the New Zealand firms carefully assessed what would distinguish their product and make it particularly valuable to their target customers. The great scope of their product and technology knowledge (built up during their rugged landscape days) has allowed these firms to recognise and then develop connections in technology and markets; these insights have been hidden from their more specialist competitors. Thanks to their flexible production facilities (see Chapter 4), these firms have carved out valuable market niches by producing small runs of highly customised product, earning them considerable loyalty from their international customers. Fred Holland describes how Nuplex survived in Asia once Asian manufacturers entered the markets:

We lost the ability to sell large volumes . . . because that was being made locally but we did pick on a few niche areas that the local manufacturers were not interested in making . . . they were a bit more complex so . . . we developed some specialist technology that needed niches.

Another consequence of being first to the international markets with these products was the ability to influence and, in some cases, set the standards surrounding the products. Considerable lobbying was needed to do this for several of the products, but the advantage of locking in (Arthur, 1996; Schilling, 1998) the new market niches to the New Zealand product specifications established the firms in their markets and, in some cases, enabled the firms to lock out many of their encroaching rivals. As we saw in Chapter 1, Tait Electronics, for example, played an important role in establishing the popular open standard for trunked radio known as MPT 1327, and supplied some of the first MPT 1327 systems. The firm was therefore able to exploit the advantages of being one of the first to market with a system that became the de facto world standard. Bill Gallagher describes some of these standard-lobbying efforts as part of a strategy to 'put tacks on the tracks of followers'.

CONSEQUENCES OF THE GUSHER

In some of these firms, the experience of large and often sudden international success (the gusher) had several consequences for their technology and innovation strategy. The gusher led to a concentration on the successful product in order to focus and grow, thus narrowing the firm's range of products. This focus set up a new technological platform for the firms, from which they then evolved a new range of product variants.

Some firms curtailed their innovation process in response to the sense of chaos caused by the gusher. Putting a hold on innovation helped them to maintain a sense of control over their destiny. These firms had to go with the flow of the gusher and concentrate on satisfying the demands it put on their resources and capabilities, often at the temporary expense of other core processes.

While courting the gusher might be perceived as a risky strategy, the alternative path, for some firms, was more risky. PEC made a conscious decision to phase its global aspirations, which constrained its rate of growth. Tidco (before it became Svedala Barmac) tried to diversify to spread the risk, but was unsuccessful.

CONCLUSION: LEVERAGING THE LOOPS

A recurring pattern is apparent in these firms' stories of innovation-based growth. There are significant links between actions taken by the firms and their subsequent management of the beneficial effects that followed. These fundamental action and reaction processes are represented as feedback loops in Figure 3.1. The firms have usually driven each of these loops and then exploited the consequences in a way that has propelled them to the next stage in their growth. In other words, the firms have grown by *leveraging* these feedback loops. There may be other loops that are not evident, but seven emerged from the histories examined here.

The first loop represents the development of their first vintage of product, which provides the platform for experimenting and developing the next product vintage. The second loop corresponds to the firms' efforts to acquire technological knowledge offshore, such as in licensing arrangements. The resulting links have often evolved into collaborative, technology-sharing peer relationships, in which knowledge flows in both directions.

Loop three embodies the relationships with customers from whom the firms can gain important knowledge, and with whom the firms can share knowledge.

FIGURE 3. 1

Technology evolution: leveraging the loops

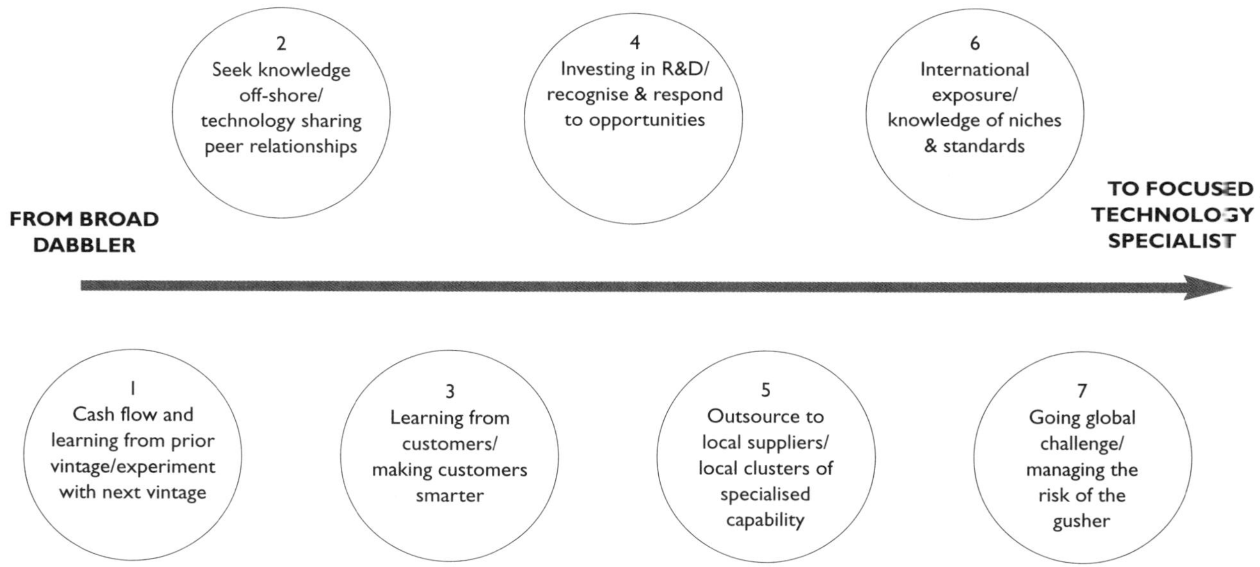

The fourth loop represents the greatly enhanced absorptive capacity that results from investing in R&D and building a significant technical skill base in the organisation. The co-evolution effect of firms on their suppliers is represented in the fifth loop. The longer-term effect of this loop, the development of clusters, could probably be mapped as an overlapping series of such feedback processes between linked outsourcing firms and their suppliers.

The final two loops are directly related to the going global process. In the sixth loop, the firm's first forays into the international marketplace confer knowledge of relevant standards and distinct market niches. The firm can then establish first-to-market benefits and both increase and cement its international exposure.

The last loop is probably the most critical to the firm's survival. Energy, concentration and persistence are needed to ride the chaos that results from the gusher.

The decision to go global drives the company to make the transition from a broad technology and product dabbler to a focused *technology specialist*. It is risky to resist the evolutionary imperatives of the gusher to focus and specialise.

A further overarching loop can also be discerned. For some firms, the process illustrated in Figure 3.1 appears to begin all over again as the firm embarks on a new dabbling phase with the next range of technologies or products, which may involve a major increase in investment and subsequent growth. Tait Electronics, for example, is agonising over whether to make the transition to digital technologies. It could be expected that surviving one gusher and consequent evolution into a technology specialist will have prepared and emboldened the firms as they seek the challenge of their next evolutionary phase.

Chapter 4

The Role of Operations Management in the Evolution of Competitive Capability

We wanted to get to the point where manufacturing was no longer a constraint on sales. (Steve Tucker, Gallagher Electronics Ltd)

This chapter examines how the management of operations contributes to the success of these exemplar firms. It is based on interviews with the CEOs, follow-up interviews with operations managers, plant tours and a manufacturing practices questionnaire in six of the firms. It also relies on the transcripts of the interviews with both the CEOs and operations managers, as well as the case studies of all the companies involved. In particular it discusses how the production interventions undertaken by the operations managers support the changes in the firms' manufacturing strategies brought on by their success and by the turbulence in their business environment.

COMPETING THROUGH OPERATIONS

Competitive capabilities in operations management

Researchers in the field of operations management describe six broad categories of competitive capabilities: cost, quality, flexibility, delivery, service and innovativeness. These have been expanded to make finer distinctions and are listed in Table 4.1 with definitions used by members of the Global Manufacturing

Futures Project. These are manufacturing-based capabilities and are not the only ways in which firms can win orders in the marketplace. Non-manufacturing sources of competitive advantage, such as reputation or design excellence, have also been discussed in Chapter 1.

An operations strategy is 'concerned with setting broad policies and plans for using the resources of the firm to support the firm's long-term competitive strategy. A firm's operations strategy is comprehensive through its integration with the business strategy' (Chase et al., 1998). In order to translate the business strategy into what it means for operations, a number of authors have suggested ways of categorising the decision areas. One of the best-known lists is that proposed by Hayes and Wheelwright (1984) and shown in Table 4.2. They suggest four 'structural' and four 'infrastructural' categories. The former are the 'bricks and mortar' decisions that have long-term impact, are difficult to reverse once in place and usually involve large amounts of capital investment. The latter are more 'tactical' in nature because they involve ongoing operating decisions and generally involve fewer 'highly visible capital investments' (*Ibid.*, p.31). The authors go on to say that 'it is critical that these decisions, made throughout the organization and at all levels, be consistent with the decisions made at other points in time and within other categories, and that their cumulative result over time is the desired manufacturing structure and infrastructure' (*Ibid.*, p. 32).

Andi Lusty at Svedala Barmac describes the changes in manufacturing strategy and competitive priorities following their change of ownership in the 1980s:

> Svedala changed its emphasis in the markets to selling the equipment through our own distribution outlets or our own houses as they call them. At that stage we became a manufacturing and support unit that became far more remote from our customers. That was a big change for us because our customers now were the houses rather than the end users. So to a degree the factory then became a manufacturing unit with not so much direct involvement in the ongoing customer contact/service. Our focus in the last couple of years has been cost reduction — how we can improve the product as a manufacturing unit. That's resulted in us investing heavily in robotics, and looking at changing how we make the product, and being very focused on how we can change and improve productivity and flexibility in the factory. Also, trying to do the same thing with less inventory, trying to do it a lot quicker and smarter with fewer people. So there's been a bit of a learning process.

The competitive capabilities of the firms studied

Terry Hill (1985) has attempted to combine competitive capabilities (Table 4.1) with manufacturing strategy decision categories (Table 4.2) and interface them with the firms' marketing strategy. He has coined the terms 'order winners' and

TABLE 4.1

Definitions of competitive capabilities in operations management

COST
Ability to profit in price competitive markets

FLEXIBILITY
Design flexibility: ability to make rapid design changes
Volume flexibility: ability to make rapid volume changes
Mix flexibility: ability to make rapid product mix changes
Breadth flexibility: ability to offer a broad product line

QUALITY
Conformance quality: ability to offer consistent quality with low defects
Performance quality: ability to provide high-performance products
Reliability: ability to provide reliable products
Durability: ability to provide durable products

DELIVERY
Speed: ability to provide fast deliveries
Dependability: ability to provide dependable deliveries

SERVICE
After-sales service: ability to provide effective after-sales service
Product support: ability to provide effective product support
Broad distribution: ability to make product easily available
Customisation: ability to customise products to individual customers' needs

INNOVATIVENESS
New product flexibility: ability to introduce new products quickly
Innovation: ability to generate sales quickly from new products

TABLE 4.2

Manufacturing strategy decision categories (Hayes and Wheelwright)

Structural
Capacity — amount, timing, type
Facilities — size, location, specialisation
Technology — equipment, automation, linkages
Vertical integration — direction, extent, balance

Infrastructural
Workforce — skill level, wage policies, employment security
Quality — defect prevention, monitoring, intervention
Production planning/materials control — sourcing policies, centralisation-
    decentralisation rules
Organisation — structure, control/reward systems, role of staff groups

'order qualifiers' to indicate the marketing priorities of the competitive capabilities. An order winner is a capability that enables the firm to differentiate itself or its product from the competitors' products. An order qualifier is a capability that the firm must have in order for its products to enter the market and be considered by purchasers. It must maintain this capability at all times or it risks losing its markets. Depending on the situation, any of the capabilities described in Table 4.1 may be an order winner or qualifier, but order winners and qualifiers may not always or exclusively be manufacturing capabilities. Hill suggests that once the firm has decided the order winners and qualifiers for a particular product/market combination, then this should guide the decisions made in the structural and infrastructural categories.

The most common order winner claimed by the firms studied is their innovativeness. This encompasses their product design capabilities, the harnessing of leading edge technologies and being first to market. Although conformance quality (low defect rates) is important, it is an order qualifier; these firms are more likely to be competing on performance quality (product features) and reliability (low probability of failure in service). Delivery responsiveness and cost-effectiveness at high mix and low volumes are other order winners common to most companies. Table 4.3 is an assessment of their order winners expressed in operations management terms.

Developing capabilities

There has been much debate in the field of operations management as to what capabilities should be developed, whether there is a preferred order and whether there are compatibilities or synergies between capabilities. Skinner (1969) argued that top management should set the operations strategy in terms of how the company intends to compete in the marketplace, that is, it recognises it has strengths and weaknesses and so can chose to differentiate itself in various ways. Put together, the decisions made in key areas result in a particular operating system with specific operating characteristics. So rather than conforming to or adopting an industry standard, the 'manufacturing task' was for managers to configure their system, through internally consistent choices, to reflect the priorities or trade-offs implicit in the firm's competitive situation and corporate strategy (Hayes and Pisano, 1994).

Hayes and Wheelwright (1984) developed Skinner's concept of trade-offs further when they stressed the need to prioritise the capabilities. They argue that any attempt to compete by offering superior performance on every capability (cost, quality, dependability, flexibility, service and innovativeness) is dangerous since the firm will probably end up second best on all of them. They believe that to overcome this risk, a manufacturing plant needs to prioritise its

TABLE 4.3

Operations management order winners

PEC	Innovation, leading technology and design skills, combination of mechanical and electronic technologies, first to market, cost-effective solutions on time
Tait Electronics	Innovation in transistor technology, cost competitive, design quality, customisation, delivery reliability
Formway	Innovative design, reliable delivery, customer service and breadth of product range, systems solutions, delivery speed (compared with overseas competitors)
Nuplex	Customised products, flexibility to do small order quantities, breadth of range, delivery reliability
Gallagher	Product features and quality, service and distribution, delivery speed, cost competitive, product range to provide customer solutions
Criterion	Design skills, precision manufacturing, quality, delivery speed and dependability
Svedala Barmac	Cost competitive, delivery dependability, product design and features, customer service
Kiwi Dairies	Low-cost manufacturing, logistics, quality
Montana	Product quality, service, distribution and innovation

competitive dimensions to suit the company's business strategy. More recently, the static nature of the trade-off model has been criticised. Hayes and Pisano (1994) suggest that a company still needs to differentiate itself from its competitors on the basis of something valuable to the customer. The way to do so is to harness the benefits of various improvement programmes, such as JIT (just-in-time) or TQM (total quality management), 'in the service of a broader manufacturing strategy that emphasizes the selection and growth of unique operating capabilities' (*Ibid.*, p. 40).

Wheelwright (1981) and Nakane (1986) first suggested the idea that capabilities could be compatible or supportive rather than being traded off against each other. Wheelwright noted that Japanese manufacturers considered quality improvement as a means and cost reduction as an end, and not trade-offs as Skinner had suggested. Nakane suggested that Japanese manufacturers who sought to offer flexibility must first address quality, dependability and then cost improvement, each depending on the next. Ferdows and De Meyer (1990) likened their cumulative model to a sand cone. Their proposed sequence of capability development was quality, dependability, speed (of product development) and cost efficiency. They also believed that progress on the development of each capability should never cease: once efforts have begun on quality, and some improvements have been obtained, work can then start on developing dependability while work continues on quality. So as each stage begins, efforts on the lower capabilities should continue. This broadens the base while capabilities are added. Baden-Fuller and Stopford (1994) also claim to have observed a cumulative development of capabilities where the sequence varies with the firm. For Ferdows and De Meyer, trade-offs could still exist but they believe that the nature of trade-off relationships is contingent upon the approach. For example, cost and quality are traded off against each other if the attention is put on the cost; however, they both improve if attention is put on quality.

In summary, the essence of the trade-off model is that there is no one way to compete. However, the sand cone model says, to some extent, there is one best way to achieve a multiple set of manufacturing capabilities. Ferdows and De Meyer (1990:175) claim that while 'different business strategies may call for different capabilities from the manufacturing function, there is still a similarity of *approach* among those who build lasting and stable capabilities'. The companies in our study do not seem to agree with either of these models. 'I think we've got to do it all exceptionally well or we don't get a living,' said Michael Chick at Tait when asked about priorities among their capabilities. Richard Allan at Nuplex described the range of capabilities that they need and how they have developed:

> So recognising the needs of the market was our particular strength and we still think it is and then we've either adapted our service-related requirements to feed the market or the technology related requirement. Going back to the bad old days, service was just something the market got, good, bad or indifferent and that was sort of a New Zealand trait. Our main strength was in providing the technology that was acceptable at the market price. These days of course things have changed and your service is paramount and technology is just one part of the service regime. I try and instil in the field people that our vision is to be the supplier of first choice to New Zealand industry. And how you do that is many things but if you don't give customers a reason to go somewhere else they won't and it's that simple. That's been a core strength from the early days right through to today.

There is much evidence to confirm that these firms have had to push ahead on all capabilities concurrently. In a later section, actual performance figures show what has been achieved (see p.72–83).

THE DRIVE TOWARDS WORLD-CLASS MANUFACTURING

At some stage in their history, these firms launched themselves onto a high growth trajectory that put their operating systems under tremendous pressure and forced them to reshape existing capabilities or develop new ones. Interviews and analysis of these firms showed a number of evolutionary patterns. Chapter 2 considered the two most common patterns, going global and the gusher, and used these to explore the configuration-threatening change that resulted from the natural evolution of the firm's own competitive capabilities.

When these changes hit these companies, it soon became apparent that the manufacturing operations could not meet the demands put on them. Gallagher, Tait and Formway, for example, found that the increased orders lowered delivery performance and caused large increases in inventory, shop floors bogged down under work-in-process (WIP) and a loss of production due to information overload. Steve Tucker of Gallagher comments:

> The evolution of the company from the late 1980s was Bill [Gallagher] saw that our information technology wasn't keeping up with the requirements of manufacturing and he looked at the MRP plus the Oliver Wight [one of the inventors of the MRP — materials, research, planning — approach] philosophy. We sort of adopted at that stage an attempt to go for the world-class manufacturing, and I suppose we got, by Oliver Wight's standards, a sort of class B manufacturing. Not in any formal sort of measurement but that's where we felt we were at. But I think [that] through to the 1990s we never really put the emphasis on manufacturing to get it to world-class capability. I mean Gallagher has got a complete product range and a good strong margin and . . . while we were trying to be a low-cost manufacturer [emphasis on world-class manufacturing] wasn't a strategy in its own right.

Initial attempts at improving manufacturing concentrated on dealing with operational complexity and attempting to solve problems through computer packages such as MRP, or kanban systems (Formway). This was the trigger for the drive towards world-class manufacturing.

When Hayes and Wheelwright developed the term 'world-class manufacturing' in 1984, they reckoned that relatively few manufacturing companies in the United States considered their manufacturing operations as a source of competitive advantage. For these authors, a world-class manufacturer was one that was better than almost every other company in the industry in at least one important aspect. In a view that echoes the resource-based view of the firm (see Chapter 1), they also noted that the 'organizational and technological skills needed to produce products better than your competitors are extraordinarily difficult to duplicate, and therefore constitute one of the soundest bases for achieving a sustainable advantage' (Hayes, Wheelwright and Clark, 1988: 20).

World-class manufacturing practices

This section compares the practices at the firms in our study with the common patterns of practices found by Hayes and Wheelwright in their 1984 American study. Additional practices that have been added by other researchers, such as process focus and use of demand-pull or JIT practices for material flow through the value chain, are also included (Voss, 1995; Flynn et al., 1999; Dean and Bowen, 1994).

Dimension	*Practices*
Workforce skills and capabilities	• extensive training and retraining beyond entry level, focusing on skills, work habits and motivation
	• cooperative arrangements with vocational technical institutes
	• apprenticeship programmes
	• internal training institutes

Typically, all the firms in this study seek out highly skilled people, people with integrity, people who are likely to be good team players, people who are dedicated, focused and interested in opportunities and challenge. They follow this with extensive training and multiskilling and often link reward systems in part to knowledge and skills developed. Criterion has developed close links with the Manukau Institute of Technology for vocational skills training. Others have similar arrangements with tertiary institutions to provide work experience and projects. This enables them to pursue the best graduates. Such is the reputation of some of these companies that they readily attract talent from overseas. People who want to work with the best in the world will seek them out.

> We don't have a large development laboratory, but our people are very skilled. Our flexible manufacturing operation also allows us to put our new technology into practice very quickly. (Geoff Swailes, Nuplex)

> We focused on staff training and we're really recognising . . . the electronics and plastics industry training organisations and we're really encouraging all our staff to work their way through the PITO [Plastics Industry Training Organisation] credits and so forth and we were the first ones to have a national certificate in

electronics for manufacturing. We were the pilot group for the ETITO [Electrical Trades Industry Training Organisation] training which is I think a spin off from PITO. So we encourage that [and] we were the first. (Steve Tucker, Gallagher)

Dimension	Practices
Management technical competence	• ensure a significant number of managers have engineering or technical degrees • train potential managers, early in their careers, in a variety of technologies important to the firm • rotate managers through various functions to broaden their experience

The managers at both senior and middle levels in the firms studied are highly qualified with a strong technical background, particularly engineers and chemists. The firms tend to promote from within and develop these managers by giving them a broad understanding of the business through a series of career moves within the company. In many cases the founders of these firms are people who started out with a fascination for tinkering with machinery and equipment. This is reflected in the people they have employed and developed as managers — people who are technologists at heart and have maintained that passion for technology.

I deal with many matters that do not fit neatly into line managers' functions. [In] my 27 years here [I have] developed the ability to adapt and do whatever task is needed to be done for the company. (Geoff Swailes, Nuplex)

Dimension	Practices
Competing through quality	• seek to align products and processes to meet needs that are important to customers • long-term commitment to quality • strong attention to product design • involvement of all functions in product design and quality improvement

The firms in our study all consider that they gain a competitive advantage through the quality of their products. They see themselves, however, competing not on conformance quality, i.e. low defect rates, but, more importantly, on product features or attributes and performance. Most have achieved ISO9001 certification and/or some industry specific standard.

Dimension	Practices
Workforce participation	• going beyond simply putting employees in teams
	• develop a culture of trust between workers in various departments and between workers and management
	• routine, close contact between management and workers
	• develop participation policies to ensure 'we're all in this together'

The development of workforce assets has been one of the most striking features of the companies studied. The careful selection, extensive training and presence of highly visible managers contribute to a positive response to change initiatives. Some companies have all employees on individual contracts; others have a unionised workforce and no interest in individual contracts. Under either system, there are high levels of workforce participation in improvement activities, as Steve Tucker at Gallagher indicates:

> And [the supervisors] have even driven a whole lot of things such as within plastics, they've come up with what they call the skills matrix ... which is all the skills that we're trying to get towards for all the staff members. And for each one of those skills they've broken down like a procedure on how you measure that skill, what the skill is and how you can practise that. Now staff can actually work through the skills matrix and we put it up on the board with who's where with regard to skill level. Yeah, the staff has really reacted to it well and they're driving towards improving their skill levels because they're being judged against others and they see it as a personal challenge. That's one thing they spun out of a leadership training that we put the staff through. So it is the people. At the end of the day as you work [up] through management you get more and more demands on you and you can't do it all yourself and people will not work for you if they don't respect you, it's as simple as that. So a lot of our success is driven by open, honest, transparent communication and respect for people that we work for. You don't last long around here if people don't respect you.

Dimension	Practices
Rebuilding manufacturing engineering	• bolster ability to perform sophisticated maintenance, process upgrades and continuous improvement of existing equipment.
	• build or invest in proprietary equipment

All the firms studied have nurtured a significant engineering capability from the start. Some have world-class reputations for their precision die-making, and sometimes contract out their expertise in this area. All have invested in sophisticated CAD to accelerate design and development times and improve ease of manufacture. At Nuplex Fred Holland talked about leveraging this practice off their base of technical competency. But these firms are skilled not only at building some of their own equipment, but also at improving the performance of purchased equipment, as Andi Lusty of Svedala Barmac notes:

> We bought a robot that was already being used by one of the factories in Sweden and these guys said, 'Well, if you buy this type of robot I can send a couple of technicians out to help you if you need it.' We bought it and didn't need them. Our biggest problem was realising how different our procedures needed to be, how different the putting the things together needs to be. We actually make rotors in the reverse order to how we used to make them [because of] how the robot works in terms of finding a position and moving. For instance, we used to hard face the product last, to build the rotor then hard face it at the end. Now we hard face it at the beginning of the process. The reason is that the whole thing warps when it gets hard faced and then the robot can't find the same spot because the warping isn't consistent. We realised that the tolerances of putting it together were far more important to the robot. We had to be within half a mil[limetre] for the robot to be in the same place every time. We used to have something like 4- or 5-mil[limetre] tolerance in our jigs for making rotors. We also made them so badly that we used to machine them to make sure that they were round and flat so now we don't even have to do that. Our jigging is now much more accurate. We hard face it first and build it backwards.

Dimension	Practices
Incremental improvement approaches	• continuous improvement in small increments
	• continually adapt to changes in customer needs

These companies have had to improve their operations continually but it has not always been in small increments. The decision to pursue offshore markets has certainly been a common reason for having smarter operations. Formway and Criterion were under pressure on delivery performance in their early stages. Criterion was awarded a model of a DC10 by one of their American customers in recognition of their willingness to use airfreight to meet delivery schedules. The reforms of the 1980s were also a trigger to action. Tait and Gallagher found themselves under considerable cost pressure during this period and introduced MRP systems and are now implementing ERP systems. Svedala Barmac has so changed the way it makes its rotors so that it is cheaper for customers to replace rather than repair a worn part. Gallagher have also developed a more formal operations strategy since they found their performance slipping in recent years.

> So Rob Booth [deputy CEO] was the catalyst along with Bill. About two and a half years ago [they were] looking at our manufacturing and saying, yeah okay we make good margin etc. but hey, you know things are slipping in manufacturing and we're missing a few orders. And we've got this continual cyclical approach every year where we're gearing production up and down. The focus wasn't on manufacturing in its own right. So Rob kicked off an initiative, about two years ago, to come up with a separate operations strategy that supported our desire to be a number of things: flexible, customer responsive, lowest cost, and quality. I suppose [they] were the four key drivers that we wanted to instill in our manufacturing environment. So we embarked on at that stage what was a formal change process within manufacturing to improve the way we address all of those factors but it started small and just sort of escalated on itself. There wasn't a grand plan at the start that had a project plan mapped out for the next few years. It was just a recognition that these four, we weren't world class in, let's get the ball rolling and let's start addressing them. (Steve Tucker, Gallagher)

Both Tait and Gallagher have set up in-house excellence programmes that work on improvement issues. All the study companies set themselves challenging improvement goals, particularly in areas like lead time reduction, quality and operating with lower WIP inventory.

> On the operations side it would be the cycle time from receipt of an order, ideally placing an order on us by our CSO [central sales office] through to us delivering the products through to them. Our target for this year is to get one week in terms of receipt of an order to us dispatching. That's our target. Our target for 2001/2002 is to get one week for it to be in their offices. That means we can only probably do it in four days and we can do it at best in four days here and the thing is it's give about three days on the frame. So we're trying to get to a week this year. That's our target, get down to a week this year. (Michael Chick, Tait)

Dimension	Practices
Process focus	• processes designed to be foolproof
	• extensive use of statistical techniques to reduce variance in processes
	• standardised process instructions given to personnel
	• information on quality and productivity is readily available to employees

All companies are reorienting their operations towards a greater focus on process. They seek to improve the physical flow of materials and products, as well as the flow of and access to information. Tait has probably adopted a more formal system of process identification than most of the others, as Michael Chick explains:

[Our] business systems [group] is going to be the glue for trying to ensure that we are process oriented. So what we've identified under our 'Paragon' process and under our Tait management system [are] four critical areas: management support, which is the least important, product generation, order fulfilment and customer relations. Under the Tait management system we have corporate owners for each of these processes and then we have owners within mobile radio [division] for each of these processes. So management support, product generation, order fulfilment and customer relations: everything we do needs to fit into one of those. We then have the people who are responsible within mobile radio for the process development within each of these sectors. So on our computer system we have the process we follow and then the engineers are working to the worksheets and the mechanical work to worksheets as a subset of them. So process developments [take place] under these guys within mobile radio and we have quality and customer interfacing and we have information systems and technologies [linking in].

Dimension	Practices
Demand-pull flow systems and JIT practices	• shop floor layout means machines and processes are in close proximity to one another
	• direct labour can stop production for quality problems
	• use a (kanban) pull system to control production
	• suppliers are certified or qualified for quality
	• have long-term arrangements with suppliers
	• vendors supply on a just-in-time basis

These firms are not averse to reorganising the physical layout to improve the flow of materials. Kanban systems are in place at Formway (particularly chair production), Gallagher and Tait. All have long-term arrangements with suppliers; call-off contracts, agreed volume contracts and consignment stocks are common. These enable the firms to operate just-in-time deliveries with local suppliers.

Where materials and components have to come from overseas, such arrangements are not possible and higher stock levels have to be held. At Nuplex, for example:

> Raw materials could be three months' [lead time] and the big stuff, like [a special] monomer, the boat comes every three months so you've got to predict how much you want off that boat because you haven't got another chance until two or three months time. [The] number of raw materials we'd use would be over a thousand just in the chemical division and each one could be an ingredient into a particular recipe. (Geoff Swailes, Nuplex)

PATTERNS OF EVOLUTION AND THE OPERATIONS MANAGEMENT RESPONSE

As discussed in Chapter 2, one of the key strategy decisions has been to focus on a market niche, narrowly but deeply (Simon, 1996), and to seek market dominance. In many cases these firms started out with a wide product range but now offer a very wide product mix, in other words a large number of variants within a narrow product range. For some, the need to operate in global markets has meant the added complexity of having to match specific country standards or requirements. As a result most firms have developed the manufacturing capability to offer high degrees of product customisation on short delivery times, with high levels of delivery dependability and product quality. Figure 4.1 gives a summary map of the impact of the decision to internationalise and focus on a niche market, and this section explains this diagram by describing the nature and impact of the production interventions that have been made in order to restore the fit between operations and the business environment.

Responsiveness and flexibility
The decision to expand into international markets and focus on a narrow market niche flowed from the realisation that these firms had leading edge products. The depth of their market niche and subsequent broad product mix of up to 1000 or more end products (variants) has required production interventions to deal with short runs overlaid by seasonal and cyclical variability. In order to achieve better customer responsiveness and to control costs, one of the most important interventions has been the reduction of manufacturing lead times. This has meant improving operational and labour flexibility and the physical flow system.

> A great deal of our time has been spent on focusing on our production cycle times. By understanding the processes our efforts have been to drive those times

down. After gains from upgrading our plant and equipment we have looked at other solutions. For instance, sourcing technology from overseas, the use of a catalyst in a range of our products reduced cycle times by almost half. (Peter Sherwood, Nuplex)

Flexibility is seen as increasingly important in operations. New Zealand managers have often cited the achievement of greater flexibility as something that has improved their firm's performance in response to the heightened

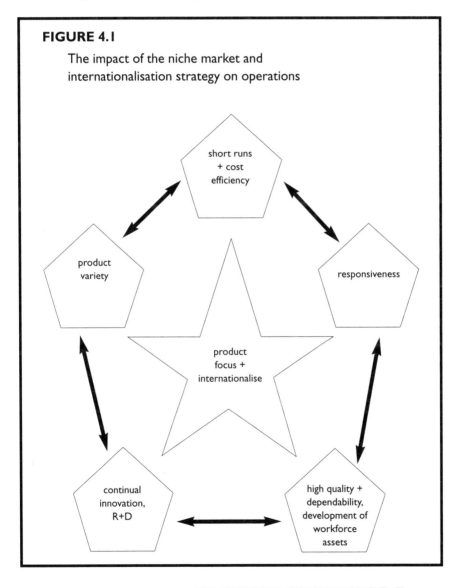

FIGURE 4.1

The impact of the niche market and internationalisation strategy on operations competition of recent years (Corbett, 1996). It remains, nevertheless, a vague concept and often difficult to measure. Flexibility is defined as the ability to change the operation or initiate or adapt to change with little effort, time or cost penalty (Upton, 1995; Slack et al., 1995). Definitions of different types of flexibility were given in Table 4.1.

In his *Harvard Business Review* article, Upton (1995) proposes some different dimensions of flexibility and notes the importance of managers choosing the right type of flexibility to compete on, or investing in suitable facilities:

- range — a more flexible plant can produce a wider range of products;
- uniformity — a more flexible plant achieves the same level of performance across the product range;
- mobility — a more flexible plant can change more quickly from one product to another within the range.

Having the right kinds of flexibility gives the firm both internal and external competitive advantages. Internally, flexibility speeds up responsiveness, saves time and improves dependability. Externally, customers see that the firm can respond quickly to an order, alter the delivery time to suit and offer a broad product range. Labour flexibility is an important contributor to firm flexibility. By this is meant multiskilling and the ability of the operators to rotate jobs through cross-training. We now consider how our sample firms have used these concepts and frameworks to respond to their dynamic business environment. Figure 4.1 shows the links between the production interventions made in these firms in order to reduce manufacturing lead time and better manage operations.

Technical control of production
Technical control of production requires two things: engineering control of plant and equipment, and management of material flow. Some would say that the latter requires the former (Williams et al., 1994). Firms in our study strive for engineering control through work on set-up times, changeovers and regular investment in more sophisticated technology. Andi Lusty of Svedala Barmac:

> I think some of that has been the fact that robotics is becoming much cheaper and much easier to programme. Whereas before you used to have to be making thousands of the same things and have them working all year at the same thing, now [batches of] tens and twenties are viable and pretty soon I think it's going to be threes and fours are viable. A robotic station used to be over a million bucks and now you can put one whole thing together for about $130,000–$140,000 and we're looking at one at the moment which is down

about $60,000 and these things will run 24 hours a day without sick breaks. So that's a big, big change for us.

The management of material flows has been achieved through attention to lot sizes, changing transfer batch sizes, changes in plant layouts, reducing WIP inventories and improving control of planning and scheduling. In some cases this has meant the use of MRP packages and, in other cases, kanban-driven JIT systems. Recently the limitations of MRP packages have become apparent and some companies have moved to ERP packages, and taken advantage of the planning, scheduling and optimising modules available with these software systems. Each intervention requires a detailed knowledge of the firm's processes and effective remedial action.

> We still have work centres where things are built at each various stage of production. But we have multiskilled teams and we shift them around and we basically make one product, get it rolling down the production lines and start another one behind it and try not to integrate a whole lot of various products you can build at once. . . . We've driven down a lot of our batch sizes and looked at them and said, 'Well hey, we were making 500 here because it was most efficient and only making 20 in the next work centre and putting the 480 in stock. Why do we do that? And then let's try and align the minimums to be consistent through the production process.' It's not always practical. There are still examples, like in plastic injection moulding, where we might make a run of 1000 but only use 200. It's just physically not economical to change the die. But we've tried as hard as we can to align all the minimums. We've reduced our work in progress. We had basically about 8000 units in work in progress in the factory and now we've only about 800 units at any one point of time. (Steve Tucker, Gallagher)

The investment of time in understanding the process details and identifying the problems is significant. This, however, is overshadowed by the investment needed in executing the solution. As these firms discovered, in order to make a significant improvement in overall factory material flow, and hence reduce manufacturing lead times, managers and operators must make hundreds of focused interventions and problem-solving investigations. They have used Pareto-type analysis — 80 per cent of the orders come from 20 per cent of the customers — to separate the 'vital few from the trivial many' and there have been some 'low-hanging fruit to be picked'. Most striking, though, is their sustained commitment to learning about their processes and continuous improvement. Table 4.4 shows the improvement in the last two years by some of the companies visited.

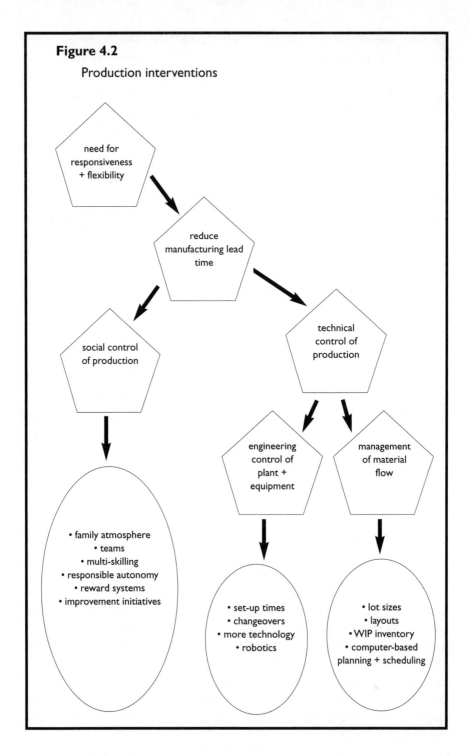

Figure 4.2

Production interventions

need for responsiveness + flexibility

reduce manufacturing lead time

social control of production

technical control of production

engineering control of plant + equipment

management of material flow

• family atmosphere
• teams
• multi-skilling
• responsible autonomy
• reward systems
• improvement initiatives

• set-up times
• changeovers
• more technology
• robotics

• lot sizes
• layouts
• WIP inventory
• computer-based planning + scheduling

TABLE 4.4

Percentage improvement in responsiveness over last two years

	Gallagher	Tait	Formway	Nuplex	Svedala Barmac
Product design time	40%	30%	20%	0%	20%
Manufacturing lead time	75%	50%	10%	10%	10%
Delivery speed	50%	15%	10%	5%	0%

Both Gallagher and Svedala Barmac can respond in five days from order to shipment if required. Nuplex can achieve one day. Tait has reduced its manufacturing lead time from 20 days to ten over the last two years and is now working on reducing it to four. Simultaneously, they have all improved on-time delivery performance from the 80–90 per cent range to the 95–99.5 per cent range.

Quality
One major benefit of reducing manufacturing throughput time has been, in the words of Steve Tucker, operations manager at Gallagher, 'our ability to detect quality problems in real time'. As a result their reject percentage during processing has fallen to 0.3 per cent and is even lower at final inspection.

> We also found a big flaw in this old philosophy of work centre management and [having] work centres, [which] was that quality issues weren't identified in real time because they were a week before they got to the next work centre. In fact it's not even true in that sense because it was unlikely that that week's production they were using was for the next week's production in the next work centre. It was probably going to put in stock to be pulled off in one month or two months' time. Whereas now we make one, well that's probably a bit of an exaggeration but we might make ten in one work centre and then they're passed on straight away to the next work centre. And while they're building the other 90 this work centre says, 'Well, hang on I've done the quality test and there's these scratches on the plastic that I don't like or whatever.' So we're picking up quality issues real time through this philosophy.

All acknowledged that they seek continuous improvement in quality performance.

We are also trying to characterise our manufacturing processes in terms of sigma or failure rates in terms of what we expect to get out of the process — a lot of this is obviously evolving. On future projects for instance we would say to the project manager we want a failure rate, we're prepared to accept a failure rate of 2 per cent, we want 98 per cent, we want it to take ten minutes to make, the reject rate has to be whatever this is. So we're trying to specify in reproducibility or in sigma characteristics what our requirements are in terms of development of the product. Of the manufacturing people we're asking them to specify what the manufacturing characteristics of our SMT [surface mount technology] machines are such that we can use those in our development to predict what is the performance we would achieve in a quality sense, in a time sense, in a cost sense. (Michael Chick, Tait)

Product innovation and development
Following their world-beating innovation, the challenge for these companies has been to maintain their innovative advantage and fend off or outmanoeuvre the competition. They spend considerable amounts on R&D, typically 10 per cent of sales per year, and consider this vital for their ongoing success. Most have made substantial investments in AutoCAD-type software and are into three-dimensional solid modeling. Many have developed extensive in-house capability in precision tooling work and product and process engineering. They believe this enables them to keep tighter control on output quality. Gallagher, for example, has become more vertically integrated because increasing volumes meant bringing back some outsourced items; this gave them better control of quality and improved plant utilisation.

In their new product developments these firms display the phenomenon of 'ephemeralisation'— developing products that are progressively accomplishing more and more functions with fewer and fewer materials and effort. The futurist Buckminster Fuller first used the term ephemeralisation in 1922, and defined it as 'the principle of doing ever more with ever less weight, time and energy per each given level of functional performance' (Fuller, 1985:792). He gives many examples of ephemeralisation. In 1520 it took Magellan two years to sail around the planet in a wooden sailing ship. Three hundred and fifty years later it took a steel steamship two months to do the same. Seventy-five years later a plane, made of metal alloys, took two weeks to fly around the planet. Thirty-five years later a space capsule, made of exotic metals, takes one hour to circle the planet. The materials used continually get lighter and stronger and more versatile. For a more current example the Internet comes readily to mind. It represents a degree of ephemeralisation that allows one individual to influence or interact with hundreds, thousands or even millions of people, with negligible resource use.

The firms in this study find they must either become more sophisticated in their use of materials (and hence use smaller quantities) or increase the performance of the products for a given quantity of material. As one manager at Criterion said, 'How much technology can you get in a piece of furniture?' Criterion's designs started out with square edges (one-dimensional machining), then they went to rounded edges (two-dimensional machining) and their latest products include desktops with rounded edges on curves (three-dimensional machining).

Some of these companies noted another aspect of this trend, namely that their rate of ephemeralisation is increasing. The development of new products is accelerating and product design times have to be shorter. A result is more emphasis on formalising new product introduction processes. This involves both the structures of the organisation and the tools used. Tait, for example, as Michael Chick explains, has modelled its product development process on Hewlett-Packard's structure and introduced much tighter timeframes on development stages.

> We're not historically a learning organisation. We're historically learning individuals. What we're trying to do is now try and get the organisation to be a learning organisation. So we want more processes in place which are key to our operation so that we can map those processes, improve those processes. . . . We have actually documented those processes and that's [where] we're trying to make a significant step up because in the past it was all in people's heads. What we're trying to do is learn from our mistakes on that. There are great people here but if the people were not here there would be significant problems. So we're trying to put a lot more into the process [of understanding] what we're doing.

The use of design for ability to manufacture easily and assembly techniques receives far greater attention in these companies than in the typical New Zealand manufacturer (Corbett, 1996, 1998). An important aim of the design process at Gallagher, Tait, Svedala Barmac and PEC has been to maximise the commonality of parts and assemblies so that market customisation occurs at the latest possible stage of the process.

Management of material flow
Process control and inventory management systems vary somewhat. Those firms with more stable demand patterns and repetitive operations, such as Formway, tend to favour internal and external kanban systems for some product lines and a requirement philosophy for others. Gallagher and Tait have distributors or selling offices in over 50 countries worldwide. They must ensure that orders placed at

various stages in their supply chain do not create excessive variability in factory demand. Svedala Barmac, Gallagher and Tait are aiming to increase their ability to forecast sales by improving feedback systems from offshore distributors and warehouses. This will lead to decreased variability in factory demand and therefore, they hope, greater ability to cope with remaining fluctuations.

> [We're] usually making for stock. We try and get as much forward notice of machines that are likely to be ordered. So we get something from marketing, which says these are all the projects we're working on and they put a percentage in, a percentage of likelihood to order. If it gets up to 90 per cent we put it on the shipping schedule as a possible for two or three months' time. The guys out here make everything that's on order and then start looking at what's the next most likely to sell. That's the order in which they make things. They're standard products so there's no real amount of tailoring that particular product to a particular order until it gets to the stage where it might need a different motor size or it might have a different starter but the main product is pretty much standard. (Andi Lusty, Svedala Barmac)

Tait aims to improve an internal kanban system to help with this. Gallagher, which has a greater seasonal demand factor, is investing in finite capacity scheduling software to be able to track what orders would be 'available to promise'.

An issue for many of the companies is the lead times for the supply of some raw materials and components from overseas. These have improved over the

TABLE 4.5

Current distribution of inventory value and percentage of parts fabricated in-house

	Purchased material and parts	Work-in-process	Finished goods	% of parts and components fabricated within plant
Gallagher	53%	10%	37%	30%
Nuplex	30%	Negligible	70%	85%
Svedala Barmac	15%	10%	75%	75%
Formway	26%	59%	15%	75%
Criterion	12%	6%	82%	70%

years as company success has increased volumes purchased, but their buyer power is still not strong. These factors have implications for where stocks are held. Also, larger stock levels have to be maintained for a raw material that arrives by ship only once a month. Results have been impressive over the last few years in some companies for which there is data: at Gallagher WIP has fallen by a factor of ten in terms of units, and several companies have reduced their total stock levels by 30–50 per cent. Table 4.5 shows the distribution of inventory value and percentage of parts fabricated in-house.

New technology systems within manufacturing and the firm
Information technology has become an important part of the manufacturing strategy for some of these firms, especially with investments in CAD and the recent development of appropriate tools and packages that fit onto ERP systems. These help to deal with complexity and variety issues. A number of companies are starting to replace MRP systems because the limitations of this package have become more obvious in recent years. When it was first adopted by, say, Gallagher in the late 1980s it proved immensely valuable in dealing with excessive inventory. The new systems are linking plants with their offshore distributors and stock points to provide faster feedback on sales, thereby improving production planning and forecasting. There has been a steady investment in higher levels of factory automation. Robotic systems, where they exist, tend to be of a simple design aimed at improved material handling and labour savings. The high-mix, low-volume type of manufacturing characteristic of these companies makes it hard to justify upgrading to state-of-the-art machines, although, as Svedala Barmac has found, the cost of suitable robotic systems is falling quickly.

Table 4.6 summarises this section by detailing the extent of each firm's investment in various improvement programme areas over the last two years. It shows the high importance given to manufacturing throughput time reduction, and the associated process redesign, selective automation and set-up time reduction. MRP and, in some companies, ERP, are receiving much attention. There has been little interest in moving to cellular layouts despite this being highly recommended in lean production and quick response manufacturing theories.

Social control of production
Management has used different ways to develop, delegate responsibility to and exercise control over workforces. There are a number of layers to this. Some of these firms are privately owned and have sought to retain a family atmosphere among their employees. Senior managers and owners are very visible and there

TABLE 4.6

Extent of firm's investment of resources (money, time and/or people) in programmes over last two years
(1–7 scale: 1= not at all, 7= to a great extent)

	Gallagher	Svedala Barmac	Nuplex	Formway	Criterion
Cellular manufacturing	3	2	2	3	5
Factory automation	5	5	2	5	3
Process redesign	5	5	4	4	4
ERP systems	7	3	1	7	5
Just-in-time	4	4	3	6	2
MRP	4	5	5	6	5
Manufacturing throughput time reduction	7	5	6	5	4
Setup time reduction	6	5	4	4	4
ISO9000 certification	1	5	6	6	5
Supplier certification	4	4	4	3	4
SPC	3	3	4	4	5
TQM	4	4	4	6	4
ISO14000 certification	1	4	5	2	2
Pollution prevention	4	4	6	3	4
Recycling of materials	4	5	5	3	4
Waste reduction	4	4	3	3	4
Workplace health & safety	6	6	6	6	4

is a lot of socialising among employees, particularly in small towns. At Criterion the company social club has an in-ground, indoor swimming pool visible from the entry foyer. There is also a squash court and bar area. Typically, in the companies studied, 5–15 per cent of shop-floor employees leave during a year. These firms are strong believers in having a highly skilled workforce. They go out of their way to recruit highly qualified people and invest heavily in their continuing education by, for example, paying for attendance at evening classes at local technical institutes.

In terms of organising production, Friedman's (1977) distinction between direct control and responsible autonomy is a useful way of examining management choice. All firms exhibit combinations of both. Managers, engineers and supervisors specify or show workers what to do, while individual workers or teams of workers retain some autonomy over exactly how the job is done, the allocation of their time and the degree of commitment to continuous improvement efforts. The firms studied place considerable emphasis on team-based working with decision-making pushed down to what was described as 'the appropriate level'. In some cases this includes responsibility for scheduling work. In all cases there is a consistent use of teams to focus on problem-solving, quality responsibility and process improvement initiatives. As Steve Tucker of Gallagher says, 'At the end of the day a lot of our good initiatives of late have been coming out of the shop floor.'

The extensive use of teams also assists control through worker peer pressure. Management retains control of plant layouts, basic time allocations and payment systems that determine the overall structure of the work (Williams et al., 1994).

Traditionally, management's influence over the labour process is challenged by independent trade unions. In New Zealand the Employment Contracts Act, introduced in 1991 and replaced in 2000 by the Employment Relations Act, reduced the influence of the unions, and the coverage of collective employment contracts. Employment practices vary in these firms. Some operate with all staff employed on individual contracts, some still have union agreements. All, however, claim they have achieved increased labour force flexibility by being able to cross-train, multiskill and deploy workers widely throughout the factory. It is, however, important to note that these firms are exemplars and had begun developing their workforce assets long before 1991: the introduction of this legislation did not initiate radical changes in their operations. Rather the senior managers felt it enabled them to make improvements and extend things like multiskilling. These forms of social control and workforce flexibility are not the cause of success or failure in our companies. When market conditions turned, or the gusher slowed down, staff retrenchment had to occur and some loyalty was lost.

INTERPRETING THE RESULTS

What do the results mean in practice?
Both the gusher and going global have been profoundly unsettling to the configuration of capabilities of these firms. They have had to make production interventions to rebalance or renew their operating system, and in particular to focus on a niche market. The temporary loss of fit with the business environment has led to changes in external architecture, including relations with suppliers and the development of more formal product distribution arrangements. In some companies the manufacturing side of the business could not

deliver the required quantities and quality to meet promises or requests. These niches required greater responsiveness to customers and some firms are moving more towards a make-to-order basis.

The changes made to develop better internal fit relationships as a result of this environmental turbulence have been discussed earlier in relation to the characteristics of world-class manufacturing. These firms have made sustained efforts to improve technical control, material flow and management of inventory (use of MRP or kanban). Particular emphasis has been placed on the development of workforce assets. Extensive training, multiskilling and use of flexible work contracts also appear to be important. These firms have continued to develop heir engineering capability and product innovation through high R&D spending. Some companies have regarded outsourcing as a complexity-reducing factor, but generally they eschew outsourcing in order to maintain greater control over quality and delivery.

TABLE 4.7
Comparison of some features of operating systems

Lean production	Quick response manufacturing	Firms in this study
Focus on eliminating non-value adding processes	Focus on reducing manufacturing throughput time	Focus on reducing manufacturing throughput time
Leading to • Improve quality • Reduce cost • Reduce lead times	Leading to • Improve quality • Reduce cost • Eliminate non-value-added waste	Leading to • Improve quality • Reduce costs for low volume, high-mix operation • Eliminate non-value-added waste
JIT deliveries	Some JIT	Some JIT deliveries within New Zealand
Outsource through network of tiered suppliers		More vertically integrated, do not favour outsourcing
Good supplier relations	Good supplier relations	Good supplier relations
Reduce all inventory	Inventory as necessary	Inventory as necessary Reduce WIP
Cellular layout	Cellular layout	Little emphasis on cellular layout

What do the results mean in theory?

These firms are generally operating in a high-mix, low-volume manufacturing environment with high levels of product line complexity. A large number of product variants is responsible for this situation, which follows from their narrow but deep market strategy. There appears to be no wholesale adoption of the 'lean production' prescription for world-class manufacturing featuring Japanese production intervention techniques. Firms are taking ideas from various sources and using what fits best with their business strategy. Indeed, because they operate in global markets from a New Zealand base, these firms will never be able to adopt fully the tenets of the lean production system. This is particularly so when offshore suppliers are interested only in orders representing about three months' sales or when it is not possible to have deliveries more frequently than once a month. The variability of market demands and of capacity means that there are many paths to improved and sustained performance on a higher trajectory. Nevertheless these firms have focused predominantly on responsiveness, flexibility and being cost-efficient at short run production. The main driver of this focus has been a determination to reduce manufacturing lead-times. For small- and medium-scale manufacturers targeting a global niche, this is a more appropriate system to develop, but it must be acknowledged that aspects of a lean production system can be incorporated into the production interventions. The configuration observed has more in common with the 'quick response' or 'agile manufacturing' concepts, though with reduced emphasis on cellular manufacturing. Table 4.7 compares these models with what appears to be the common pattern in our companies.

Dealing with complexity

Complexity in manufacturing is a function of the number of product variants, how the product is constructed and the route it follows through the factory. The high-mix, low-volume manufacturer faces particularly high levels of complexity. A number of authors (Kotha and Orne, 1989; Frizelle and Woodcock, 1995) have addressed the issue of complexity in manufacturing organisations. Frizelle and Woodcock describe a way of measuring complexity associated with a product and process. Frizelle (1998) and Khurana (1999) give more details on ways in which it can be managed using theoretical and case study examples. Structural complexity arises from the structure of the factory, to which both products and processes contribute. Each work centre or operation that the product must pass through represents an obstacle to the flow through the system. Each work centre may be required to handle a number of products and tasks. As Frizelle says, 'the structural complexity comes from the way *the product structures map to the resources that are there to carry out the work.* . . . One important and surprising consequence is that [many] product variants do not have to mean a complex

FIGURE 4.8

Route map for management of complexity
(adapted from Frizelle, 1998)

	Structural complexity	Operational complexity
	Simplification	Management + control
Prevention	Better design	Improved reliability
Cure	Process analysis	Enhanced planning

internal structure' (*Ibid.*, p.56, Frizelle's italics). Operational complexity concerns what happens on a daily basis on the shop floor. It is related not only to the planned flow of a product through the factory, but also to the impact of random events or disturbances, such as breakdowns, which throw the schedule out of kilter and require operator or management action. Frizelle suggests a route map for dealing with complexity as shown in Figure 4.8.

Many of companies studied have travelled the route in a repeated reverse or clockwise process. In other words, one of the first investments made was in an MRP system to enhance production planning and scheduling; only recently have they been putting more emphasis on beginning with design for manufacturability (DFM) tools and techniques. Part of the reason for this is historical: advances in formal DFM tools and analysis are more recent, and MRP packages were seen as necessary to deal with the planning and scheduling problems arising from accelerating sales.

Simultaneous development of capabilities

There is little evidence that these manufacturers follow the quality-delivery-cost-flexibility sequential model of capability development proposed by Ferdows and De Meyer. It is also unlikely that these firms could afford the trade-off between capabilities that Skinner suggests. Rather, they found it necessary to push ahead on developing many capabilities simultaneously to restore their configurational balance as quickly as possible. They also maintained their development of new products and managed the rapid increase in size of their organisation; and the need for customer responsiveness has required a reduction in lead times for both new products and manufacturing.

Chapter 5

Human Resource Management and the Acquisition of Organisational Agility

INTRODUCTION

'In a business climate characterised by unprecedented, unparalleled, unrelenting and largely unpredictable change, competitiveness is a moving target. Under such circumstances, organizations stumble and sometimes fall because the rate of change in their external environments simply outpaces their organizational capacity to keep pace.' Dyer and Shafer (1999:148) go on to say that organisations which survive and prosper in these circumstances can be thought of as 'agile organisations', which 'strive to develop a built-in capacity to shift, flex and adjust, either alone or with alliance partners, as circumstances change, and do so as a matter of course'. Organisational agility is not an either/or proposition, but 'a state of becoming rather than being'. It represents an ideal state of affairs — aspiration rather than reality.

As the previous chapter showed, the quality of agility has been central to the evolution of global leaders in New Zealand. As they expanded into overseas markets, they were forced to meet increasingly varied specifications for local markets, yet sought to retain production in the one (New Zealand) site to retain economies of scale. The result has been a distinctive emphasis on workplace flexibility. Regional leaders, too, have needed flexibility to service their broad product range. And all these organisations have continued to succeed in markets that have changed frequently, substantially and rapidly. They have responded to those changes and have sustained themselves, often in very adverse circumstances.

This chapter explores the ways in which human resource management (HRM) strategies have fostered flexibility and agility, using as a guide the template offered by Dyer and Shafer. They propose that agile organisations (AOs) need employees who:

- take initiative to spot threats and opportunities in the marketplace, reconfigure the organisational infrastructure to focus resources to deal with serious threats and opportunities, and learn (no waiting for permission or instructions to act);
- rapidly redeploy whenever and to wherever there is priority work that needs doing (eschewing TIMJ — 'that isn't my job');
- spontaneously collaborate (even in virtual teams or organisations) to pool resources for quick results;
- innovate (moving beyond old solutions unless they truly fit); and
- learn rapidly and continuously.

The next step is to identify the human resource management policies and practices that encourage the development of these attributes. The HR activities Dyer and Shafer define as critical in acquiring agile attributes are work design, staffing, training and development, performance assessment and reward management, and employee communication.

WORK DESIGN

By far the most important HR policy area for acquiring organisational agility is work design, which refers to the principles that underpin the allocation of tasks in the workplace. In AOs, all employees are expected to see themselves and others 'as owners of fluid assignments with responsibility for results (rather than as occupants of fixed positions who are simply responsible for carrying out tasks)'(Dyer and Shafer: 168). As Bridges observed, in developing the concept of 'dejobbing', employees 'no longer take their cues from a job description or a supervisor's instructions. The signals come from the changing demands of the work project itself. People learn to focus their individual efforts and their collective resources on "the work that needs doing"'(quoted Dyer and Shafer: 168).

Work design principles that encourage organisational agility include cross-trained teams, flexible job profiles and task allocation, and the integration of previously discrete tasks (the remarriage of conception and execution). Staff at all levels of the organisation, working in teams, are encouraged to take responsibility for decisions in their area and to consider its relationship with other parts of the organisation. Work design is crucial in AOs because it sets parameters to the range of possibilities in other HR policy areas (Dyer and Shafer: 160).

The firms in our study almost uniformly demonstrate these principles of work design. When Criterion adopted a new cellular manufacturing philosophy in the early 1990s, it meant a radical change to work design. The company installed a flat, team-driven organisation structure so the 140-strong manufacturing company now has just one layer of eight managers between the managing director and the production staff. Staff are organised into self-managing 'cells', each of which has established performance indicators and activity-based costing systems; rewards are linked to performance improvements. Montana has organised its one bottling plant in Glen Innes into a series of production teams whose supervisors report directly to the plant manager. The teams operate as autonomous business units: they are responsible for scheduling their work and, for example, can decide themselves whether overtime needs to be worked. Teams are responsible for their own quality assurance. It is very important to the team's sense of autonomy and task commitment that a 'white coat' does not descend from on high to check their work.

In 1989 Formway introduced the Fast Cycle Manufacturing Programme aimed at reducing lead times, increasing manufacturing flexibility and improving delivery reliability. This was supported by a flattened hierarchy and the introduction of Fast Cycle Product Teams. Each team was put in charge of one product from the start to the end of its manufacture. Each worker had a skill or task with which they were most familiar, but all learnt new skills to improve their flexibility so that they could fill in for each other to ease bottlenecks. The introduction of delivery windows simplified the production planning process, freeing up more management time and allowing decisions to be made at the operator level. Formway seeks involvement from staff by providing them with an environment in which innovative behaviour is the norm. As Rick Wells explains, employees are encouraged to participate in decision-making through the team-based culture.

> Obviously, being involved in decision processes makes a real difference as to how people view the organisation, so in that sense it's very much a part of our culture. We want a company where all the players have an understanding of what the customer wants, and who focus on how we individually and collectively can better serve that need.

Formway's systematic focus on innovative design has generated products that have built it a valuable reputation, but these assets are not easy to imitate.

PEC took a similar approach. It established multilevel, cross-functional teams and encouraged them to be continually innovative rather than leaving innovation solely to the R&D team. HR practices provided and retained a pool of competent staff and the culture created an environment that prized creativity and innovation. Ironically, PEC found that its own success during the 1990s jeopardised its innovative capacity. The company had to cater for a diversity of customers, so major efforts were focused on tailoring current systems to suit different customer requirements. By 1995 staff numbers had doubled to cope with customisation, but no new products were invented during this period. From 1997 PEC re-emphasised the importance of product innovation by placing cross-functional teams at the centre of the product design and problem-solving process, and by constantly encouraging staff to suggest improvements.

Svedala Barmac has a flat, team-based structure with the supervisor of each team reporting directly to the managing director. Decision-making authority is pushed down to the teams whose members take personal responsibility for quality. Andi Lusty explains why:

> In South Africa, where they have very low operating cost, they have a huge QA [quality assurance] department where the stuff keeps getting sent back to be redone. They end up doing the QA like you wouldn't believe. You get the stuff out and the QA is 30 per cent of the cost of the product. Whereas we don't have any QA inspectors because everybody is responsible for their own QA. If you're passing it on to the next guy then he's going to give it back to you, because if his work goes through and it's still bad, then it becomes his problem.

Initially Bill Gallagher found that going only halfway in work redesign was counter-productive. Gallagher introduced work centres in which staff had considerable discretion as to how they operated but were highly specialised and able to work only in that centre. The company found this was impeding its capacity to respond quickly to new orders as particular work centres were bound up with their own work programme. Accordingly, Gallagher, like others in this study, moved to a cross-functional, multiskilled team structure. Bill Gallagher learnt that, having established the team structure, senior management must respect the jurisdiction of the team members: 'if someone has a problem it's easier for the boss to blurt out the answer. I learnt a long time ago, that if you are going to make all the decisions around the place, you have to keep making all the decisions.'

Many of the distinctive HRM features of these organisations are the legacy of workplace reform initiatives in the early 1990s. Workplace New Zealand, a management/union organisation, was set up to spearhead workplace reform initiatives which encompassed everything from team working, multiskilling and flat management structures, through to new style industrial relations. Workplace reform aimed to empower employees to find better and smarter ways to work, and it met with particular success in manufacturing organisations. New ways of working brought improvements in quality, productivity and flexibility.

But not all the firms in our study have adopted these work design principles. Nuplex has clung to a traditional model and attributes this to the relatively unchanging nature of the technology. Nuplex's commercial manager Geoff Swailes comments:

> . . . we're making now some of the basic polymers that were made when I started in this industry 40 years ago. Okay, we're making them very much smarter and better but we are still using many of the early raw materials and they're doing the same jobs, they're still making paint.

STAFFING

The need for employee commitment leads the AO to seek stable, long-term staffing relationships. 'Most AOs, contrary to what might be expected, lean toward a so-called closed internal staffing system (i.e. while they realise the futility of life-time employment and careers in this day and age, most have yet to subscribe to the currently fashionable free-market notion of the employment contract)' (Dyer and Shafer: 169). In their selection of staff, AOs give weight not only to technical criteria but also to personal competencies such as problem-solving and interpersonal skills. A key selection criterion is commitment to organisational values. AOs tend to hire at entry level and promote from within, which places a high premium on succession planning. Nonetheless, in some circumstances, such as when a firm needs the injection of specific expertise or to serve as a catalyst for a change of direction, an AO may hire selectively from outside to senior positions. Because AOs wish to be flexible on all dimensions, they tend to use contingent employees. But such employees are very difficult to integrate into the value system of AOs. And firms may incur significant transaction costs and loss of quality from employing them. Another staffing dilemma is that a preference for a flat organisational structure may limit career opportunities and give able and ambitious staff good reason to leave.

The fit between this model of staffing and the policies of the firms in our study is considerable, though not as close as that with the AO model of work design. The firms do take account of both technical and personal competencies in selecting employees. The technological sophistication of many of their work processes places a high premium on the employment of technically competent staff. PEC developed a highly qualified team of about 120 drawn from a variety of disciplines. This team deployed not only the latest technological knowledge in microelectronics and mechanics, but also the know-how accumulated from historical learning and experience. The latter was a key dimension of PEC's technological capability. For Gallagher, the implementation of MRPII in 1988 necessitated the hiring of suitably qualified staff. This combination allowed the company to achieve ISO9000 accreditation. As we have seen, a mining qualification is required before anyone can join the Svedala Barmac sales team.

On the other hand, AOs stress the importance of personal competencies, sometimes rating these even more highly than technical competence. Although Formway has always sought skilled staff, it has also opted for team players with integrity, energy and initiative. It is unlikely that any firm would consciously seek staff lacking these qualities, but not all companies give them the same degree of formal priority as Formway. Kiwi Dairies' HR manual states that recruitment criteria will include not only technical skills but will 'look to the future by seeking people who have the personal attributes and share the values that will make the company strong for the future'. Gallagher has recruited able graduates from Waikato University but has found that most lacked the maturity and people skills to perform well in managerial roles. Today Gallagher looks for a mixture of graduate recruitment and experience. PEC specifically sought staff who embraced the company's culture and core values.

There is a clear tendency for hiring decisions to be made at the level at which the appointee will work. Montana and Svedala Barmac have devolved responsibility entirely to the teams, and senior managers resist involvement in hiring decisions. As Andi Lusty of Svedala Barmac puts it: 'They're responsible for hiring their own staff and they live and die with the staff they hire. I don't get involved . . . usually until they want to lay somebody off. Maybe one in five, or one in ten doesn't work out.'

Kiwi Dairies has also devolved hiring authority but HR does advise the teams. Gallagher had contracted early candidate selection to consultants but is in the process of bringing that back into the firm. Other firms appear to regard recruitment decisions as too important to be done by recruitment specialists.

Not all firms have embraced devolution to the same degree, however. PEC retained significant senior management participation in all hiring decisions. The company carried out at least three interviews before hiring — one by the CEO, one by a senior manager and another by a team capable of assessing the required competencies of each job applicant.

The firms in our study demonstrate a mix of attitudes towards traditional employment relationships. It is certainly the case that they promote from within. At Nuplex, succession planning has ensured the steady flow of technically qualified staff into management positions. All but one of the current plant supervisors began their employment with the company in the laboratory. They also assign a high priority to long-term employment: employee turnover is low.

But the firms display a range of views on the use of contingent employees. None show any interest in the more radical models of the so-called flexible firm, touted in some quarters as the key to success. These models of a JIT workforce, comprising a relatively high proportion of temporary or casual workers, and an extensive reliance on outsourcing and the use of consultants, clearly hold little appeal for our firms. Nonetheless, Formway has made considerable use of consultants to supply it with management knowledge as well as technical advice. It has drawn upon the expertise of design, ergonomic, and health and safety consultants. More recently, Formway has also worked closely with a design firm on both marketing and graphic design concepts with the aim of developing an integrated marketing strategy. PEC had a similarly positive attitude to outsourcing. To cope with rapid growth, the company subcontracted much of the manufacturing process and deliberately limited the number of staff to between 90 and 100 (until a period of even more rapid growth in the early 1990s). This subcontracting strategy aimed to preserve what the firm saw as key aspects of its competitive advantage. As John Williams put it: 'We believed that innovation, quality employee relationships and efficiency all begin to decrease when numbers grow beyond this figure. We had seen so many factories lose innovation as their size grew.'

Gallagher, on the other hand, which has outsourced in the past, is now highly committed to an integrated model. Bill Gallagher observes:

> . . . part of our philosophy is we are a very integrated manufacturer. A lot of companies around the world are going away from that and outsourcing a lot of their manufacturing whereas we are going perhaps the other way and are recognising that we aren't huge production runs by world-class standards and if you want to keep an in-house control over quality where you've got small production runs, going to Asia to have your circuit boards made is not a smart move for our type of manufacturing.

Gallagher also has moved away from the employment of temporary production staff. Instead of paying its production workers overtime, it has 'rolled up' all overtime and penal payments into a base hourly rate, which the workers are paid for every hour worked, regardless of whether they work 40 or 50 hours in a particular week. This allows the company to increase production quite substantially at short notice without incurring the transaction costs and the potential loss of quality involved in employing untrained and uncommitted casual workers. It also boosts morale and fattens the pay packet of its own staff.

As indicated in Chapter 1, most firms in our study have created an architecture of workplace relationships based on goodwill, trust and the expectation of mutual benefit for both firm and employee. As the AO model suggests, to acquire these attributes, both firm and employee must expect the relationship to be long-term. This is the norm in these organisations.

When these firms have been forced to downsize, they have done so reluctantly. In the case of Nuplex, downsizing followed the acquisition of the poorly performing Australian Chemical Holdings. In another case, downsizing followed a life-saving takeover at a time of financial crisis. The CEO was seemingly aware that decisive action was vital, but appeared unable or unwilling to act if it involved laying off his staff. His successor observed:

> . . . the boss didn't want to lay anyone off because he was the type of man that he wasn't about to lay his people off. Had it gone a lot longer, I don't think he would have taken the hard decision and probably the bank would have taken over. I don't know how close they were to putting us into receivership, I really don't, but they must have been thinking about it. He was sitting amongst the works and he would just keep boxing on, hoping things would improve.

For the founding CEO of a firm that exemplified 'family' values, the sacrifice of 'his' workers to save the firm was a choice he could not force himself to make.

The new managing director did not show a similar reluctance to act on a subsequent occasion but the significant and negative impact this laying off of staff had upon the local region was of great concern to the company and gave it a major incentive (if such was needed) to ensure that this would not happen again. Gallagher downsized hugely (from 400 to 150 employees) in the early 1990s as part of a large-scale upgrading of the firm's manufacturing operations. This had a very positive impact on its cost structure. Other companies such as Montana have been fortunate enough to be in continuous expansion and have not had to downsize. For Kiwi Dairies, downsizing resulted from success and the takeover of Tui; the experience was difficult and acrimonious. For all companies, downsizing of any significance poses a challenge to employee morale and motivation and may call into question core values such as mutual commitment and reciprocity. Each organisation has to manage this process so that it does not irrevocably rupture the bonds of trust that have been developed.

TRAINING AND DEVELOPMENT

Organisational agility requires high levels of technical and personal competencies. Accordingly, AOs place great emphasis on competency-oriented training and its application in the workplace. Continuous learning rather than competency-based pay is the key to competency development. Although competency-based pay can be used to develop specific expertise, circumstances in AOs change much more quickly than such pay programmes can be redesigned. AOs ensure that opportunities for training are evenly distributed throughout the organisation. Typically, training programmes concentrate on business imperatives and awareness of the organisation's market situation; the organisation's vision, core values, and performance objectives; and, to a much lesser degree, managing change. Dyer and Shafer (1999:170) argue that, in their training programmes, few AOs achieve an appropriate focus on the development of agile attributes.

The firms in our study all fit closely with the AO training and development model. Their training and development programmes focus on technical and personal competencies and on embracing organisational vision and values. Since the late 1980s, Formway has invested in training its staff in brainstorming techniques and problem-solving methods. At Gallagher, training in personal competencies includes literacy programmes and effective workshop thinking (EWT). These are courses designed to challenge employees' thinking styles, empower staff to add value to the workplace and make the job more interesting. The induction programmes at Kiwi Dairies and Montana stress the importance of new recruits learning and embracing the core vision and values of the firm. The Montana induction programme states that:

> Successful integration of a new employee requires that they not only understand the specific technical issues that relate to their new position, but also that they develop an understanding and appreciation for 'the way things are done at Montana' or the culture of the business.

Montana lays great stress on a programme of personal development for its employees. It has worked for more than ten years with a consulting company, Human Synergistics, which operates as the firm's HR arm. Human Synergistics provides training in personal development rather than an exclusive focus on technical skills. After two to three months new employees undertake a self-assessment questionnaire, designed and applied by Human Synergistics, which measures their motivational patterns, how they relate to others and how they make decisions. After six months, the second part of this self-assessment exercise involves other employees giving feedback on the new employees' behaviour patterns. The induction programme at Montana also places great emphasis on inculcating the unique history, culture, language and ritual of the wine industry. All employees are taken on a winery visit (wine tasting included) and in the first three months of employment, they all complete levels one and two of the Wine

Industry Appreciation Programme and are encouraged to complete levels three and four within two years.

The technical sophistication of most of the firms in this study requires them to focus on the development of technical competencies and on continuous learning. In recent years, Criterion has invested heavily in upgrading the skill level of its staff. About 60 staff attend company-subsidised evening classes at the Manukau Institute of Technology. Selected courses include graphing, mathematics, English and effective communication. Criterion's HR staff are working with the New Zealand Furniture Industry Training Organisation to develop a unit standard training and assessment system for the whole industry. In-house training courses include job instruction, workplace relations, performance reviews and company values. The HR unit also offers counselling services to employees. The result has been a radical upskilling of the workforce. Criterion believes it should have begun the change a decade earlier, and that it may take a generation to turn around cultural attitudes to further education in the local community.

At Kiwi Dairies all new staff are encouraged to undertake a training needs analysis with their manager and agree on training objectives. They are then responsible for implementation of their personal learning and development plan. Kiwi Dairies supports all production staff completing the Diploma in Dairy Technology at Massey University and the National Diploma in Science. (The company pays fees and wages.) Gallagher invests in a range of on-site training in personal and professional development. It has adopted the industry-training framework for both plastics and electronics. It encourages all staff to work their way through the PITO credits and it agreed to operate as the pilot for the development of the electronics framework. Technical training focuses on production planning systems, CAD, manufacturing tools, R&D, surface mount technology and electronic mail.

Not all learning takes place in formal programmes. The use of cross-functional teams fosters learning through staff interaction. All the firms focus on continuous learning as a source of competitive edge. The scrutiny of customer complaints is a valuable learning process. Geoff Swailes explains the system in use at Nuplex:

> Yes, to mention customer complaints, it's used as a means of continuous improvement. We don't just fix every customer complaint and put a Band-Aid on, then say that's it done and it won't appear again. What we do is to receive the complaints, put them in the database, and then analyse the root causes of the complaint. These could be many steps away from the actual complaint event. We then go back and discuss the root causes amongst ourselves and fix the root causes. It works.

PEC, for whom research expertise was critical, regarded personal networking as an important dimension of learning; its staff share many employment conditions with academics. By reading selected technical journals, by attending conferences in New Zealand and overseas and by interacting with experts in their field, PEC's staff gained up-to-date knowledge of the latest technological developments in many fields.

Skill development is not always sought for its own sake. A limited range of skills may do the job just as well, as Andi Lusty of Svedala Barmac explains:

> Remember we don't have qualified welders here. What we have are guys off the street who we teach to weld and who learn how to weld only one way, which is down hand, the easy way when at full speed. So they'll be able to weld something for us and they'll do an absolutely bloody marvellous job as long as it's down hand and full speed. If we get a qualified guy in here they get so fussy and they don't do anything like such a good job. But they can do it upside down, on their ear or backwards and forwards, whereas our guys can't; but they're bloody good at what they do which is down hand at full speed.

PERFORMANCE ASSESSMENT AND REWARD MANAGEMENT

AOs undertake regular performance reviews but recognise their limitations in flat organisations with fluid assignments which are experiencing rapid change (Dyer and Shafer, 1999: 171). In such organisations, there may be no person qualified to review the performance of many staff and, given the pace of change, a regular six or twelve-month review cycle is too long to wait for the correction of deficiencies. Although 360-degree performance reviews may seem to provide the answer, in practice these tend to be too cumbersome for AOs. Consequently, most AOs focus on setting clear goals and establishing the right of all employees to give and receive feedback on their and others' performance. Employees at all levels are involved in establishing performance objectives, assessing progress and taking corrective action where necessary.

> The manner in which agile organisations operate tends to ensure that employees secure considerable intrinsic rewards from their work. However, AOs also stress extrinsic rewards. It is argued that compensation policies which encourage organisational agility tend to include: broad-banding; market-based pay levels; selective reliance upon competency or skill-based pay in order to encourage specific learning; and contingent forms of compensation (Dyer and Shafer, 1999: 171).

In these firms, performance management and reward and recognition are inextricably linked. They all assign a high priority to performance review and attempt to link performance to reward. There is, however, considerable variety in how they do this.

Gallagher is sceptical of formal performance reviews. The company sees its staff as a team of flexible highly qualified and experienced experts. Performance is measured and rewarded, but is not controlled. Bill Gallagher has disdain for what he calls the 'control techniques' of hierarchical management: people should 'feel free to express themselves and should enjoy a satisfying job'. Although job descriptions are non-existent at Gallagher, the company uses key performance indicators to evaluate staff performance. The company's profit-sharing plan is linked to employee personal performance. Kiwi Dairies has no formal performance review system for either production workers or supervisory and managerial staff. In only the former case, however, is this a deliberate policy choice. Three attempts to introduce a performance assessment system for managers have failed; a fourth attempt is under way.

PEC exemplified a highly formalised system, as it did in other HR activities. The firm's performance management system aimed to ensure that evaluation processes were compatible with the organisation's culture. The reward system was set up to recognise and reward all employees based on individual improvement in their knowledge and skills, and the application of both. A minimum of two job analysis interviews was planned annually to discuss an employee's goals for the next twelve months. These interviews integrated business goals, which flowed down from the corporate planning process, with personal development goals. Similarly, Montana has a formal Performance Development and Review System for all managerial and supervisory staff. For production workers, however, it entrusts performance review to the teams themselves. Performance issues are dealt with in the regular team meetings and management becomes involved only if the team cannot agree.

Svedala Barmac is trying to enlarge its database in order to effectively assess individual performance via teams. This recognises that, notwithstanding collective effort, employees want to be rewarded for their own contribution.

> We do a staff survey every year to try and [gauge attitudes to] having a money bonus: 'Do you think it works as an incentive? How would you like to see it operate?' Every man in the place wants a bonus based on what they do and not what the next bloke does. So [we'll go] first to individual departments, and then we'll go to work groups, and then we'll go to individuals. So at least they can have some sort of direct input into their bonus scheme and how it works.

A perennial issue in team-based organisations is whether individual performance assessment, and reward based significantly on this assessment, threatens the team culture. Svedala Barmac's Andi Lusty does not think so: 'while they're still involved in both what the department's doing, and what the company's doing, they're also still involved [as an individual]. They still know what the strategy of the company is and how the company's doing and everybody gets to see these results.'

As the AO model suggests, these firms make extensive use of contingent or at-risk compensation. Criterion's employees all participate in a company profit-sharing scheme. Formway's bonus structure for management requires the company to meet its overall profit objective before anyone is rewarded. Because of the cyclical nature of the industry, bonuses have been earned in only two recent years. Formway applies a gain-sharing scheme that allows production employees throughout its Gracefield plant to benefit from improvements in efficiencies. The number of hours employees work determines how much of the pool they get. This system is designed to motivate teams. The motivation of individual employees is left to peer group pressure within those teams. In the sales area bonuses are three-quarters team-based and a quarter individual-based. Gallagher's profit-sharing plan is linked to staff's personal performance. All staff share a minimum of 15 per cent of the company's annual profits. PEC, too, had a profit-sharing scheme involving all staff, until the gusher put such pressure on funding growth that the scheme had to be reluctantly set aside.

Informal processes of recognition can also be important. At Criterion, the two brothers who founded the firm have found that they had not spent enough time applauding other people's accomplishments. Like their workforce, they are working to learn new styles of behaviour. At Formway, senior managers secure employee commitment through broader recognition of staff achievements than just financial reward. The key reward is the opportunity to take initiative and be credited with having successful ideas. Its cooperative structure prevents Kiwi Dairies from having an employee profit-sharing scheme, but the firm exemplifies the AO's emphasis on new forms of employee reward and recognition. It supports a Kiwi employees' club by allowing members of the club committee paid time off during work hours for club duties and also provides administrative support. Kiwi Dairies has several other forms of recognition. Oscars, awarded quarterly, recognise 'any outstanding work performance that greatly exceeds the expectations or the usual requirements of the job or any behaviour that strongly reinforces the company values'. The Chew Chong Awards, named after the founder of the dairy company from which Kiwi Dairies grew, reward creativity and innovation in the workplace. Employees are honoured for continuous service of 10, 20, 30 and 40 years, and the firm has established a 20 Year Club with an annual members' dinner to present all company service and retirement awards; this is hosted by company directors and general managers.

COMMUNICATION

Communication is the glue that holds everything else together. To achieve and sustain organisational agility, all staff members must have the information they need to do their job and must be able to impart information that others need to do theirs. AOs aim for seamless information flows and an open-book management style that fully communicates the current market situation. They also emphasise vision, values and common performance objectives (Dyer and Shafer, 1999: 172). Regardless of what the core values are, the key requirement is that these values are widely disseminated, understood and adhered to throughout the organisation.

Communication is not a separate activity. An organisation that communicates solely by way of readings from tablets will communicate effectively, but the message will be quite different from what is intended. By contrast, communication permeates all other HR activities in our firms. The application of work design principles aims to ensure that every voice is valued. In Bill Gallagher's words, 'nobody has the sole rights on being right'. John Williams's motto was: 'I believe that any good idea from any PEC staff member must always be given a chance to be fairly evaluated'. Team-based operation supports the efficient communication of necessary information. Training and development programmes are vital in establishing mutual expectations between employees and the organisation. Performance assessment allows the evaluation of past performance and expectations of future performance to be communicated among staff members.

Firms can institute specific vehicles or forums of communication that complement HR-based forms of communication. For example, to foster team spirit, Formway's senior management conducts monthly team briefing sessions with managers, who then hold sessions with the employees.

John Williams held 'news' meetings for 10 per cent of the staff on a rotating basis. He used these to ensure that everyone was aware of the company's vision, core values and beliefs, and the reasons behind them. As the company grew, the news meetings were superseded by focus meetings held every four months, in which all aspects of the company's affairs were discussed. A regular *PEC Network News* publication also disseminated important information.

Svedala Barmac holds an annual 'no holds barred' retreat to which a cross-section of the workforce is invited. Problems can be aired without fear of repercussions. The objective is to ensure that the communication bridge between management and staff is strong and wide. In 1999, Svedala Barmac also brought managers together for the first time, as Andi Lusty explains:

> This year for the first year we've had a factory managers meeting where we're all beginning to talk about sharing technology and how we need to do things

together and try to ensure continuous improvement. That's a tiny step forward and we've been asking for that for a long time.

CONCLUSION

The firms in this study demonstrate a range of HR policies and practices, but it is possible to identify some important common factors that are significant in acquiring organisational agility.

The strongest similarities lie in work design and in training and development. Most firms display a strong commitment to cross-functional multiskilled teams that operate with considerable autonomy and decision-making discretion. All firms are committed to training programmes that combine the development of appropriate technical and personal competencies with the articulation of the organisation's core values.

There is more variation in performance assessment systems and associated reward structures, but most firms articulate performance objectives consistent with the organisation's goals, and then assess progress towards them, though the degree of formality with which they do this varies considerably. Reward structures incline towards an element of at-risk compensation and a link with performance at either the organisational or individual level. Most variation was observed in staffing policy and practice. Although all firms show a commitment to long-term stable employment relationships, their use of contingent staff varies considerably.

Chapter 6

Leaders and Owners

The competitive development of the New Zealand enterprises in this study cannot be explained adequately without reference to the people who have led them, and to the individuals, corporations and co-operatives who have owned them. This chapter looks at those leader and owner characteristics that contributed to the capabilities presented in Chapter 1, and to processes of transition such as the gusher and going global. The objective is to show how leaders and owners have made direct contributions to the relationships, reputation and innovations of their firms, and to the attributes of balance, scope and coherence that characterise competitive capability.

LEADERS' INFLUENCE ON COMPETITIVE EVOLUTION

The exceptional people who lead these New Zealand firms are unusually gifted and well-rounded people, but the intent here is to focus only on those personal attributes that clearly contributed to the development of competitive capabilities in their firms.[1]

Innovators

As discussed in Chapter 3, leaders — global leaders in particular — have often played an important role in initiating and fostering the innovations that have launched their firms on a trajectory to global success. Sir Angus Tait is probably the outstanding example of this trait. He has been excited by the potential of radio technology all his life, beginning with wartime involvement with radar in Britain, and progressing through several generations of mobile radio technology as first the transistor and then solid-state electronics transformed the industry.

Although Tait has passed on the design of his radios to very large teams of highly qualified engineers drawn from all over the world by his company's reputation, he continues, in his eighties, to be briefed on the technical side of his business.

Angus Tait is but one example of the passion for innovation. Bill Gallagher senior was an inveterate inventor. Driven by the shortages of the Depression, his fertile imagination produced a steady stream of inventions, first for his farm and then, after the war, for sale. The absolute source of Gallagher's global leadership in electric fences was the farm's horse, which had an unpleasant habit of relieving itself over the family car. A well-placed wire and a spot of current soon fixed the problem, and battery-powered electric fences remained a staple of Gallagher's business from the beginning. But Bill senior turned his hand to many other products including trailer-mounted top-dressing units, gas producers and other agricultural machinery. Thirty years after the company's founding, Bill senior was still 'tinkering' (to use his son's word) in the firm's workshops in the 1960s as Gallagher worked on the commercialisation of mains-powered electric fencing, the product that was to transform the company into a global leader. Paul Tidmarsh at Tidco and John Williams of PEC also applied their natural talent for engineering to launch and expand their businesses.

But innovation is not always product-related. Over 20 years the board of directors at Kiwi Dairies has steadfastly pursued a strategy of consolidating milk flow from as far as distribution systems can carry it to the company's Hawera site. This is now the world's largest dairy factory, with economies of scale second to none in the global dairying industry.

The founder's passion for technology can also distort the balanced development of the firm's capability portfolio. A business model that puts technology at the centre of the company's competitive advantage can sometimes forget to pay enough attention to the other requirements of business success, such as customer acceptance and profitability. Once again, Angus Tait's experience illustrates the point. His first business, A. M. Tait Ltd, fell into receivership because, as Sir Angus puts it:

> I was convinced that technology was the shining gold that would solve all problems. I'm not a numerate person. I hate numbers. I was overoptimistic. I pretended there were no goals in life other than technology. I very rapidly found out that this thing called payday came round once a week. It [receivership] was a ghastly experience.

The tradition of technological innovation remains fundamental to Tait's competitive strategy, and balances can still be disturbed by its power. The company's globally successful T2000 radio was an elegant piece of engineering design, but a devil to manufacture. The radio's curved glass screen had to be specially ground, and gold alloy had to be used internally to insulate key components.

Dynamos of energy and resilience

Another attribute of the entrepreneurial personality is boundless energy, and leaders of these exemplar organisations display the trait to a fault. Leaders with a particular responsibility for offshore sales and marketing, such as Andi Lusty and Bill Gallagher, have gone for years spending more than 100 days annually overseas, working with dealers and sales offices, keeping the relationships fresh and sustaining pressure to produce results. To exchange the comforts of a successful lifestyle for hub-and-spoke air travel and synthetic hotel rooms, these men must clearly have considerable reserves of energy and enthusiasm. In the time we spent with them, they never seemed tired. And these leaders may have physical advantages: Andi Lusty was a professional squash player as a young man, and Bill Gallagher a keen diver.

Energy is also expressed in the will, drive and determination to embrace change constantly, or indeed to create it. In the relatively brief life of Formway Furniture, Rick Wells has stimulated a steady stream of strategic innovations in his firm. The Ergo Station workstation of the mid-1980s was used to bankroll the development of the Zaf chair at the end of the decade, which in turn became the platform for the company's move into the Australian market and offshore assembly and marketing. The 1990s saw the company move into systems furniture and widen its market reach into North America. Energy has become a central attribute of the Formway culture.[2] These leaders have earned many laurels for the success of their businesses, but they are not used for resting upon.

Another expression of the life that is so strong in these leaders is their resilience in the face of disappointment. Angus Tait has never allowed himself to forget the humiliation of going into receivership with his first business, but neither has he let it hold him back from having another go. 'You have two options. Go and hide from the world, which some people do and never come up again. Or you can try again.' At the age of 48, Tait took the second option, and three decades later, Sir Angus is still driving himself to stay on top of the complex issues that confront the global development of Tait Electronics:

> I am very fortunate in being surrounded by some very bright and competent people. I have got to read what they write, and listen to what they say. When you are 80 it is bloody hard. Sometimes if I haven't slept very well. . . . But I come in anyway. I am very lucky because I am forced to keep up with what's going on. It's very hard work. I am grateful for the pressure they place on me.

A leader's reserves of energy are drawn upon especially during the intense periods of change when the coherence of the firm's configuration of capabilities is disturbed and the organisation — and especially its leader — are thrown into sustained efforts to re-establish a new balance for the business. Both the gusher, and the huge step of going global from a tiny New Zealand base, produce balance-breaking pressure. It is during these, relatively brief, periods that new capabilities are created. Without the leader's energy, these transitions would not happen. There are many examples:

- Bill Gallagher's intense efforts over three to four years in the late 1980s to win official approvals for use of his new electric fence systems from the Byzantine layers of European bureaucracy, and to establish a network of distributors before a Danish competitor could get established.
- Andi Lusty's construction of a distribution network for Tidco in the United States and Canada over four to five years in the 1980s, in a race against two other Barmac licensees.
- Angus Tait's habit of being the first to get to market with new technology: with transistorised mobile radios in New Zealand in the 1970s, and again with MPT1327 compliant systems in Europe in the 1980s.

International outlook

These leaders, some doing business in 50 to 60 countries around the world, have always been able to put their New Zealand-based business in a global context. Several leaders are in fact imports: Andi Lusty and Fred Holland both hail from Britain. Andi Lusty's early career with squash took him all over the world, including New Zealand on one occasion. (He met his Matamata-born wife at a squash tournament in Canada.) Fred Holland, a chemical engineer, came to New Zealand in 1962 to set up the polymer plant for a joint venture between his British employer, Revertex, and a New Zealand-owned partner. The venture eventually grew into Nuplex Industries. Holland has continued to draw insight from his global network of contacts in the chemical industry. For example, during the years of export incentives in New Zealand, his caution in the use of these funds was guided by trends he saw overseas:

> People thought the good times were going to last forever. We used them to develop our markets in Asia . . . but we didn't structure our whole company on them because we knew it wouldn't last. If the thing didn't make good business sense, then just doing it because of the tax doesn't make good sense to me . . .

Everybody thought that their happy little environment in New Zealand was going to continue. I suppose, because we were exposed globally with our contacts and we were very much involved with the world all the time, we saw these trends happening, we saw the changes, and we thought: How do we survive?

And New Zealanders are great travellers. As mentioned above, Bill Gallagher continues to spend one-third of each year offshore touring his widespread network of dealers. The global perspective contributes to people's willingness to take on the challenges of internationalisation. For Angus Tait, it was not at all strange to make his first move the British market, as far away from New Zealand as you can get. Having spent many years there during the war, he was more familiar with Britain than with most places in between.

'A man who fits well'

Perhaps the most distinctive characteristic of these leaders is their affinity with the people who work for them. Particularly for the owner-operated businesses, the owner-manager feels a sense of responsibility and commitment to his employees that can be stronger than any quest for return on investment. When Tidco ran into difficulties in the late 1980s, Paul Tidmarsh resisted moves to restore profit by shedding workers in a small township that was already struggling with recession. Eventually, it took a change of owner to sever bonds that Tidmarsh could not bring himself to break. As Andi Lusty recalls, 'We tended to have some old-timer people that he looked after. He was very much a people-friendly person.' Likewise at Criterion, the Smaill brothers have considered moving their production offshore to lower-cost countries; but as Wally Smaill puts it, 'Actually I didn't really want to do it. My lifestyle and I like New Zealand. Why should I desert all these people?'

In several cases, the founders of these businesses have taken the view that the workforce should participate quite fully in the success of the business. As Bill Gallagher recalls of his father,

In Father's day in the 1950s, he used to spend a large proportion of the profit on staff bonuses. I can remember the factory when it still had a dirt floor. It was a really good year and the staff were all smiles because he gave about half of it away. I guess in earlier years our biggest cash expense in the business was staff bonuses, and we still run it.

Clearly, the balanced development of a business can be distorted by the strength of the personal ties these owner-managers have with the people who work for them. On the other hand, the leader's commitment to the employees clearly calls forth a reciprocal commitment from them to the success of the enterprise. Comparing himself with some icons of business who have accumulated far bigger 'bags of gold', Angus Tait puts his position this way:

> I suppose I take refuge in the reality that my competence compared to the smash and grab guys is minuscule and the only thing I have to offer is my willingness to work with people and to create an environment in which they are willing to stay. . . . Clever devils — one admires their achievements and says they are light years ahead of me intellectually. But in the final analysis, if personal relationships are not right, it will all go. You can be all those clever things, and have titles next to your name, but if you can't make your way. . . . Where there is resounding success, there is a man who fits well.

With attitudes like this, it is no surprise that leaders often inspire familial levels of affection and loyalty in their employees. To give just one example, the affection that Tait employees feel towards Sir Angus has a symbolic embodiment in the foyer of the company's corporate office. When he was knighted in 1999, every one of the 1000 employees in the company signed a scroll with their personal good wishes. A couple of employees were on leave in out-of-the-way places, and huge efforts were required to get their signatures, but they were determined not to be left out. Obviously the whole firm was proud to see a man they had respected and admired for so long being acknowledged in this way. Warren Rickard comments: 'Angus is a great listener and that's probably what endears him so much to the people. He is a father figure to the company. . . . So that's the thing he has. I can't really put my finger on it.'

Many of these leaders are clearly the source of the behavioural norms that support high-quality, long-term relationships, both within the organisation and with business partners beyond the firm. The trust, goodwill, integrity and cooperation, and dependency involved are direct expressions of the leader's own norms. In this way, many leaders make direct contributions to the social, and therefore strategic, cohesion of their organisations.

It is probably important to leave the last word on these rather weighty issues to Bill Gallagher: 'It's not the sort of thing you want to talk about . . . I've still got Father's principles, but I guess I've had more fun!'

A willingness to grow

Processes like the gusher and going global create huge transformations in a business. A three- to four-year gusher, during which sales double every year, produces a company ten times bigger than when it started, with a vastly more complex range of challenges and issues. If they are not to limit the enormous growth of their firm, leaders must be willing to grow enormously too.

As the longest-serving leader in our study, Angus Tait offers a particularly good example of what is involved in growing with the company. Tait describes his style of business when he started out in 1950:

> There was no planning. I did most things. I worked ridiculous hours. I had people on the production side. The technology was my prime concern, but I was also the salesman. I spent the day rushing around, and I went all over the country selling things and generally dissipating my energy with varying degrees of success. . . . There was a competent lady [who] did the mechanical things like sending out bills and getting in the money, [and] calling out to me the size of the overdraft and what was I going to do about it . . .

In those days, Tait designed his own radios, which were proudly displayed taking up most of the boot of a car and considered as wonders of compact design. Production required 'lots of girls with soldering irons and nimble fingers, and it took anywhere from four to five to six hours to build a radio'.

Contrast this with Angus Tait's current role, 50 years later, as executive chairman of a global enterprise employing 1000 people and active in over 80 countries. His radios are now designed by an R&D staff of 200, and can fit into the palm of your hand. Radios are made in a highly automated facility that has reduced the labour content per radio to just twelve minutes.

Earlier we discussed just how much hard work is involved in keeping up with this scale of growth. It is perhaps inescapable that personal growth on this scale would also be painful. Angus Tait is ruthless in reminding himself of the demise of his first business.

> It failed because it deserved to fail. How about that for bluntness? It certainly failed because I was a commercial bum. I was. I was so naïve. I was a technologist at heart and I said to myself, technology's what matters and money's not important. It will look after itself.

Tait swallowed this bitter medicine and learnt from it. He was prepared to acknowledge the limits to his interests and, as he puts it now, 'If you don't know something about a facet of business, you had better get somebody who does know.'

Given the inevitable limitations of the human condition, a willingness to share responsibility for the growth of the business is a clear prerequisite for balance and scope in the evolution of a company's capabilities. Angus Tait's humility, which makes him such a good listener, also contributes to his own, and his organisation's commitment to learning. 'I keep saying to the young men around me, everyone should go through receivership. It's a great ego-adjusting experience.'

Table 6.1 summarises this section. It shows leaders' contributions that have contributed to the evolution of competitive capability in their businesses. The full scope of leaders' contributions will surely extend beyond what has been apparent to this study. This is an initial offering towards a very new question.[3]

TABLE 6.1

Leaders' contribution to the evolution of competitive capabilities

	Innovators	Energy	International	Interpersonal	Personal growth
Capabilities Relational external		√	√		
Relational internal				√	
Relational reputation					
Technology innovation	√	√			
Technology multiple tech					
Learning					√
Portfolio Scope					√
Portfolio Balance	?			?	
Portfolio Coherence		√		√	
Evolutionary processes Going global		√	√		√
The gusher		√			√
Focus & grow					
De-/recoherence		√			√

√ = evidence of a positive contribution
? = evidence of an impediment

OWNERS' INFLUENCE ON COMPETITIVE EVOLUTION

For the firms in this study there have been many episodes in which the owners have had a demonstrable effect on the development of competitive capability. We can compare the effects of these contributions across a range of owner types (Table 6.2). We explored the causal links between owners and evolution through the perceptions of the managers involved. When explanations have common ground within the same owner type, and differ across owner type, it strengthens the proposition that owners have influenced the competitive development of their businesses in distinctive ways. When there are different experiences *within* owner types, the reasons for those differences have been investigated. In several instances, this has produced further insights, uncovering the effect on capability development of influences other than ownership.

For this part of the study we held additional conversations with managing directors (MDs) of a group of companies that collectively span a wide range of owner types. Nuplex and its predecessor corporate entities have been listed on the New Zealand Stock Exchange since 1956, and Fred Holland has been MD, or has reported to the only previous MD, for much of that history. Until 1991, however, the company's shareholding was controlled by a succession of offshore owners: British-based Revertex from 1962 to 1981; United States-based Monsanto, through its Australian subsidiary, from 1981 to 1988; and finally Kerry Packer's Consolidated Press Holdings from 1988 to 1991. Fred Holland is thus uniquely well qualified to assess the pluses and minuses of offshore ownership — in several of its national permutations — as against public stock ownership.

Further insight into offshore owners is offered by Andi Lusty's experience with Svedala Industri, the Swedish owners of Svedala Barmac. His point of comparison is to the private owner-manager Paul Tidmarsh, whose company Tidco built up and consolidated the global Barmac business. Other current MDs also have personal experience of more than one of these forms of ownership and have offered their own comparisons of how each type has contributed to the competitive development of their business.

Five of our firms are privately owned, and were managed by their owners for the period covered in this study. We do not believe we could have found better exemplars of this form of corporate governance, so widely used in New Zealand, than Angus Tait and Bill Gallagher. Finally, Kiwi Dairies is a fine example of the co-operative mode of governance that has played a powerful role in the development of the country's agricultural processing industries.

The following pages set out distinctive influences that owners have had on competitive evolution — both positive and negative — for each of the owner types identified in Table 6.2.

TABLE 6.2

Ownership types

	Public stock corporation (PSC)	Owner-managed enterprise(OME)	Multinational subsidiary (MNS)[4]	Cooperative-owned enterprise (COE)
Kiwi Dairies				#
Nuplex	#		#	
Svedala Barmac		#	#	
Gallagher Group		#		
Tait Electronics		#		

Multinational subsidiaries (MNS)

Going global

As shown in Chapter 2, internationalisation has been a powerful driver of the development of competitive capability in these firms, so multinational corporation (MNC) owners should be expected to contribute distinctively well to this process in their subsidiaries (MNS). This indeed has been the case at Svedala Barmac (see also discussion on p.41). Immediate access to a global network of sales organisations, so-called Svedala houses, has given the New Zealand subsidiary an unprecedented period of growth since it was acquired in 1990. This advantage has been so strong that the company has missed an entire cyclical downturn in this very cyclical industry. Tidco had already built a global network of independent and owned distributors, and many of these were replaced with the local Svedala house. But access to markets not already reached by the Tidco dealer network has been enough to give the company a good decade of profitable growth.

A feature of international ownership is that the MNS's business is seen within the context of the parent's global strategy.[5] In Svedala Barmac's case this contributed to the capability development that accompanied internationalisation. By the late 1980s Tidco had effectively completed its consolidation of global Barmac licences and, finding its sales dominated by the Barmac product, it had attempted to diversify into other ventures to spread its risk. The lack of success in these ventures was one factor that brought Tidco to a crisis and change of ownership. The new owner, Svedala, with some 2000 product lines of its own, had no need to diversify, and its strategy for the New Zealand subsidiary was to focus on the Barmac business and extend its global reach. Hence a broadly based MNC parent, through its established global distribution and marketing network, and its preference for focus and grow strategies, can make distinctive contributions to the processes of going global, relative to other owner types.

The contribution is not automatic, however. It all depends how the MNS fits into the parent's strategy. When the subsidiary has a product with global potential, as with the Barmac, the incentives for both parent and MNS to go global will be strong. But without that potential, when the MNS seeks a position of regional leadership based on a broader range of products and technologies, offshore ownership can impede the process of capability development. While under the control of Monsanto, Nuplex's competitive evolution was constrained in two ways:

- Monsanto encouraged Nuplex to take a leading role in rationalising the New Zealand industry, but it was not allowed to take the same role in Australia, where Monsanto had a subsidiary, to which Nuplex reported;
- Nuplex's steady accumulation of multiple licensed technologies, and networking with technology partners, were retarded once the company came to be seen as a part of the global Monsanto empire. Partners who were happy to share technology with a small regional player were much less inclined to do so with the subsidiary of a global giant.

When the strategic development of parent and subsidiary come into conflict, it is to be expected that the parent's will win. Fred Holland: 'They were getting out of the sort of areas that we were in. . . . Monsanto was changing direction, and if you are not in that direction, you don't get any capital.' In this case Monsanto's acquisition of a controlling interest in Nuplex was primarily defensive, and there was little incentive for the offshore owner to contribute to the competitive development of its subsidiary.

Management systems
Less equivocal is the contribution made to MNSs by their parents in the areas of management systems. Both Andi Lusty and Fred Holland cite their offshore owners as a source of managerial capabilities that were important to the development of their organisations. Fred Holland's assessment of Monsanto is that:

> . . . they came in at a very good time because we had been growing quite rapidly and we were very much seat of the pants people. . . . Monsanto brought to us a more structured business format and we needed it. [Monsanto contributed] in

the areas of safety and health, environmental protection, because we were now with an American company in the eighties and they were paranoiac about it. So this put great pressure on us to get our act together and improve, which was good . . Also in the area of budgeting and forecasting and financial control. . . . I enjoyed the period. I personally learnt a lot. They were the best management consultants I've ever had.

In a very similar experience, Andi Lusty cites the excellence of Svedala's financial reporting systems, which require full financial statements every month, within five days of month end. Formerly Tidco had taken up to six weeks to close accounts, and only on a quarterly basis. The style of the Swedish parent is to leave considerable autonomy to its subsidiaries, providing they stay on budget.

> They use a system where they agree a budget for a year. . . . If you're on 100, you are on budget; 120 is good news; 97 or 98 is bad news. It's like a traffic light, if you go to orange . . . you've got to improve.

Providing returns track against budget, the MNS is pretty much left alone to run its business. Andi Lusty normally sees his Swedish boss in Matamata once every two years, and would expect to see him more often only if the company's performance weakened, 'but we haven't had that problem yet'. Biannual visits to Sweden allow time to review performance and budgets.

Both executives agree, however, that there is a price to be paid for the disciplines of these excellent management systems, namely a more time-consuming and bureaucratic approach to decision-making. Fred Holland recalls that, though he learnt a great deal from his Australian bosses during the Monsanto days, 'they learned something from our entrepreneurial style'. Andi Lusty notes that decisions now taking up to eighteen months might have taken only minutes during the Tidco days.

Management systems are one element in the creation of an effective learning organisation, and MNCs have clearly made contributions here that, as we shall see below, have been less automatic in the case of owner-managed firms. There are, however, other expected elements of MNSs learning from their parent companies that have not eventuated in these firms. Andi Lusty does not believe he has gained any distinctive insights into global industry trends from his association with overseas owners.

A source of capital?
From the perspective of a business based in a tiny economy at the edge of the world, the large multinational owner holds out the promise of a distinctively

massive source of capital. As we have seen, experiences of very rapid growth put enormous pressure on the firm's capabilities, one of which is financial resources. The experience of MNSs in this study suggests that realisation of this promise will depend on the parent's global strategy, and how the subsidiary is perceived to fit into it.[6]

Andi Lusty's experience with Svedala Industri has been unreservedly positive:

> I think the way the Swedish run their businesses is terrific. I'm just glad we didn't end up with somebody who just wanted to put money in and get it all out in a year or two. Prior to Svedala, a lack of cash flow had been a major constraint to growth .... But there's been no blocks for us to spend any money to advance the business.

Svedala Industri allocates funds on the basis of expected return on investment and, providing a target rate of return can realistically be expected, funds are forthcoming. After years of struggling to secure funds from banks, Andi Lusty found his relationship with Svedala liberating: 'We just kept writing to them "we need more money". And they just kept sending it — it was wonderful!' It is to be recalled, however, that the focus and grow strategy of global expansion for the Barmac machine was one that MNS and parent agreed on.

Fred Holland's experience with parental funding was far less munificent. Neither Revertex nor Monsanto was a generous funder of the Nuplex business. Revertex provided initial capital when its joint venture in New Zealand was first established in 1962. After that, all funds for growth of the business had to be internally generated. The same was true for Monsanto, and for Packer. Contrasting Nuplex's 30 years of offshore control with its present position, Fred Holland comments:

> We did everything out of our own resources. Now we have been able to go outside of our resources, and now we have a much more robust balance sheet. We have taken on a lot more debt [in order] to grow, so we have added a bank discipline ... in addition to the sharemarket.

The experience of these companies suggests that access to a multinational parent's superior funding capability will be contingent on the MNS strategic development path. As long as this is consistent with the parent's view of the business, funding may be distinctively easy to reach. If not, the offshore parent may underfund the development of the business, relative to other owner types.

Sources of competitive capability
The question remains whether an offshore parent might offer distinctive access

to the various sources of competitive capability presented in Chapter 1, or contribute to the scope, balance and coherence of the overall portfolio. The experience of these firms suggests that the distinctive contribution of this owner type is more likely to be negative than positive.

Access to leading global technology is often cited as one of the benefits of multinational ownership. It might therefore be expected that the MNS would have an advantage in innovation capability. But the experience of Nuplex suggests that, once again, it is the strategic match between the two businesses that will determine whether the parent's technology is of distinctive value to the MNS. Revertex did provide the forerunner of Nuplex with the technology to produce polymers when its joint venture in New Zealand was established in 1962. Furthermore, the New Zealand company's contacts with other Revertex businesses in Malaysia and South Africa initiated its network of technology partners, which it retains to this day. But since then Nuplex has had little help from its owners, and in some instances has been impeded by them. Nuplex's strategy of branching into a broad range of resin- and polyester-based chemicals quickly outgrew Revertex's more focused technology, and the company turned to a network of licensees to extend its technological scope.

By the time it took control of the company, Monsanto was moving out of the kind of chemicals that are the core of Nuplex's business. As noted above, the Monsanto connection also put a cloud over the development of Nuplex's network of technology partners. Today, Nuplex differentiates itself from large, global chemical corporations on the basis of the breadth of its technological experience. Firms such as Monsanto have been following a different strategic trajectory, towards specialisation. As long as Nuplex's destiny was controlled by a company moving in the opposite direction to its own, its competitive development was impeded.

There is also a downside to an MNC giving its subsidiary access to its global distribution network. On the positive side, the parent's capability can quickly substitute for the slower construction of a network of business partners around the world, or the even slower development of a network of company-operated sales offices. This has undoubtedly given Svedala Barmac a decade of strong growth as the Barmac is promoted in countries it had not formerly reached. The downside is that Svedala houses have more than 2000 product lines to promote from Svedala subsidiaries around the world. The mutual dependency that characterised the relationships between Tidco, a small isolated producer in New Zealand, and its local dealers dependent on the manufacturer's product, has gone. Svedala house managers do not have the time even to talk to all the manufacturing subsidiaries whose products they sell so the MNS cannot build the kind of high-powered relationships of reciprocal trust and commitment evident in owner-managed enterprises. (See below for the distinctive strength of the OME in forming high-powered business relationships.)

As the Svedala Barmac experience shows, the extent to which an MNS is constrained in developing high-powered business relationships will depend on how much autonomy it is allowed.[7] In the Barmac case, Tidco already had an extensive network of dealers and distributors in key global markets. At the parent's behest, these were replaced with local Svedala houses wherever possible. It should be reiterated that the arrangement has produced a decade of strong growth for the Matamata company, but it has not been based on the kind of relationships that can give a company its own appropriable source of competitive advantage. Indeed local management believes the company could have grown faster had it been able to select which dealers were to be replaced with houses, and which were to operate alongside the local Svedala house.

Owner-managed enterprises (OME)

Long-term relationships
The most notable characteristic of the five OMEs in this study is the distinctive emphasis they place on relationships of all kinds. Relationships are important in any business, regardless of its owner type, but in the OME they acquire a special importance, compared with PSCs and MNSs, because the organisation is small and relies on others to make its way in the world. This is particularly true when the firm is operating on a global scale, and early in its history.

Bill Gallagher offers a good example of the creation of competitive capability through external business relationships. His construction, in the late 1970s, of a European network of dealers for his world-beating electric fencing technology locked in the company's initial innovation-based advantage. He recruited his dealers personally and has visited them on average twice a year ever since. He selected people he could relate to personally, often in family-owned and operated businesses like his own. With only a very few exceptions, all the dealers he recruited 20 years ago are still with the Gallagher Group today.

Bill Gallagher has developed some deep insights into what it takes to turn such networks into engines of competitive differentiation, and he believes that OMEs such as his own have distinctive advantages. He notes first that dealership arrangements with autonomous businesses outperform the few direct sales subsidiaries Gallagher has established:

> Failures have been where we've had fully-owned [sales] subsidiaries. . . . I don't believe they have had a direct enough connection between results and payment. The real successes, the big successes, are the ones where we have the local

entrepreneur and we are the backseat driver, where we own between 10 per cent and 40 per cent, and the local guy runs it like us, but we can grow them from the backseat.

By dealing through an autonomous business, Bill Gallagher captures a number of valuable assets. These include the dealer's whole-hearted commitment to the development of the business, coupled with sufficient autonomy to make the best of his or her local knowledge, and to adapt to changing local conditions (see Chapter 2, p.41 and Chapter 1, pp.10–11). But these benefits will flow only if the dealer is willing to commit a significant proportion of his or her business to Gallagher. Only when the dealer's livelihood depends on Gallagher can the latter 'grow them from the backseat' and achieve the unity of purpose and coherence of strategy that produces competitive advantage.

But getting an autonomous business to accept this level of dependency requires making long-term commitments. And these are particularly credible when they come from an OME, as Bill Gallagher explains:

> . . . one of the things that we have really stood [firm] upon is loyalty to our distributors. I get criticised because we still work with the poor-performing, to try to make a go [of them], rather than firing them and starting again. I remind them that we work with them. I put up with a bit of poor performance rather than go around and chop off heads. I see my competitors going around chopping off heads. The result? Nobody would ever get 70 per cent of [a dealer's] business on their product because they don't trust them not to get cut off. I've got people with their whole livelihood depending on us. I might be able to cut off just one or two heads. But I wouldn't get people [putting] 80–90 per cent of their business depending on us.

Would this level of dependency be possible had Gallagher been a corporate owner such as a PSC or an MNC?

> No, because nobody would trust us. You wouldn't know who the general manager was this year. Nobody in their wildest dreams would ever get 50 per cent of their [the dealer's] business. They would be too vulnerable.

So an OME is more able than other owner types to commit itself to a long-term relationship of reciprocal dependency. It is one reason why the trustworthiness and integrity evident in these leaders have contributed to the competitive advantage of their businesses (see p.107).[8] As we have seen, these same traits of commitment and trustworthiness have also contributed to the creation of high-quality workplace relationships within the firm, and to a coherent and supportive culture.

Balanced goals

Because their owners are directly and personally involved with the major constituencies of a business (its employees, customers, bankers, suppliers, distributors), and because OMEs are typically small compared with corporate entities, they are more aware of their dependence on these external parties. They are hence more likely to strike a sustainable, but evolving, balance between these interests than are the forms dominated by a single constituency (such as the PSC, MNS and COE). By ensuring that all are catered for equally, OMEs work to secure the continuing commitment of each constituency. And, as Bill Gallagher points out, for the business to succeed over a period of years, all constituents must be satisfied, and more than satisfied.

> If you look after your customer and you look after everybody in the line to the customer, then you generate wealth. [Is there an order?] Money is number three. Satisfaction really, it is fun and exciting, that's number one. Number two is the people thing: the people you work with, the customers, the distributors. And then generally wealth, that's a scorecard . . . and if you don't do that then you really can't do the first two. So which order do you put it? I personally put it at number three; but you are well to put it at number one. If you don't make money, all of a sudden money becomes number one.

Warren Rickard of Tait Electronics points out that the balance between these interests changes in response to the evolving pressures on the business. In recent years Tait has had to focus on profitability to fund extensive R&D investments and other constituents have not always received the attention they needed. As electronics technology has increased the creative and knowledge content of the product, the company has had to concern itself with the needs of its large number of engineering and software designers. Tait's Statement of Corporate Objectives shows the balance the company seeks to strike between its primary constituents (see Table 6.3).

If the OME strikes an inappropriate balance between the needs of constituencies, return on capital will suffer. OME leaders derive many forms of satisfaction from their relationship with their business. Money is only one of these and, in these relatively wealthy individuals, it is clearly subject to the law of diminishing marginal returns. As discussed, owners will at times sacrifice their own financial return to other constituents, but this is no more sustainable than short-changing any other constituency. Strong returns on capital are needed to

To benefit customers
To provide communication products and services for the benefit of customers by successfully designing, manufacturing and distributing quality radio communication equipment.

To benefit employees
To provide secure, challenging and rewarding employment, benefits and prospects for all employees.

To benefit the community and the country
To help generate wealth and enlarge the pool of technical and commercial resource within the country.

To ensure the continuance of these benefits
To evolve an organisation which is robust, profitable and progressive in order that it can thrive and grow in its ability to meet these objectives.

finance the challenging development of an OME. As Bill Gallagher notes, reflecting on his father's time, 'Well of course, making money was not really a driver at that time. It took me a few years to work that out. But if you make money you've got a whole lot more options available to you.'

The willingness of OME owners to accept modest cash payouts from their businesses may give them a temporary advantage in the financing of risky and long-horizon investments such as R&D. Angus Tait certainly links his company's ability to sustain high levels of R&D spending to his own preference for technology ahead of money. But, as he discovered when his first business collapsed, ignoring the financial dimensions of a business can only be pushed so far. Indeed, OMEs have a particular need to remain profitable, as the major source of funds to grow the business is internal. As Warren Rickard of Tait explains:

We do have some fairly rigorous financial key performance indicators that we measure. The upside of not being a public company is that you don't have to go to your shareholders and worry about your share values; and you don't have to worry about general public sentiment. The downside is you can't trot out to make a two for one issue to raise more money. So the only source of money for our R&D is the profit we make.

Because innovation requires a steady flow of investment, the OME tolerance for weak returns will ultimately be a disadvantage, even though the willingness to reinvest profits may help in the short term.

Finally, these balanced goals can find expression in a commitment to the community at large. Andi Lusty at Svedala Barmac wants to keep the business thriving for the sake of the small rural community of Matamata, of which he feels very much a part, and to which he feels considerable responsibility: 'The biggest driver for me is that if we don't change and keep improving here, then why the hell should they keep a manufacturing unit here in New Zealand?'

Warren Rickard sees similar motivations in Augus Tait:

> He feels very strongly — he is totally committed to Tait being not only a New Zealand employer, but a Canterbury employer. He gets extremely upset by companies . . . that 'take their bag of gold and run', to use Angus's expression.

Because they see themselves, their business, and their financial success as depending on a community, these leaders appear to regard the achievement of personal wealth at the expense of the community as a kind of theft.

Learning and adaptability

If the strengths of the OME form stem from the long-term involvement of the leader, so, too, do its relative weaknesses.

Among these is the reliance such firms inevitably place on the talented individuals who own and run them. A well-known transition in the evolution of an OME is the need, quite early on, to delegate responsibilities to professional managers (see Greiner, 1972). Also well known are the difficulties that talented people face in sharing the care of their enterprise with others. If OME leaders resist this difficult transition, they will limit the scope of their enterprise, and the organisational coherence that results from effective management. This was the primary lesson Angus Tait took with him from the demise of his first business: 'If you don't know something about a facet of business, you had better get somebody who does know'.

It is symptomatic of the difficulty of this transition that professional managers rather than owner managers first introduced the disciplines of financial planning and reporting (including one of the earliest installations of EVA (economic value added)-based[9] accountabilities in New Zealand) to Gallagher (Neil Richardson) and to Tait (Martyn Gall).

It is one thing to delegate functional responsibilities to professional managers, and all OMEs in this study did this many years ago. It is much harder to hand over general management responsibility, particularly while you are as full of energy, and as valuable to the enterprise, as these leaders are. Typically, the owner-manager finds it very difficult to hand over the reins. Angus Tait has had more than one attempt at this, his most recent beginning in 1998. Both he and his new CEO, a long time Tait manager, feel it is going well. Warren Rickard offers some valuable insights into what is involved in making this transition effectively:

> The key to the whole thing is probably my relationship with Angus, which is excellent. There is a level of mutual understanding and respect that is great. . . . The positive thing about the situation here is that Angus acts as a mentor. . . . Angus totally lets me have my head in terms of the way we want to go. . . . he doesn't take the CEO role. . . . He gives his opinion, which obviously people listen to, but he doesn't take a directive role. I don't ask his permission to do anything; but I keep him informed. We have lots and lots of discussions about strategies. I find that extremely valuable, just to sit down and talk with someone.

At some stage, of course, OME founders have no choice but to hand over direction of the business. Bill Gallagher and Angus Tait have thought deeply about the options here. And Paul Tidmarsh's experience at Tidco offers another perspective. The options can be quickly listed:

- Pass the business on to the next generation, as happened with great success when Bill Gallagher senior handed over to his sons, and when Reg Williams handed over to his son John;
- Hand over to professional management, and separate management from the ownership of the business, as Angus Tait has done by establishing a foundation to hold the ownership of his business;
- List on the stock exchange, an option not attractive to either Gallagher or Tait, who see the sharemarket as inimical to the long-term philosophies of their business;
- Sell to another firm, as Tidmarsh did when Svedala Industri bought up Tidco;
- Involve current management in the ownership of the business, an option Tait feels may have helped him to retain valued managers he has lost, but which Gallagher worries 'never yields a good return for the shareholders'.

Each option has its drawbacks. If these delay the transition, the result is extra demands on the leaders, possibly at a time in life when they are less able to meet them. These people have been able to grow with their firms, but at some stage the demands of the growing enterprise must be too much even for the most adaptive and talented individual.

Neither does the OME form find it easy to make use of an independent board of directors. Tait and Gallagher have constructed boards with a mix of professional skills, including law, accountancy and (in Gallagher's case) marketing, as well as senior experience in relevant businesses as CEOs or managing directors. Both boards have been with their respective companies for about four to five years. Gallagher has established regular direct reporting from operating divisions of the company to the board; hence, in Bill Gallagher's words, 'they can go round the CEO if they wish'. Both boards are small, with four to five people, and have a majority of external non-executive directors. Angus Tait has the position of executive chairman.

The use of external directors is encouraged in the PSC as a means of providing an independent challenge to the thinking of the executive. Gallagher does use his board primarily for this purpose, but Tait finds his board has a limited ability to really challenge the thinking going on inside the company:

> The difficulty in seeking an external view is that a technology company, having been in business 30-odd years, the people inside have a particular view, a depth of understanding. I find it difficult for someone external to our bit of the industry to come here and say 'Why don't you do so and so'. . . . My experience is that these external views are always disadvantaged by the limitations of their understanding of what's going on.

And in the final analysis, the OME boards have only limited influence over the affairs of the company. As Bill Gallagher puts it, 'The role of the directors is normally to hire and fire the chief executive, and that's not on; you can't do that!'

So, compared with other corporate forms, the OME form of ownership does not change its top management frequently and so cannot renew itself as readily.

Surfing a tsunami

The other enormous challenge for the OME is riding the powerful waves of change that transform the small, broad-range, domestic enterprise into a focused global leader, or even to a leading position on a regional scale. Transitions such as going global or the gusher place heroic demands on organisations and leaders. And these organisations have experienced a number of other, less dramatic episodes that have powerfully disturbed the coherence of the firm's strategy and capabilities, placing great pressure on the leader to find a new basis for the firm's competitive advantage.

As we have seen, leaders respond to these episodes with exceptional reserves of energy and commitment and an unusual capacity for personal growth. It might further be argued that, because they are small, OMEs have no choice but to adopt the focus and grow strategy. But a single OME leader will not be able to respond to these challenges as often as other corporate forms that can cycle several CEOs through the top job in the same timespan.

In the companies we have studied there have been occasions when the owner-managers have clearly chosen to avoid the pressures and the risks of the expansion paths confronting them. At PEC, John Williams made a conscious choice to phase growth from leading Australasian supplier to global supplier, by introducing a multiregional stage.

> So in 1990 when we developed the 8850 product we said we've got to become a credible world regional supplier. . . . It would have been obvious to go to America or Europe or Japan, . . . there were other companies there making far less sophisticated products but it's very hard to break down the relationships between say Deutsche Shell, Germany and [its suppliers]. . . . We went around the world and when we came back we said, the Southern Hemisphere is the place to start for our oil industry retail products.

Paul Tidmarsh, feeling his business to be exposed as the Barmac came to dominate Tidco's turnover, chose to diversify his risk in a series of new product developments. Quite apart from the removal of scarce capital from the Barmac, and the lack of success of most of these ventures, the strategy took Tidco in a direction opposite to the focus and grow strategy demanded by the company's world-leading technology.

An even more common response is for owners to find their personal goals diverging from the needs of the business. Bill Gallagher senior and Paul Tidmarsh reached a time in their lives when they wanted to enjoy the fruits of their labour. Gallagher built two large cruising boats and introduced his sons to diving. Tidmarsh chose to take up farming. These very natural choices distracted management attention and scarce capital from the insatiable needs of the business. Although all these entrepreneurs have reinvested energetically in their businesses, the huge demands of building a global or regional business from a tiny domestic base place enormous demands on the OME's ability to finance its own growth. When personal needs conflict with the needs of the business, competitive evolution is impeded.

Public stock corporation (PSC)

Professional management
Historically, the public stock corporation was invented to overcome the limitations of OME governance. By separating ownership from the management of the firm, the PSC greatly expanded the contributions employees could make to the

direction of the enterprise. Typically, multinational PSCs add professional systems of management planning and control to the OME companies they acquire. As well as providing a foundation for organisational learning, such systems make important contributions to the overall coherence of the enterprise. By moving beyond the limits of the individual owner-manager, the PSC is designed to enhance the scope and balance of the firm's configuration of capabilities. A steady flow of managers through the organisation, at all levels, gives the PSC constant access to new perspectives, and new sources of initiative and energy.

Almost the entire weight of management studies over the last two decades has been devoted to diagnosing the limitations of the PSC. These include its excessive delegations and hierarchy (see Jacques, 1990), its predilection for spending shareholders' money on diversification that produce jobs for managers but poor returns for owners, and its tendency to trap thinking in 'dominant logics' (see Bettis and Prahalad, 1995) and 'architectures of simplicity' (see Miller, 1993) that inhibit change. But the fact remains that the bulk of global production continues to pass through PSC hands. Any balanced assessment would still have to conclude that the PSC has been a great institutional innovation.

The experience of our companies suggests that many of the distinctive advantages of the PSC have indeed been realised. The PSC, in its MNC variant, or in the form of professional managers and consultants brought into the firm, has been the origin of professional management systems introduced to OMEs.[10] Nuplex Industries, which has the longest share listing history in our study (indeed one of the longest surviving listings on the New Zealand Stock Exchange), has developed a remarkable range of 2000 products and an extensive range of markets in which it is active. This breadth of scope is now the basis for the company's competitive appeal overseas. Integral to this evolution has been the development of many general management roles within the firm, roles that span marketing and HR as well as technology. Fred Holland comments on the distinctive nature of management in New Zealand:

> The fact that we are small means that individuals get a much broader view of any business at a very young age. We travel overseas, or my staff do, and when we go to some of these big companies, about ten different people have to come in to cover a range of things that we want to talk about. And we are not experts yet we do know our business pretty well in all those ten subjects. . . . We've exposed people to things very quickly, very early. I mean, I had a boss that gave me that opportunity and I give my staff the opportunity too. Some of them don't make it, but a lot of them do. And then they are very, very strong valuable people. Having just acquired a company in Australia I've transferred quite a lot of middle to upper management over there to run the show . . .

Fred Holland has drawn on this pool of general management talent to head up acquisitions as the company has led a strategy of industry rationalisation, first in New Zealand and then in Australia.

Under Fred Holland, the Nuplex board has also been carefully constructed to provide a breadth of relevant expertise and an independence of view. Fred Holland is the only executive director. External directors include:

- a senior accountant, whose expertise in receiverships has been helpful in guiding Nuplex's strategy of industry rationalisation;
- a production engineer with experience in East Asian markets, a region of growing importance to Nuplex;
- a Sydney-based lawyer with experience of the chemicals industry in Australia, having been chair of one of Nuplex's acquisitions there;
- and an Australian-based former CEO of a chemical company, with extensive global experience in the industry.

Mindful of the disciplines of sharemarket listing, Fred Holland has chosen a board that provides rigorous, independent governance. 'I wanted a board who's going to contribute, and they contribute. They are confrontational. . . . They are challenging. I've chosen to be challenged.'

Nuplex divisional managers report direct to the board on a rotational basis, and members meet with key managers. Fred Holland sees the board's primary roles as providing him with challenge and advice on the strategic development of the business, monitoring performance and ensuring that the firm has strong financial planning and control systems. The Nuplex board clearly contributes more to the governance of the firm than is possible within OME forms. The fully independent board is also a considerable improvement over the days when Nuplex was controlled by Monsanto. As we have seen, differences in strategy between parent and MNS characterised this relationship, and were expressed in boardroom battles where Bill Campbell, Fred Holland's predecessor, would argue vigorously for the company's own strategic direction on behalf of minority shareholders and against the controlling share. Fred Holland was not on the board in those days, but recalls the broken ashtrays being cleaned up afterwards.

A channel for capital?
The other great rationale for the PSC has always been its superior access to capital. There is no question that Nuplex's liberation from controlling offshore interests in 1991 has been a boon to the company. In Fred Holland's words:

We were free to develop the company in the way the company needed to be developed. And we had pretty good support from shareholders, raising capital when we needed it. . . . We came to the market with a pretty strong balance sheet, and have used it to grow the business in the way we wanted to do.

Part of the new freedom is the ability to raise debt capital, within limits of prudence. Access to debt capital can be important when commercial sensitivities preclude a new public equity offering, for which the purpose of the issue must be disclosed. Compared with its former life under MNC control, Nuplex is clearly much freer to set its own strategic direction, and to finance its growth. As a result, it has been able to take a leading position in consolidation of the Australian chemical industry through its 1998 acquisition of the largest player in that industry, Australian Chemical Holdings.

There are, however, a number of reservations about New Zealand's capital markets as a source of capital support for globally competitive enterprises based in New Zealand. As was shown in Chapter 2, transition to global leadership typically involves world-leading innovations and very large-scale growth on a limited domestic base of operations. These transitions typically grow the business ten-fold over the course of a few years and require a major expansion of the firm's capital base. These transformations are very difficult for even the most mature venture capital markets to support. For several of the companies in this study, approaches to the local venture capital market have been brief and unimpressive. In the experience of Wally and Brian Smaill of Criterion,

> The DFC for us is the reason we are here. If it hadn't been for that, we would have never, ever got off the ground. . . . [And it was done] without giving away our heart and soul. I mean, we wanted to retain control of the company. We didn't actually feel that comfortable . . . getting a venture capitalist in and sitting on our board. I'm sure they could give us good value, but in the end we've given away our business and our ideas. When's the right time to do that?

With the exception of Kiwi Dairies, all the global leaders in this study made the going global transition during the years of interventionist economic management regimes, and many benefited from export-encouraging investment and technology supports administered through the Development Finance Corporation. Whether local capital markets, deregulated now for fifteen years, have improved their ability to support transitions on this scale is a question that remains to be answered. But these transitions remain extremely risky, and PSCs may face particular difficulty in making them.

In the experience of firms in this study, capital markets are not good at valuing and supporting the long-lived and intangible assets of goodwill and reciprocity that create sustainable advantage from relationships and reputation. Governance structures dominated by just one constituency, as the PSC is dominated by the interests of capital markets, will find it harder to strike a sustainable balance between the interests of all contributors to a successful business.

Furthermore, market valuations in New Zealand as elsewhere are subject to considerable variation. They respond to self-reinforcing herding behaviours among investors that produce wide fluctuations in the valuation of underlying assets. Warren Rickard refers to the influence of 'general public sentiment' on equity valuations and Fred Holland sees fashion playing a strong role:

> Small or medium capital New Zealand businesses in 1997 were very fashionable and everyone went rushing into them. . . . Our share price rocketed up. And then it becomes unfashionable and all the way down again.

Fred Holland prefers to work with EVA-based valuations of his company, and get on with 'providing the value'. As we have seen, the risk of takeover created by sharemarket volatility is not a risk that OME leaders such as Angus Tait or Bill Gallagher are willing to take. In Gallagher's words:

> My objective is longevity of the business. How do we achieve longevity? Going public? We decided that's not it, because once you go public you get raided . . . and that's a relatively short future.

Cooperative Enterprise (COE)

Over the last 20 years, Kiwi Dairies has transformed itself from one of several Taranaki-based cooperative dairy factories into an enterprise that integrates the entire production of dairy products in the lower half of the North Island. It has consolidated production in the largest single-site dairy factory in the world, producing 6 per cent of New Zealand's total export earnings. The company has built a world-leading production facility, and in recent years has established the high-quality workplace relationships that characterise many other firms in this study. But the portfolio of capabilities developed by Kiwi Dairies is more focussed than in most of the other firms, and this is due to the distinctive structure of the dairy industry, where the industry's offshore marketing is concentrated in the New Zealand Dairy Board, and much of its R&D in the New Zealand Dairy Research Institute. In addition, the internationalisation that has been a powerful force for capability development in other companies happened for the New Zealand dairy industry over a century ago, before Kiwi Dairies even existed.

Kiwi Dairies stands out in our study for the smaller scope of its capability portfolio, and the narrower range of its evolutionary experiences. This means there is less scope to observe any distinctive contributions of the COE ownership form to the historical evolution of the business.

Relationships
The salient feature of the producer COE is, of course, the very close relationship between the enterprise and its owner-suppliers. The intensity of this relationship is more evident at Kiwi Dairies than in any other form of business relationship seen in this study. Farmers, along with dairy industry executives and directors, dominate the board of directors; the board has never included a member from outside the industry. On the other hand, representation within the industry is structured very carefully, with major geographic regions and different farm sizes being represented. Membership of the board is by election, with thirteen wards, each electing a member. Each ward represents an equivalent production of milk-solids. The company's crucial relationship with the Dairy Board is given effect through its representatives, the current CEO and the current deputy chairman.

Like the management of the company, Kiwi Dairies' board is firmly committed to the principles of co-operative enterprise.[11] These define a cooperative as follows:

> A cooperative is an autonomous association of persons united voluntarily to meet their common economic, social and cultural needs and aspirations through a jointly owned and democratically controlled enterprise.

A brief statement of the internationally accepted cooperative principles is shown in Table 6.4. Kiwi Dairies managers contrast their commitment to these principles with other, more 'corporate' styles of governance elsewhere in the industry. The strength of commitment to these principles within the company is exemplified by John Young, Kiwi Dairies' former board chairman: 'The cooperative principles are worth fighting for'.

The principle of democracy is stronger here than in the PSC corporate governance model. Although it lessens with size, owner-suppliers have historically expected a much more direct involvement with the management of the firm than is usual in a PSC.

Clearly, the strength of the ties established between the COE and its supplier-owners differentiates this form of ownership from all others in the establishment of mutually beneficial long-term networks with the firm's suppliers.[12] An inseparable part of Kiwi Dairies' capture of world-leading economies of scale has been its ability to persuade dozens of smaller dairy COEs to merge and pool their production capacity.

TABLE 6.4

Cooperative principles

- Voluntary and open membership
- Democratic member control
- Member economic participation
- Autonomy and independence
- Education, training and information
- Cooperation among cooperatives
- Concern for the community

Goal balance

On the other hand, the very close relationship with just one stakeholder has made it difficult in the past for Kiwi Dairies to give equal attention to engaging the enthusiastic support of other stakeholders. Until Craig Norgate took over as CEO in the early 1990s, farmers' interests were the only focus for executives' concern. As explained in Chapter 5, continuing expansion of the Hawera site eventually convinced management that they would not achieve the production efficiencies they sought with a 'command-and-control' workplace ethos. The company has since developed high-quality workplace relationships that contribute directly to its leading competitive position in the global industry. While this experience illustrates that producer-owned COEs can grow to embrace the needs of other stakeholders, it also shows that such developments can easily be impeded by the predominance of one stakeholder group. PSCs also confront this problem, but the unusually close control imposed on COEs makes them particularly vulnerable to this limitation.

The board plays a key role in moderating this imbalance, explaining to owners the needs of the business, and winning their support for strategic developments. The board members' insight into the needs of the business stems from their greater overview of the enterprise and its context. The Kiwi Dairies board promotes its vision through an extensive programme of area forums with owner-farmers. These air contentious issues and help the board to assess the extent of support and resistance to its initiatives. The emphasis on education enshrined in the fifth cooperative principle is partly a recognition of the challenge of remaining committed to cooperative enterprise. A well-known saying among cooperatives is 'a cooperative without education will last a generation and a half'.

Despite the constant pressure for payouts, and the resistance among some

TABLE 6.5

How different owner-types contribute to or impede the development of competitive capability

	Multinational subsidiary MNS	Owner-managed enterprise OME	Public stock corporation PSC	Cooperative enterprise COE
Capabilities				
Relational in/external reputation	? will depend on autonomy of MNS	√ mutual dependency with suppliers & distributors √ balanced goals	? due to short-run focus ? imbalanced goals	√ good link to suppliers ? imbalanced goals
Technology Innovation Multiple technology	? will depend on strategy fit to parent	? due to owner's tolerance for low profit √ firm driven by technologists		
Learning Management systems Board of Directors	√ MNC owners are source of management systems	? will depend on owner delegating to professional management	√ company run by professional management √ with independent board	
Portfolio Scope Balance Coherence	? MNC owner may restrict scope, balance, coherence	? will depend on owner delegating to professional management	√ company run by professional management	
Evolutionary processes Going global The gusher Focus and grow De-/ recoherence	? will depend on fit of MNS strategy to parent	? due to limits of • capital • energy • personal growth • personal goals		

√ = evidence of a positive contribution, distinctive to the owner type
? = evidence of an impediment, distinctive to the owner type

farmers to capital spending, the Kiwi Dairies board has successfully steered the company through the 30-year venture to consolidate milk production into the huge Hawera facility. The lasting relationship inherent in the cooperative form of governance has contributed to the board's ability to pursue the strategy for so long. In this sense, COEs have something in common with OMEs, which can also take the long view. The Kiwi Dairies experience shows, however, that COEs are unusually reliant on the quality of the board.

Conclusions on ownership

Table 6.5 gives a very brief overview of the distinctive influence that the four different owner types have had on the competitive evolution of their firms. No one type is inherently superior. Each has its distinctive strengths:

- MNS and PSC in the contributions that professional management makes to systems of organisational learning, and to the pursuit of a broad, balanced and coherent portfolio of capabilities;
- OME in the creation and sustenance of long-term relationships of reciprocal dependency and benefit;
- COE in the creation of very close relationships with one supplier group.

The distinctive strengths of each owner type has channelled the evolution of the firm's competitive capabilities to take advantage of these strengths:

- The Gallagher Group's exceptional network of offshore distributors, and its 'family' culture in the workforce;
- Tait Electronics' commitment to innovation;
- Kiwi Dairies' leveraging of high-quality relationships with owner-farmers into a world-leading scale of production;
- Nuplex's use of a pool of experienced general managers to grow into multiple technologies and multiple markets;
- Svedala Barmac's rapid internationalisation under its Swedish parent.

But each type of owner also has its inherent weaknesses. The development of these businesses indicates that firms have been able to offset the inescapable limitations of a given owner type by borrowing from, or mimicking, the strengths of others:

- OMEs have imported management systems, often embodied in experienced managers, to offset the OME's reliance on the single owner-manager;

- MNSs do better to the extent that they are given the autonomy to develop their strategy and capabilities in ways that OMEs take for granted;
- COE boards work to offset the inherently imbalanced goals of supplier-dominated governance.

By evolving in a way that makes best use of the owner's strengths, and by adapting to moderate the weaknesses inherent with each owner type, these firms have all achieved positions of leadership in their chosen markets. The problems have arisen when these processes of evolution and adaptation have been impeded:

- An MNC parent imposing its strategy on a subsidiary;
- A dominant owner-group impeding the development of other long-term relationships;
- An owner-manager whose personal goals start to depart from those of the business.

The success of these examples lies, in part, in their ability to avoid or escape these problems.

Chapter 7

Managing with a Piece of No. 8 Wire: National Culture as Competitive Advantage

Right, the reasons why we were lucky and why we did well. My father decided to set up business in New Zealand and I mentioned you were lucky if you're in New Zealand because you've got all these innovative Kiwis here and Kiwis are the most innovative people in the world and you've got the toughest customers in the world. So that's a good start. (John Williams, PEC)

INTRODUCTION

Kiwi ingenuity, commonly symbolised as the ability to improvise and innovate with nothing more than a piece of No. 8 fencing wire, is a central theme when the CEOs of our companies talk about capability. This study has centred on a shared question: 'How do you grow world-class competitive capability?' This chapter focuses on the 'New Zealandness'[1] of the companies — on national culture as competitive advantage. Hugh Fletcher joined many other comment-ators when he recently argued that a national 'game plan' for New Zealand must 'focus on what is unique about New Zealand' (Fletcher, 1999: 80).

Without being asked specifically about national culture, the CEOs chose to raise this issue themselves in various ways. In looking for links between individual competencies and organisational capability, we first asked CEOs how the 'people factor' contributed to competitive capability. What are New Zealanders especially good at? We then asked if the CEOs saw anything unique about New Zealand companies — did 'New Zealandness' make a difference to capability? While analysing what the CEOs had to say about Kiwi ingenuity, we realised that a wider sense of national identity shaped the ways they described their commitment to their companies and to New Zealand itself. These commitments were evident in such strategic issues as company ownership and location, as well as relationships with New Zealand customers and suppliers.

KIWI INGENUITY: THE NO. 8 WIRE FACTOR

In spite of the fact that metrics spelled the end of No. 8 wire, it lives on as a symbol of Kiwi ingenuity, another familiar expression that proposes a kind of unique national competence. Max Bradford, a former Minister of Business Development, has defined Kiwi ingenuity as 'thinking outside the envelope of convention . . . our readiness to adopt innovative solutions to new challenges, our refusal to be bound by the constraints of tradition and a willingness to stride ahead of the pack' (Bradford, 1997:18). In their analysis of various forms of New Zealand national identity, Wetherell and Potter have pointed out that 'nationalist discourse takes the familiar things of the small-scale and writes them large as a global "corporate identity" for 3 million people' (Wetherell and Potter, 1992:142). In this way expressions such as 'No. 8 wire' and 'Kiwi ingenuity' link individual and organisational experiences with national culture.

How did the CEOs in our study talk about a uniquely Kiwi competence? Frequently there were two or more related ideas in a single statement, as in the statement from John Williams of PEC quoted at the beginning of this chapter, there are several linked ideas:

> Right, the reasons why we were lucky and why we did well. My father decided to set up business in New Zealand and I mentioned you were lucky if you're in New Zealand because you've got all these innovative Kiwis here and Kiwis are the most innovative people in the world and you've got the toughest customers in the world. So that's a good start.

First and most important, this speaker describes the New Zealand location as positive, 'lucky'. This positive interpretation of national culture creates a good news scenario for both the speaker and those who share or who are persuaded by this story. Barry Jones is a former Australian Minister of Science and Technology, and influential writer on changes in the nature of work (Jones, 1990, 1991). In a recent speech to the Australia and New Zealand Academy of Management, he argued that negative aspects of national culture hold Australia and New Zealand back from creating smart countries (Jones, 1999). In other words, the competencies are there but they are not mobilised because our cultural frameworks exclude the possibility of economic success founded on a widespread capacity for innovation. Statements such as 'Kiwis are the most innovative people in the world' challenge these frameworks, whereas expressions such as 'colonial cringe' and 'tall poppy syndrome' reflect the ways that these post-colonial settler societies struggle within cultural limits. Barry Jones calls this problem the 'Richard Pearse syndrome'. Richard Pearse was a New Zealander who is believed to have carried out the first heavier-than-air flight before the Wright brothers. But because he was located in New Zealand, his invention never took off commercially. Jones ascribes this failure to a cultural 'syndrome' that lacked either the attitudes or the material infrastructures to realise the potential of this breakthrough. When CEOs can see this kind of potential, have the confidence that New Zealand staff can make it happen and can convey this confidence to others, they help to create the conditions for competitive advantage.

John Williams sees New Zealanders as world-class innovators who are also fortunate to be partnered with 'the toughest customers in the world'. In this way his sense of Kiwi capability links Kiwis as workers to Kiwis as customers. The customer relationship is discussed later but here it is worth noting that a positive spin on Kiwi national culture can create a virtuous circle in which various strategic players, such as customers and staff, are linked.

In talking of Kiwi culture we are inevitably referring to a set of specific historical and geographic circumstances. Being able to specify these can help to answer the question: 'What creates the innovative capacity of a nation?' (Birchfield, 2000:62). Here is how Angus Tait sees the issue:

> I'm very wary of the old Kiwi ingenuity, I'm very wary about that because there are also a lot of smart people in other parts of the world. But I will say this. There is a better phrase than Kiwi ingenuity and that is simply that we are able to do more with less. That is the truth of our situation. It's been bred out of us, it's been bred out of us and in another generation or so we won't be very much smarter than the rest of the world because the isolation that gave us the advantage of doing more with less is going away.

Several points are made here:

- there's nothing intrinsic about Kiwi ingenuity (it is not in our DNA);
- it is the product of a particular combination of geographic and historical circumstances in which isolation has forced us to 'do more with less';

- those circumstances have changed, and so we will lose, are now losing, this source of advantage.

The paradox then is that the forces of globalisation — technological, economic, political — that bring our markets closer may also take away the unique capabilities developed in response to isolation. Our CEOs identified two main components of Kiwi ingenuity: 'all-rounderness' and 'having a go at doing that ourselves'.

All-rounderness

The *Dictionary of New Zealand Archive* quotes the familiar claim that 'New Zealanders live off their reputation as super-competent all-rounders who can . . . play Mozart on a tea-chest with a length of No. 8 fencing wire' (New Zealand Dictionary Centre). Fred Holland of Nuplex explains 'all-rounderness' this way:

> I suppose one of the strengths that I recognised in New Zealand companies was people, you know, educational standards, the general innovativeness of people in this country, the fact that we are small means that individuals get a much broader view of any business at a very young age. We travel overseas, or my staff do, and when we go to some of these big companies, about ten different people have to come in to cover a range of things that we want to talk about and we are not experts yet we do know our business pretty well in all those ten subjects. Yet over there, you ask them something, 'Oh, I don't know, Joe Brown's there' so Joe Brown will have to come in and talk about that. So New Zealanders at a very early age get a very strong, almost general management overview of a business. I guess it depends on the philosophy of the company, too, but I mean that's certainly how we've developed here. We've exposed people to things very quickly, very early. I mean, I had a boss that gave me that opportunity and I give my staff the opportunity too. Some of them don't make it, but a lot of them do. And then they are very, very strong valuable people.

In this view the small size of the country creates a very broad hands-on training that supplies the textbook environment for innovation. This environment offers opportunities to try a range of new experiences and to integrate a range of knowledge types to create new knowledge, which can then be shared among staff who interact across loosely defined professional boundaries. This knowledge generation process is supported by good basic national educational standards, as well as by the philosophy of the company — in other words, by the ability of managers to foster this innovative environment and to create benefits from it.

How can this kind of all-rounderness continue to be fostered when companies go global? In the Svedala Barmac case, the close relationship between customers and on-the-spot all-rounder Kiwi engineers fed constantly back into innovative product development. Acquisition by Svedala partly broke this link, and the New Zealand management has lobbied hard to reinstate it as a component of their unique capability. The idea that Kiwi engineers have distinctive skills recurs in the literature. For instance, in a 1996 example, headlined 'Singapore group buys Kiwi ingenuity', the chairman of New Zealand's Winterfield Telecommunications Group, Ron Hayward, described the advantages of Kiwi engineers: 'A Kiwi telecommunications engineer is not like one working in a big US corporate where he trained for doing just one part of a job. Because we are a small country, most of our engineers do a lot of things.' He suggested that these skills are especially useful in Asia-Pacific markets where infrastructure is still undeveloped (Inder, 1996: 43).

'Having a go at doing that ourselves'

'Let's have a go at doing that ourselves' (Criterion). This phrase expresses the attitude of inventing, reworking and adapting technologies to get the job done. Again this attitude is seen as a product of isolation: 'As we grew on, we said the problem is that we just cannot get the technology overseas, we have to do it ourselves and we just made sure we had the right people to do that' (Wally Smaill, Criterion).

Smaill is also clear that there was no point in inventing for the sake of it, or inventing where you can modify:

> We said why reinvent the wheel, if there is technology available elsewhere, and we can obtain it, it is a lower cost way of doing the same job. But you still have to have the capability of modifying it to suit your own market . . .

Fred Holland of Nuplex makes a similar point:

> We've modified a lot of things. We've taken processes that have been designed to some specific need and then we've adapted them to meet the needs that we've identified to make our product better. I think that goes even through the systems and things like that, that we've incorporated in our business as we've seen fit.

In managing Kiwi ingenuity, these CEOs talk about relating invention and adaptation to strategy. Wally Smaill of Criterion also stresses the value of sharing the knowledge that is created:

'There's got to be an easier way' [is] really just a way [of thinking] in everything we do. I suppose that's the way we are. We're always trying to go the next step and if you like, record the way it's done so that we can improve on the results that we achieve as we go through.

How does Kiwi ingenuity mesh with an organisational culture of innovation? John Williams of PEC:

We create an environment for innovation. . . . We created a caring environment for our staff members which encouraged innovation and with anyone's idea on anything fairly evaluated and adopted if appropriate.

Hitting cultural limits

But as well as providing a resource for imagining desired new futures, national identity has limitations that constrain what those future successes can be, and who will share in them (see Table 7.1).

In a discussion of new versions of national identity in the new millennium, Anthony Hubbard has argued that many of our 'favourite legends' of 'national character' are 'comforting fantasies' that 'won't fit the new chaos' of our current situation (Hubbard, 2000: A1). In particular, he points out that 'the versatile Kiwi —the fellow who can do anything with a piece of Number 8 wire — has deep roots . . . in pioneer culture'. This is a rural figure of the past — 'the laconically humorous rural man who can turn his hand to anything. He dislikes women but he knows exactly what to do with a sheep' (*Ibid.*). It is clear that there are aspects of Kiwi ingenuity that belong inevitably in a rural, isolated past. The pioneer settler mentality can have mileage in terms of what Bradford calls 'our refusal to be bound by the constraints of tradition' (Bradford, 1997:18), but it can also perpetuate an attitude of superiority over not only the old colonial powers, but also the tangata whenua.

Can the most enabling frameworks for Kiwi ingenuity be reworked for the present and future, and how? For instance, No. 8 fencing wire skills and Kiwi masculinity have traditionally been inseparable. A recent collection on Kiwi masculinity has the 'male' symbol in No. 8 fencing wire on its cover (Law, Campbell and Dolan, 1999), and the tradition of 'blokes in sheds' lives on as an image of Kiwi innovation (Hopkins and Riley, 1999). Not only does this masculine image continue to marginalise women in a range of industries, it tends to reproduce masculine cultures which value 'hard' technical skills most highly and discount 'soft' skills that characterise contemporary knowledge work. Similarly, policy initiatives to improve national capability tend to centre on science and technology rather than commercial skills such as marketing and information

TABLE 7.1

How No. 8 fencing wire Kiwi ingenuity works to both enable and constrain a vision of Kiwi capability

ENABLING	CONSTRAINING
• creates empowering links to existing, embedded narratives of Kiwi capability • can be reconfigured for competencies of the future, e.g. as knowledge work • can be rewritten for new industry contexts, e.g. film, fashion • emphasises that working in small distributed locations encourages innovation rather than standardisation • focuses on existing 'hard' technical skills	• is located in a nostalgic past of rural and engineering-based industries • is limited to masculine 'Kiwi bloke' identities (the bush engineer hiding out in the shed) • is limited to neo-British settler identities • emphasises 'doing it ourselves' — risks failure to look for outside expertise • marginalises 'soft' skills

systems (Hooper, 1999), or cultural industries (Creative New Zealand, 1998, 1999) such as film and fashion, which have already proved to be world-class.

Thus several traditional dominant themes of New Zealand national identity are limiting for the future. Rather than making a futile attempt to reinvent national culture from nothing, it is time to bring into the picture the marginalised aspects of national culture and consider what they have to offer. The power of such themes as 'Kiwi ingenuity' can be reworked to include new industries, and to emphasise the increasingly smart and knowledge-intensive components of our traditional industries.

'BEING PREPARED TO LISTEN'

I have used the phrase 'being prepared to listen' to symbolise what CEOs describe as the kind of open, curious, even naïve, approach to business relationships characteristic of New Zealanders. This approach is especially effective in relation to customers, both locally and overseas. John Williams (PEC) puts the issues together this way:

> Well, the biggest advantage is that we're developing products and trying to sell them initially to New Zealand customers. We are prepared to listen — New Zealand is a classless society so our hardware designers and our software designers are quite prepared to go and work on a service station and talk to the

service station proprietor. You wouldn't get an American software designer going down and getting his hands dirty talking to a service man, that would be below his monetary class. But we're a smaller group of people and we like listening and we are prepared to listen to other people and all these good ideas get incorporated into our new products.

In this example Kiwis are not only prepared to listen, but to do so cuts across conventional professional boundaries. It is not only service or marketing staff, but also engineers and designers, who go out and create knowledge-generating relationships with customers. This working 'outside the envelope of convention' (Bradford, 1997:18) is again a source of an 'all-rounder' approach that fosters innovation. In going global, these open attitudes also help to create good ongoing marketing relationships.

Being prepared to listen, and to learn, is associated in a number of stories with a naïve attitude to business. This naïveté or ignorance allowed for openness and a willingness to take risks and to build capability by making sure that they 'had the right people to do that' (Wally Smaill). Rick Wells of Formway:

> I suppose the advantage of ignorance was we decided that we would get hold of some people that knew something. So the first real decision was to get a designer involved and I suppose what we had was a certain intellectual capability even if we didn't know a lot about furniture, also an interest in production and design which has grown but was there.

The advantage of being 'seat-of-our-pants, Kiwi cowboys' (Fred Holland) is an openness to new possibilities. But the 'intellectual capability', in Formway's terms, has to be there so that the more specific competencies can be learnt.

Listening to local customers is mentioned repeatedly as a source of learning and innovation:

> Where we couldn't license technology we started to develop it, in conjunction with the customers. And again, in a small environment like New Zealand the relationship between us and the customer is very close and we work together to develop what the customer wants to achieve from the product. (Fred Holland, Nuplex)

Here we have the combination of a small market with close customer relationships, the willingness to listen and innovation. A number of CEOs also argued that the New Zealand market is especially smart and demanding, and so is an excellent ground for learning and innovation. John Williams (PEC) linked the smartness of the local customer to national culture:

We only expect our yachties and our rugby players to be the best but we are the best at anything, let me tell you. One of the toughest markets in the world in which to sell your product is right here in New Zealand because our customers are more technologically aware than any other customers in the world. There are more Internet users in Wellington, New Zealand, per head of population, than anywhere in the world, and many of your New Zealand customers will always check the Internet before they decide to make a purchase. New Zealanders know what technology should be able to deliver, and they absolutely demand that you deliver it plus. The other thing they don't give to you easily is business just because they went to the same school as you. They want to use their dollars wisely and not just to meet their needs now, but for the years ahead. So if you can meet a customer's needs in New Zealand and Australia . . . you'll have a world-class product bar none. Our toughest market is New Zealand. It gets easier in Australia. It gets easier in South East Asia and in Europe it's a dream, I can tell you.

Others also mentioned New Zealand's reputation as an early new technology adopter, but the excellence of our more traditional industries as the platform for innovation was also seen as an advantage. According to Bill Gallagher, this excellence enables companies 'to be number one in the market of the most demanding customer and that's what we say New Zealand agriculture is today'. Svedala Barmac's Andi Lusty similarly explains that 'Most of the ideas come from the quarries themselves . . . [You have to be] out there seeing what product managers say — "Try this and see how this works" — and you pick up an idea that you can develop on. Without them you wouldn't know.' Here the reference is not just to the local market, but also to the global range of customers that Svedala Barmac has worked alongside for decades.

It is now an accepted tenet of innovation that what Porter calls 'demand conditions' drive 'pressure and incentives to innovate' (Porter, 1998b). Ironically, unlike the CEOs in our study, he believes that 'New Zealand customers are still not demanding customers' (*Ibid.*). Several of our companies saw the local market as a positive resource. Furthermore, they had thought about how to manage it most effectively, through creating relationships, being prepared to listen and to learn, and knowing how to draw effectively on the knowledge created. They not only perceived local customers as smart enough to be worth listening to, but they were also willing to listen. Many saw that capacity as related to national culture.

This low-key and open, even 'naïve', Kiwi approach can also be seen as a plus in creating global customer relationships. In a discussion of OE (the traditional overseas experience gained by Kiwis in their 20s), Inkson, Thomas and Barry

(1999) argue that the very unstructured and open quality of self-managed OE can be a source of national competitive advantage. As opposed to structured 'expatriate' experiences, OE provides 'a unique opportunity to operate autonomously and flexibly and to try new experiences' (*Ibid.*, p. 60). This argument relates to the CEO's comments on being prepared to listen. First, it highlights the value of a kind of Kiwi learning experience that is not generally recognised as adding value to organisations or to national capability. Second, Inkson et al. suggest that there are ways to learn more effectively from this kind of experience, that learning from our experiences is too important to be left completely to chance. Our national experience can be seen as a source of tacit knowledge (Polyani, 1967) that we can find articulate and share.

The Kiwi OE learning stems from our unique historical and geographic situation: many New Zealanders are driven by the smallness and remoteness of their country to go overseas to learn. This drive generates a global perspective and confronts us with other cultural possibilities. For the organisations in our study, going global was a requirement for success, and their marketing OE, approached with openness and a willingness to learn, can be seen as a source of national as well as organisational competitive advantage.

'I LIKE NEW ZEALAND'

When is a New Zealand company no longer a New Zealand company? In choosing our case study companies, we tacitly made an assumption that New Zealand companies were those established and grown here. We also assumed a continuity of identity for our companies, namely through time in the concept of 'evolution', and within the 'elastic boundaries' (Anderson, 1991) of nationality. Not all of them are New Zealand-owned, and it is possible that more will become mainly foreign-owned and move their headquarters out of New Zealand, or become just another branch of a multinational. Does it matter? To some of our CEOs, yes it does. In several examples we see that strong, personal commitments to New Zealand make a difference to strategic direction. As Wally Smaill of Criterion pointed out, a commitment to New Zealand's people and lifestyle was a strong factor in decisions about location:

> Question: You've never thought about setting up offshore in the States, for example?
>
> But actually I didn't really want to do it. [I like] my lifestyle and I like New Zealand.

In this example lifestyle and commitment — not 'deserting' New Zealand — are stronger factors than personal enrichment. In the case of Svedala Barmac, a commitment to keeping its base in Matamata and contributing to the local community is written into the company objectives. This commitment again springs from the personal values of successive CEOs and senior managers. To date purchase by the Swedish company Svedala has not threatened this objective, but Svedala Barmac must maintain its world benchmark manufacturing performance to retain its relative autonomy. Andi Lusty describes the Matamata location as combining several advantages: increased independence from the parent company, a stable workforce, local buying power and strong supplier relationships.

> . . . if we're in Italy, a Swedish manager can easily hop on a plane and be there every day and go back at the weekends. He doesn't do that here. He comes once and says, 'It really is a long way away!'. . . I think the stable workforce is very much a plus. In fact I think it's also a plus for us in terms of our buying power because we are one of the bigger players in terms of purchasing steel in New Zealand, and in terms of purchasing other inputs. So I think we do quite well. I think for all the malignment that Kiwis get, I don't think our suppliers add on such a huge margin. . . . We found in going to Svedala purchasing conferences that we're probably one of the best buying companies in the world. . . . So that has to be an advantage.

The CEO's perspective will determine whether location is viewed as a strategic plus or a minus. A personal commitment to a location or culture is likely to create a positive frame of mind. Some, for instance, see the small size of New Zealand companies as a bonus:

> What advantage have we got against our competitors? If you take why were we [successful] globally, I think we were much more receptive and flexible than our competitors. (Wally Smaill, Criterion)

Formway's Rick Wells, too, regards the flexibility of a small company as an opportunity to diversify:

> If we were in Europe we probably would have been only a seating manufacturer. It's almost [unheard] of for companies in Europe to be a systems manufacturer and a seating manufacturer. We decided that in this part of the world where flexibility and small markets is the name of the game that we need to be offering a broader range of products so we can capitalise on the relationships we built in the marketplace.

The examples in our project show that national culture informs who we are and the choices we make. Some of the CEOs we interviewed were very clear that their own sense of who they were and the choices they made were inseparable from their sense of New Zealand identity, whether or not they were born here. In most cases these personal choices translated into organisational strategies, the decision to remain a New Zealand company being a key one. From a business perspective, the questions revolve around such considerations as 'Can my business flourish from New Zealand?' and 'Could I personally do better if I move and/or take the company overseas?' Having decided that their business can do well from New Zealand, a number of the CEOs are committed to some sense of national identity or loyalty that makes the difference. In the current climate there is open tension about these issues as they translate into individual choices to leave or stay. National political debates on the brain drain —'Are New Zealand's skills going down the gurgler?' (Springall, 2000:14) — underscore the strategic importance of such choices for the country as a whole. When successive governments in the 1980s and 1990s have openly fostered a culture of competitive individualism, John F. Kennedy's 1961 call to young people to 'ask not what your country can do for you — ask what you can do for your country' (Kennedy, 1961) seems almost incomprehensible.

It is likely that the personal sense of national identity and commitment expressed by these CEOs has the flavour of a particular generation. If the positions of national cultural identity are to flow through successive generations, we have to find ways to renew and rework them. New Zealand's recent period of competitive individualism has also seen the counter-example of 'peoplehood nation-building' (Fleras and Spoonley, 1999, p. 76) in the form of the Maori renaissance. This renaissance incorporates moves towards economic and cultural success built on a strong and unique cultural identity ('Brand Maori') combined with a global focus (Hunter, 1999; Tapsell, 1997). There are lessons to be learnt here, and Brand New Zealand tends to look to Brand Maori for its distinctiveness. As The Knowledge Economy report puts it:

> Maori culture is unique to New Zealand. Maori participation in the knowledge economy provides an opportunity for New Zealand to explore how this uniqueness can be used to distinguish New Zealand from other 'western' states and economies. (Minister for Information Technology's Advisory Group, 1999, p. 21; see also Fletcher, 1999)

National culture is a perspective that links deeply felt personal identity, organisational strategy and national economic and social policies.[2] Capability works on all of these levels. For some companies national identity also has a particular link with international branding. This is most explicit in the case of Montana:

We said, 'Hey, we really do have something which is a bit different here.' The question is, would the rest of the world like it? . . . We determined very early on that our first attempt to sell wine in the USA was not to sell wine but to sell New Zealand, and therefore we had to sell what New Zealand was, and what were the values of New Zealand.

Branding exercises may draw on national culture, but is national culture more than a brand? Advertising guru Kevin Roberts has been deeply involved in various campaigns designed to sell New Zealand to the world. In these he and his colleagues have made a conscious effort to rethink and rework the traditional themes of national culture to create a new New Zealand story that will work well for the future (Roberts, 1998). As Roberts puts it, 'The management of Brand New Zealand sits at the core of our nationhood and sovereignty.' Here he puts his finger on the place where questions of national culture and questions of economic development intersect. Nationhood and sovereignty are much bigger concepts than the idea of the brand or even of economic success. To be able to draw on national culture to create successful organisations is not the same as collapsing national culture under the heading of a brand. The brand idea is taken to an extreme when Roberts suggests that all New Zealanders must contribute to a massive global tourism effort that will be the country's economic salvation. Such a campaign will depend on the New Zealand people and culture, not just the scenery. Even in the course of our daily lives we are to contribute to Brand New Zealand, as Roberts (1999) explains: 'Yours is the most important task in the whole process. You provide the compelling, memorable, quality experiences.'

Taken to this extreme — national culture as theme park — the concept of nation-as-brand starts to crack. How far can or should national culture be socially engineered at the organisational or at the national level? Is national culture a resource or a commodity? Who can own or control it?

DISCUSSION

We have competency in everything in New Zealand. We are probably the most innovative people in the world, bar none. I told that to Jenny Shipley and Bill Birch [then Prime Minister and Treasurer] yesterday and I really hammered it in saying, you people are letting us down by not telling us and the world how good we are. But some of the people round here didn't believe me so I started quoting. (John Williams, PEC)

A range of very disparate, often conflicting, commentators on New Zealand agree on one point — that we need to talk up the capability of New Zealand

and New Zealanders (*Bright Future*, 1999; Kelsey, 1999; Porter, 1998b; Roberts, 1999). In its editorial of May 2000, *Unlimited* argues that:

> The reason we don't have an Ericsson or a Lego or indeed another Glaxo is due to a lack of imagination — New Zealand can create global companies and brands. But, first we need to believe we can find markets that have no end and believe we can serve them, from here (Heeringa, 2000, p. 5).

This proposition emphasises the achievement of companies like the ones in our study. New Zealanders *have* already created global companies and brands, and served global markets 'from here'. It also points to the importance of national culture in generating the 'imagination' (Roberts, 1999) and the 'vision' (Porter, 1998b) that will draw on and develop the culturally embedded competencies found in this country. This means that it is unnecessary, and probably undesirable, for us to swap areas of traditional excellence like pastoral management for cellphone manufacture (Porter, 1998b).

Many of the issues currently confronting New Zealand companies are expressed in terms of responses to globalisation. Globalisation itself works like a story that intersects with the stories of national culture in various ways (Grice and Fleming, 1999), creating a series of critical questions for New Zealand companies (James, 1993):

- Does it mean encouraging foreign ownership and investment?
- Does it mean becoming a 'branch economy' of elite and well-educated knowledge workers employed by multinational knowledge-intensive industries?
- Does it mean becoming 'another Glaxo', translating global success into leaving New Zealand and the New Zealand economy behind?
- Does it mean, as our study exemplifies, creating unique products for global markets and serving them 'from here'?

These options flow from two contrasting ways of looking at national culture:

- national culture is a unique source of national competitive advantage and therefore a resource to be nurtured and developed; or
- national culture is an obsolete way of looking at things, and is even the source of 'insular attitudes' (New Zealand Treasury, 1990:31) that stand in the way of a 'borderless world' (Ohmae, 1991) and the inevitable 'homogenisation of all human societies, regardless of their historical origins or cultural heritages' (Fukuyama, 1992: xiv).

Michael Porter raises the question: 'What creates the innovative capacity of a nation?' Reg Birchfield argues that 'Managers here [in New Zealand] should in turn be asking what they must do to create a work environment that builds their individual organisation's innovative capacity' (Birchfield, 2000:62). On the basis of our case studies, this chapter has argued that national culture can be regarded as a resource to create positive scenarios for New Zealand companies and foster capabilities for innovation. But drawing on this resource is a skilful matter; there can be no five magic steps for managing cultural identity. Furthermore, national identity is not separate from organisations or from the individuals who manage and staff them: they are both products and producers of national culture (Knights and Morgan, 1991). Cultural understandings and skills form part of the tacit knowledge of New Zealand managers, and their staff. Processes that will help articulate and develop that tacit knowledge could contribute to both national and organisational capabilities. Stephen Hill, then director for Australia's Centre for Research Policy, has argued that:

> The power to assert a local cultural voice in the economic world arises from an alignment between global and local knowledge at a local level. . . . Across the whole development spectrum there is therefore a new advantage emerging for the 'small player' who plays their local cultural strength and its knowledge linkages most harmoniously (Hill, 1995:108).

The national programmes that are needed now, according to Hill, are both technical/scientific and social — 'both technical and social analytical abilities are implied within all levels of education' (*Ibid.*, p. 109). This chapter has drawn on a small group of CEOs to open up some questions about the 'social analytical abilities' that are needed to enable a small player like New Zealand to identify and develop 'local cultural strength' and thus to align local and global knowledge. A useful next stage would be to ask New Zealand managers and business people directly how they see national culture within their future vision. It is undoubtedly true that, in the words of Prime Minister Helen Clark, the recognised cultural industries 'define and strengthen us as a country, as communities and as individuals... [and the cultural] sector expresses our unique national identity' (Clark, 2000). But national culture is also being played out every day in sectors that are not marked cultural, and in ways that make a major difference to our national capability. All our sectors are sources of 'cultural capital' (Harley and Volkerling, 1999).

The CEOs in our study have demonstrated cultural knowledge and skills that are evident in their views of the relationship between organisational success and national culture, and are reflected in their own commitments to New

Zealand. It could be argued that by agreeing to participate in such a study they have demonstrated an unusual degree of collective commitment to the success of New Zealand businesses, and are therefore unrepresentative of local CEOs. But my references to the popular New Zealand management literature show that their concerns and commitments echo those of others and are central to current debates on the role of government in relation to business, knowledge and culture. These companies also demonstrate that it is possible to run a very effective local company that responds and contributes positively to the way we see national culture and capability — who we are, who we can be.

Chapter 8

The Role of Government

The organisations involved in this study went through their formative years at a time when government played a far larger role in the economy and society at large than it does now. We deliberately selected companies with a long history because previous work suggested that history casts a long shadow over the development of an organisation's distinctive attributes. We also had a specific interest in seeing how the reforms of the mid-1980s affected the evolutionary process.

The regime of economic management in New Zealand is now radically altered, and the environment these companies grew up in has gone. It is well beyond the scope of this study to assess the merits and demerits of that change, but we could not adequately describe the development of these businesses without exploring the government's influence. This chapter does so, drawing on the company histories that were written for the project.

From a policy perspective, the influences noted here should be of interest in highlighting areas for policy debate; however, we do not attempt to participate in that debate. At the most, we point out those areas where past policy has supported the evolution of competitive capability, and thus specify areas where the new regime needs to be assessed.[1]

WORKPLACE FLEXIBILITY

As has been shown in Chapters 2 to 4, workplace flexibility has been integral to the advantages our organisations have established. Global leaders have sought to balance the conflicting demands of economies of scale with the need for multiple product variants for their diverse national markets. They have done this by consolidating production in one New Zealand-based facility, and by adopting a range of strategies to make its operation flexible and capable of producing the variety required. Workforce flexibility has been central to this effort. Regional leaders have the same imperative, but for different reasons. For them, product variety stems from the broader range of products they offer for their regional markets.

In the pursuit of flexibility these firms adopted strategies of multiskilling and the erosion of demarcation boundaries, years before the Employment Contracts Act (ECA) was introduced in 1991. The ECA did not make any appreciable contribution to the competitive evolution of these firms because they had already achieved much of the flexibility the legislation was designed to produce. On the other hand, the reintroduction of restrictions to workplace flexibility has the potential to impede practices that are central to the competitive success of many of these enterprises. They are watching the progress of the new labour law with interest.

Even the supposedly employer-friendly ECA produced its frustrations. Andi Lusty is not alone in railing at the time and expense it involved:

> But honestly you'd be crazy to set up in business at the moment because nobody can comply with, nobody can even take the time to read and try to understand all the Acts that we have to comply with in business now. It's absolutely impossible the duress you're under. You can't fire anybody any more. . . . You can go through any number of warnings, verbal and written. . . . and you have to give them a chance to improve; and if they don't improve, then you have to give them another chance and another warning and go through the whole thing again. Nine months later you're in deeper strife than you ever were before, but you still have a disruptive person in the organisation, and you still can't get rid of them. I guarantee when you finally take the decision, you will be taken to court, then you'll lose. . . . Well we don't have the time to do that. We just absolutely don't have the time or the inclination to do it. So our lawyers say 'If you get into that situation just let me know and we'll negotiate and it will cost $15,000 to $20,000 now but at least you don't have to go through all this stuff', and no more problem. It is indeed a cost, but under the new legislation [the Employment Relations Bill of 2000] the primary judgement will be re-instatement. In future we will have to live with the disruption a cancer causes. I just wonder if you're going to have an industry [left]. Are we really encouraging businesses to grow and entrepreneurs to employ? (I'm not saying subsidies or anything like that) but you've got to make the environment [right for] somebody to want to employ somebody else, who wants to grow their business.

INNOVATION AND TECHNOLOGY

As seen in Chapter 3, innovation has been the ultimate source of the differentiation that has created global leaders from tiny, isolated New Zealand enterprises. Companies like Tait Electronics and Gallagher, among others, were supported in this by a range of government programmes and incentives.

The basic work on mains-powered electric fencing was done at the government-funded Ruakura Research Centre in the early 1960s, and was the ultimate source of Gallagher's world-beating innovation. The company received further support during the long eight-year process of commercialising the technology. As the following recollection from Bill Gallagher shows, the lure of a technology development grant played an important role in transforming the company's approach to R&D from amateur dabbling into professional technology:

> At that time R&D was really knife and fork on the kitchen table kind of stuff. . . . We never measured the amount of money. It was sort of every night and weekends. . . . What really took us from the kitchen table knife and fork was an R&D grant when we got paid 50 per cent of the increased expenditure on R&D . . . . That made sure you were doing it properly, not doing it on a shoestring and that really made quite a difference.

Tait mobile radios would not have been possible without the investment of the government-run New Zealand Post Office in a national network of transmission stations. The early development of this network fostered the creation of a mobile radio industry in New Zealand, from which Tait eventually emerged triumphant and went on to take his world-class devices into the much larger British market, and thence the world.

The New Zealand economy is a follower in many broad areas of technology, and is subject to the inefficiencies and technical imperfections of small scale. Do the kind of market signals that emerge from such an economy give enough incentive for the innovations that have created global leaders among these New Zealand firms? The evidence of the major global economies is that knowledge production is a locationally sticky activity. In other words, it grows best in integrated clusters of technologically advanced firms where pools of information, talent and informed financing develop for the benefit of all, and where specialisation — what we have called 'focus and grow' — is encouraged (see Porter, 1998). Isolated from these engines of innovation, countries like New Zealand must find their own ways to transform a generous supply of 'dabblers' into focused technology leaders. Remove these transformations and the country's innovative potential will not get much past the stage of 'blokes in sheds'. As we saw in Chapter 3, government has made useful contributions to this transformation in these firms in the past. Whether or not the scaling back of these contributions has improved matters, and released a stronger flow of world class innovations, is an open question.

EXCHANGE RATES

A key part of the process of going global for these New Zealand firms, as described in Chapter 2, is the focusing of product scope onto the innovative product that is impelling the firm into global export markets. The alternative (regional leadership) strategy is to retain a broader product scope and concentrate on Australasian markets.

In the experience of the Smaill brothers at Criterion, the exchange rate can influence this strategic choice:

> Strong New Zealand dollar: narrow market, broader products. Weaker New Zealand dollar ... wider markets, narrower focus. If you want to be world competitive you must have a narrow focus, as narrow a focus as you possibly can.

For a firm of a given size, the tighter margins produced by a strong currency remove profitability for marginal global markets, and encourage the firm to defray fixed overheads over a broader product range. Conversely, the stronger margins produced by a weaker currency increase the firm's potential geographic scope, and allow greater product focus.

CAPITAL MARKETS AND GOING GLOBAL

This study has highlighted the unprecedented scale of internationalisation when undertaken from a tiny New Zealand home base (see Chapter 2). It has also highlighted the very significant risks attached to this transition, as the balance of the firm's configuration of capability is disturbed and great pressure is brought to bear on the coherence of the firm's overall value offering in unfamiliar markets. When the firm involved is owner-managed, the personal pressures involved are extreme, to the extent that some entrepreneurs understandably recoil from them (see Chapter 6). As if all this were not enough, these transitions have in every case been motivated by the global potential of the firm's proprietary innovation, as yet untried offshore.

The risks attached to financing such propositions would give even a highly sophisticated capital market pause. In the years when these organisations went through this transition there was certainly nothing close to the venture capital market required, and the government-run Development Finance Corporation made useful contributions to many of these firms, contributions that are acknowledged to this day.[2] Wally and Brian Smaill of Criterion are particularly firm in this acknowledgement:

> The DFC for us is the reason we are here. If it hadn't been for that, we would have never, ever got off the ground. . . . [And it was done] without giving away our heart and soul. I mean, we wanted to retain control of the company. We didn't actually feel that comfortable . . . getting a venture capitalist in and sitting on our board. I'm sure they could give us good value, but in the end we've given away our business and our ideas. When's the right time to do that?

The theme of control is prominent in discussions on this issue. Typically, entrepreneurs feel, like the Smaills, that funders are too greedy in their expectations of an equity stake in the business. In discussing these perceptions with providers of capital, we have been told that small businesses have quite unrealistic expectations about what constitutes a reasonable equity stake in return for venture funding. These very informal perceptions suggest that the current position is one where the two sides of this market are talking past each other, with little profitable business being done in between.

Our study has shown that the financing of the going global transition is a distinctively risky proposition when done for the small New Zealand base. Whether current venture capital markets are meeting this challenge is a question worthy of exploration.[3]

FOREIGN OWNERSHIP

The contribution of MNC parents to the evolution of competitive capability in their subsidiaries has been explored in depth in Chapter 6. This study has been fortunate to be able to compare and contrast a range of experiences with this form of ownership. Its conclusions suggest that offshore owners woo New Zealand businesses with a mixed bouquet.

Svedala Industri has undoubtedly supported its Barmac subsidiary by giving it ready access to funds and to its global distribution network. In the very early days, Revertex also contributed technology to the company that grew into Nuplex Industries. But the Nuplex experience also shows that these benefits are dependent on the fit between the parent's strategic direction and that of its subsidiary. Usually, the second becomes submerged in the first and Fred Holland is perhaps rare for having escaped to tell his tale of impeded development. Svedala Barmac's experience also shows that the benefits of an MNC relationship will be limited if subsidiaries are not given autonomy to develop their portfolio of capabilities. We have reached these conclusions by looking at the subsidiary's experience of the relationship. Similar conclusions have been reached by those who have looked at the relationship from the parent's end (see Goshal and Bartlett, 1995; Birkenshaw, Hood and Jonsson, 1998).

Offshore capital offers many appeals: managerial expertise, funding and access to the parent's extensive portfolio of capabilities. Our study suggests that these offerings should not be accepted uncritically. Their realisation will depend on the degree of autonomy and strategic alignment between the parties. When absolute control is ceded, it is the parent alone that determines the nature of the relationship.

It seems unlikely that government in New Zealand will again interest itself with the national origins of capital. After all, when seen purely as finance, all money is the same. But it is apparent from the experience of these firms that when money buys control, the positive contributions of foreign owners to the evolution of competitive capability are far from certain.

RUGGED LANDSCAPES AND NATIONAL COMPETITION IN NURTURING ENTERPRISE

All the companies involved in this study grew up under a regime of border protection, when government enhanced the natural economic protection provided by the country's isolation. The result was a local economy characterised by many tiny market niches, protected from the full force of global competition. Biologist Stuart Kauffman has evocatively christened ecological environments with these characteristics 'rugged landscapes'.[4]

Companies in this study used these conditions in three ways to develop competitive capabilities that are now a foundation for their global and regional success. First, they have had the scope to 'dabble' in a range of technologies and markets as they sought to identify the areas where their distinctive capabilities would have most value. Before a company can focus and grow it must first sow and reap by making a number of forays into products and markets that seem to hold promise for them.[5] Rugged landscapes offer many sheltered opportunities for sowing and reaping. Hence Gallagher produced a wide range of agricultural equipment before it focused on the one product of electric fencing. Montana explored a number of market segments in its Cold Duck days, before targeting the premium quality market segments that are the basis for its present success. Scott Technology's entrée into the engineering of whiteware production lines was via the production of whiteware itself. Thus a phase of experiment has been important for these firms in identifying a distinctive advantage for themselves. Rugged landscapes provide a rich environment for such experiment.

TABLE 8.1

How to make (and unmake) a rugged landscape

- Take a sheet of paper.
- Crumple it up into a ball.
- Uncrumple it until it is about two-thirds of its original area.
- The complex topography of valleys and hills models the variety of protected market niches offered by an isolated economy.
- To simulate the effect of deregulation, flatten the paper out smoothly.

Second, these firms have used the protection of the local market to build, on a small scale, the balanced configurations of capability that later allowed them to capitalise on their world-leading innovations and take them global. As we saw in Chapter 2, the experience of Bendon in attempting this transition with an inadequately balanced portfolio led to disaster.

Third, companies like Nuplex have been able to spread into a range of products and markets which has given them a breadth of expertise that is now the basis of their competitive appeal offshore.

New Zealand's experience with the regime of protection, on the scale that it was practised, proved to most people's satisfaction that the costs attached to this particular form of intervention were too high. But the benefits of the regime for the encouragement of new enterprise and the development of competitive capabilities have been forgotten, if indeed they were ever apparent. When deregulation swept away 30 years of protection, it effectively flattened the country's competitive landscape into the fabled 'level playing field' (Table 8.1, step 5).(The words of Thomas More in Robert Bolt's *A Man for All Seasons* spring to mind: 'Who will stand in the winds that would blow them?') Without any other form of support for nascent enterprise, it is important to ask whether current conditions provide a level of support competitive with that offered by other nation states.[6]

Angus Tait offers his opinion on this question:

> We grew the roots of our business before 1984. By 1984, we were quite well advanced in terms of experience … in selected export markets. … We had nourishment flowing up those roots, so when things became difficult for a normal domestic-based manufacturer, we were not affected by that. … When this landscape was flattened, for someone to start then, to grow the roots, it was very difficult.

What have we got out of the last fifteen years? The reality is, not very much. We have a very cost-competitive economy but we haven't got much beyond that. . . . For fifteen years, in terms of growing an alternative economy we haven't done anything. . . . We have flattened the field and watched the crops grow. Well, not much has sprouted.

THE EFFECTS OF DEREGULATION

One of the reasons we chose to examine businesses whose history straddled the reforms of the mid-1980s was to see what effect this significant change had on their evolution. The effects were various:

- For those firms well established offshore, with the bulk of their revenues coming from overseas, the removal of border protection had no appreciable impact. Svedala Barmac, Criterion and Kiwi Dairies were of this type.
- For some, the impact was indirect and delayed. Formway's sales were only affected after the 1987 stockmarket and property collapse eventually led to a marked drop in sales of office furniture in 1991; by this time, however, the company had established its Australian business and was, to a degree, insulated from the downturn.
- For Nuplex, deregulation hastened a process of industry consolidation that the company had already decided to lead, and a transition to a position of regional industry leadership.
- For Tait Electronics and Gallagher, deregulation exposed a lack of cost competitiveness, which both companies energetically corrected in the late 1980s.

In summary, these firms responded to deregulation much as they have dealt with other dislocations: they struggled to recreate, in the new environment, coherence and balance in their configurations of strategy and capabilities. In the process, the companies most challenged by the reforms, such as Tait and Gallagher, created new capabilities of low-cost manufacturing by moving to more automated production and adopting the range of operations strategies described in Chapter 4.

Just as these companies had drawn advantage from the legacy of government protection of rugged landscapes, they created new advantages from New Zealand's leadership in the removal of protection. Nuplex began its strategy of industry consolidation in New Zealand almost a decade before the same forces were unleashed in Australia, and it has used its experience at home to take a leading role in rationalising the Australian industry also.

The ability of these firms to deal with the reform dislocations of the mid-1980s included a determination not to be fooled by the previous regime of distorted price signals. Several of these executives cited the names of prominent firms that had allowed themselves to become reliant on a diet of subsidies, and paid the price once those subsidies were removed. Fred Holland of Nuplex was determined not to be among them:

> People thought the good times were going to last forever. We used them to develop our markets in Asia, . . . but we didn't structure our whole company on them because we knew it wouldn't last. If the thing didn't make good business sense, then just doing it because of the tax doesn't make good sense to me. . . . Everybody thought that their happy little environment in New Zealand was going to continue. I suppose, because we were exposed globally with our contacts and we were very much involved with the world all the time, we saw these trends happening, we saw the changes, and we thought: How do we survive?

For economics-trained Andi Lusty, the objection is more generic:

> I think that all subsidies are just a waste of taxpayers' money. . . . I think any subsidy destroys and distorts a market. I'm totally anti subsidies of any description. But if you dangle a subsidy in front of me I'll spend half of my time trying to get it because it's the easiest money I'll ever get. So you're just distracting me from what I should be doing and I'll go for the free money every time. Just look at some European farmers . . . .

A ROLE FOR GOVERNMENT?

A study of ten organisations, all of whom have excelled in the development of world-class competitive capability, cannot be the basis for a comprehensive or balanced assessment of alternative policy regimes. The experience of these firms shows that they did receive valued contributions from the former regime of government intervention. But this study has no way of offsetting these positive contributions against the damage done to other firms through distorted price signals and resource accumulations.

And if these firms have created advantage from government interventions, is that because the interventions were perceptive, or because these firms are very good at creating advantage in any environment? It is quite legitimate to conclude from the experience of these firms that it does not matter what government does: they have constructed competitive advantage from the former regime of government intervention and rugged landscapes, and again from the dismantling of that regime.

But other conclusions are equally legitimate. The experience of these firms raises a number of questions that merit attention in any government's process of policy development:

- the desirability of supporting flexibility in workplace relationships;
- the adequacy of New Zealand's tiny venture capital markets to support the innovations, and the going global transitions, which have been central to the evolution of competitive capability in these firms;
- the mixed bag of costs and benefits held out by foreign ownership;
- the adequacy of current conditions for fostering the early growth and development of nascent enterprises.

This study cannot reach any conclusions on these questions, but it can point to their importance in the development of competitive capabilities from a New Zealand base.

Yet another interpretation would be that New Zealand's distinctive attributes have been, for these firms, the ultimate basis for their differential appeal offshore. For example:

- Nuplex's development of broad technical and market knowledge from its early growth in a rugged landscape;
- Gallagher's development of world-leading farming equipment, and Kiwi Dairies' creation of the largest dairy factory in the world, from their sophisticated local markets in the Waikato and Taranaki;
- Tait's development of mobile radio on the back of the early deployment of a national network by the New Zealand Post Office;
- Montana's development of international reputation on the basis of the sauvignon blanc grape and Marlborough's distinctive terroir.

The origin of these advantages is far too subtle to be easily identified. And these firms have, for the most part, been isolated in their global success rather than springing from an industry cluster of world-class businesses.[7] So there is nothing in the experience of these firms to suggest that government can play any useful role in picking winners.

But the resource-based view of the firm (see Chapter 1) would predict that a New Zealand-based enterprise must differentiate itself in some way from its offshore competitors. It would also predict that the most likely source of that differentiation would be whatever attributes from its home environment a firm can turn into global advantage — as these firms have done. New Zealand business is likely to make a rather poor copy of American, European or Asian models. What these firms have done is find their own paths to create global advantage from their distinctive New Zealand context. As previous chapters have shown, the smallness and isolation of the local market have meant that these paths seldom have parallels in management theory developed for larger economies.

With our economy now more open to the forces of globalisation, it is a moot point whether this pattern will continue in future. On the one hand, the opportunities for global advantage are more apparent in an economy where domestic prices approximate global values. On the other, global homogenisation of New Zealand's commercial, cultural, social and governmental practice would erode the distinctive attributes on which competitive advantage can be built. To the extent that government plays a role in influencing the development of the country as a whole, this study suggests that there may be economic value in finding distinctively New Zealand solutions to distinctively New Zealand problems. The search for global advantage may best be served, at all levels, by avoiding the uncritical adoption of all things foreign, and by celebrating what is distinctively New Zealand.

Chapter 9

The Evolution of Competitive Capability: a Biological Perspective

INTRODUCTION

As often happens with discussions of strategic management, this research project has been suffused with biological imagery: evolution, viability, life cycle, adaptation and growth. This chapter extends the biological metaphor beyond its everyday organisational use, examining the extent to which such imagery can help us explain why the New Zealand companies in this study have reached a position of competitive capability in their distinctive markets, and how they got there.

Transferring ideas from biology to business is by no means unproblematic, yet there is no shortage of organisational models that profess to do exactly that. In many of these the central issue is adaptation of the organisation to its environment. Corporate evolution is portrayed as a gradual process of organisational change as the firm responds to (and sometimes precipitates) flux and transformation in the environment. And competitive capability is seen to reflect the degree to which the firm is adapted to prevailing external circumstances.

The process through which a system comes to know the outside world is usually referred to as *cognition*. And since it is arguably *the* key adaptive mechanism in biological systems, especially those with a nervous system, cognition assumes some importance when applied to organisations. This has been acknowledged by management and organisational scholars who are increasingly looking to explain organisational phenomena in terms of basic cognitive processes (see, for example, von Krogh and Roos, 1998; Sparrow, 1998).

Two perspectives on cognition inform the discussion in this chapter. The first is the classic open systems perspective in which cognition is largely taken to be an information-processing activity carried out by a goal-directed system that has direct access to, and can extract information from, the external world. The second perspective emphasises the autonomous, closed and circular nature of biological systems. Here cognition is a much broader process associated with the whole process of living. Its origins are to be found in experimental work in neurobiology (see Maturana, 1983; Maturana and Varela, 1987) and in the new sciences of complexity (see Capra, 1996). As yet there are few organisational applications.

HUMAN COGNITION: A COGNITIVIST PERSPECTIVE

The most widely promoted and current account of the human nervous system considers it to be an instrument through which the human being obtains information from the environment. From this the nervous system constructs a model of the 'outside world', which is then used to compute behaviour that is adequate to ensure survival. This is known as *cognitivism* (see, for example, Varela et al., 1991). The organisation's viability depends upon there being an 'accurate' or 'realistic' symbolic imprinting of the environment within the nervous system; the organism behaves in accordance with these representations by initiating an appropriate response. The process is a bit like using a road map to plan a route. There is a destination, there is a map that accurately represents the terrain and there is action that is governed by intent.

But how does this apply to organisations? Is this, for example, how strategic management works? Evidence from our companies suggests not.

> ... I would debunk another myth. Many people will say a successful business starts from a business plan [so] you know where you are going and you know what you are going to do. That's rubbish ... [take Sony's Morita] ... he didn't know what he was going to do. He did all sorts of silly things until he found something that worked. (Sir Angus Tait, Tait Electronics)

> We tried to have a path but we have had a lot of debates about those paths. I think that's very helpful and I think that we have had quite a few changes along the line. (Rick Wells, Formway Furniture)

The haphazard, spontaneous developmental paths and indeterminacy about which Angus Tait and Rick Wells speak (and we shall return to these later) are reflected across all the companies studied. Yet company executives told us about many actions that *were*, in true cognitivist fashion, deliberately designed to move the companies closer to desired targets. Chapters 3, 4 and 5 provide many examples of this in relation to technology strategy, manufacturing systems and human resource management respectively. Furthermore, all the companies have experienced periods of often very intense focused planning and activity in support of particular goals:

> . . . everything we did was about achieving those ends; everybody in the company knew, they always had this idea in mind. (Rick Wells)

> there was an absolute insistence on the need for cooperative agreed future focused strategic planning . . . we agree on the world and then make decisions on how you get there. (John Williams, PEC)

Although the cognitivist perspective would almost certainly not completely explain competitive capability and corporate evolution, it might have *some* explanatory potential, so we decided to take a more detailed look at how its basic principles have been extended through the organisational literature. We wanted to identify a suitable benchmark, rooted in cognitivist thinking, that would allow us to interrogate the companies according to this particular line of thought.

We chose the viable systems model or VSM (Beer, 1972, 1979), which is used extensively in organisational analysis, and in designing organisational structures that have a built-in capacity to survive in highly complex, dynamic environments (Beer, 1985; Espejo et al., 1995). Since most of the companies in this study operate under such circumstances, the VSM stood out as a logical choice.

A template for viable organisational systems

Based on cognitivist thinking, the VSM is derived primarily from an observation of the way in which the human body — a 'known-to-be viable system' — is organised and controlled by its nervous system. The main focus of this model is on how organisational systems manage the interface between the operational elements that interact directly with the external environment.

This is done through largely structural means. All viable systems, so the argument goes, share five basic properties:

- autonomous operational elements that interact directly with the external environment — these enact the identity of the system;
- coordination functions that ensure that the operational elements work harmoniously;
- control activities that maintain and allocate resources to the operational elements;

- intelligence functions that consider the system as a whole — its strategic opportunities, threats and future direction;
- an identity function that conceives of the purpose or raison d'être of the system, its soul and place in the world.

A viable system requires all five functions to be in place and working in unison. It also requires an effective and efficient system of communication and information flow.

The so-called law of requisite variety is vital to the system-environment relationship. Named after its founder W. Ross Ashby, Ashby's law asserts that managing complexity requires matching distinctions in an action (for example, a market) domain with appropriate internal distinctions; hence the maxim 'complexity is necessary to fight complexity' or 'only variety can match variety'. This is another way of saying that organisations exist and are embedded in a pre-existing environment that is full of challenges and opportunities. For every opportunity and challenge that exists in the environment there has to be an internal response capability. Variety outside the system must be matched by variety inside the system. The better organisational systems respond, the more they survive and prosper.

Knowing the customer
The extent to which these New Zealand companies have sought to understand the specific needs of their customers is quite remarkable. Certainly this is not always straightforward. As Fred Holland of Nuplex puts it, '... we try to give the customer what the customer wants, but finding out what the customer wants is the trick'. Often this goes way beyond simply asking the customer. For John Williams at PEC the trick is to 'put yourself in the customer's head and think about what he would think of us at any time; instead of what we thought of the customer'. Formway's Rick Wells goes even further:

> Observation of the marketplace by an expert who is highly focused on looking for opportunities, will produce a different result from a user or customer who is just there experiencing things and just relating to you their current experiences and possibly some thoughts that they have from that . . . being market responsive is not good enough, it is only when you go beyond the market that you end up in a unique position.

When the breadth of customer requirements is combined with almost continuous change — this being particularly apparent in high-technology firms such as Tait, Gallagher, PEC and, arguably, Formway — it is almost inevitable that there is more variety in the environment than in the company. This can make it necessary to *attenuate* (reduce) environmental variety. Sometimes this is a conscious strategy, as in the focus and grow developments that have taken place at Gallagher and at Tait. Sometimes, as in the case of Svedala Barmac and Nuplex, attenuation has been imposed by international owners. Although Formway has continued to manufacture a broader product range, there have been periods when, for business reasons, it focused its attention on one or two key product lines rather than spreading itself too thinly.

Having decided on the market in which the company is going to operate, these companies, without exception, have developed highly effective conduits for information about existing and potential customers. Typically these conduits involve a combination of mechanisms that include direct physical contact with, and involvement of, customers, employing people from the industry/market being served and fostering networks with distributors, collaborative partners and external experts. These outsiders are particularly important. Although they are not employed by the organisation, they are integral components of the organisational *system.* This is an important point. In thinking about competitive capability, the key unit of analysis is the system of which the company is a part; it is not just the company itself.

> . . . our technology relationships are a networking set up where we exchange ideas . . . and work on a joint project . . . (this provides the opportunity to) . . . globalise without the investment. (Fred Holland)

> . . . in a sense, the architects, health and safety people, physiotherapists and other experts that we have developed relationships with are an integral component of the company even though they are not employees as such. (Rick Wells)

> . . . we wanted to get into red wine . . . (and) . . . we realised that enthusiasm was not enough . . . there also needs to be skill . . . so we built a very long-term and lasting relationship with a chateau in France . . . (Peter Anderson, Montana)

These firms are willing to think of themselves not as companies with fixed and rigid boundaries, but as systems with noticeably flexible and indeterminate boundaries, where outsiders often fill key roles. Here the distinction between employees and outsiders becomes blurred.

Having the capacity to deliver
An ability to identify existing and future market needs is one side of the complexity-matching equation; the other is having the capacity to deliver.

These companies have used a range of strategies to amplify (increase) internal variety. Some of these are dealt with in more detail in earlier chapters. In general they include introducing flexible manufacturing processes that support customisation, maximising internal knowledge capability and technical competencies and, importantly, giving autonomy and problem-solving responsibilities to operational units.

Since autonomous operational units allow staff to respond directly to external circumstances without always having to seek approval from higher level managers, they can fulfil an important amplification function. And this logic applies at different levels. At the company level, for example, the Swedish owners of Svedala Barmac adopt a largely hands-off approach and allow the local operation a good deal of autonomy. In contrast, Nuplex operated for many years under the constraints of an overseas ownership structure that failed to provide the freedom local managers felt was necessary to meet customers' needs.

Within Nuplex itself, however, the various operational units are given autonomy although, as Fred Holland admits, this depends upon the experience and performance of local managers. At PEC there was a deliberate strategy to give business unit managers enough freedom to concentrate fully on satisfying the needs of their own markets, although this was not an entirely satisfactory arrangement, as we shall see later.

Autonomy is evident in varying degrees at managerial levels, but the best examples are to be found at the coalface of these firms. At this level most adopt some form of the self-managing team concept to deal with such activities as work scheduling, quality assurance and, in a number of cases, recruitment. Where control systems are in place, they tend to be relatively unobtrusive.

Once again, collaborative partners are important in enhancing the organisational system's capacity to match external variety. They have a dual function: they act as an important conduit for information about the environment, and at the same time offer skills, expertise and knowledge that enable the system as a whole to deliver in the marketplace.

The wider organisational system

This process of matching complexity with complexity applies not only across the organisation-environment boundary but also within the organisation. If a company is to provide the customer with high-quality, multi-specification products in a timely fashion, the whole organisational system must support, and be able to sustain, such levels of performance. Chapter 1 stressed the importance of balance. Here we can reinterpret that idea by saying that the complexity embodied in primary activities must be matched by an equivalent amount of complexity in non-primary activities.

Sometimes these firms have forgone a good business opportunity in order to maintain the balance between operational complexity and that of the wider organisational system. According to Rick Wells at Formway, 'there have been times when we wanted to do things but have not been able to . . . what is very common is we know that there is an issue out there about something but at this stage we do not have the resources to focus on it'. At PEC it was John Williams's fear that the company's innovative capacity might be under threat, rather than a lack of resources, that led him to pass on the opportunity of going global with the company's highly successful petrol pump technology. This may have been a wise move. There are many tales in New Zealand of companies experiencing serious problems because of an imbalance, often during times of economic buoyancy, between operational activities on the one hand and strategic/ intelligence activities on the other (see Brocklesby, Cummings and Davies, 1995).

Chapters 4 and 5 provide good examples of the importance of internal complexity matching, showing how the companies have found ways of matching human resource policies with the flexibility that is built into operations and manufacturing systems, which in turn match external demand for the product.

Coordination, control, intelligence and identity
In terms of viable systems logic, the most important aspect of internal complexity matching is ensuring that the system as a whole has mechanisms to manage and support the high levels of autonomy given to operational units. Specifically the theory states that there is a need for adequate mechanisms for coordination and control ('inside and now'/day-to-day management), intelligence ('outside and then'/future-focused management) and, importantly, a mechanism that provides an overall sense of direction.

One noticeable feature of these companies is the mix of formal and informal mechanisms used for control and coordination across primary activities. Although formal mechanisms such as official reporting lines, job descriptions, and performance appraisal systems do exist, albeit with varying levels of development and sophistication, in most of the companies it is the informal mechanisms that stand out. The planned and unplanned movement of employees across job boundaries, internal promotion, direct interaction between employees and the long service tenure of relatively large numbers of staff, all offer insights into how these companies operate. The use of informal mechanisms facilitates communication and reduces the potential for serious coordination difficulties. The combination of long-term employment relationships, peer control exercised through teamwork and appropriate recruitment processes can be highly effective.

The complexity matching processes associated with operational activities are mainly what is often referred to as 'inside and now' management. 'Outside and then' or intelligence functions are just as important. Companies such as Tait, PEC, Gallagher, Criterion and Formway operate in highly dynamic environments, where company viability depends on constant innovation. By New Zealand standards these companies spend relatively large sums of money on R&D, much of which has been made possible through a private ownership structure that has allowed profits to be fed back into the organisation.

Arguably Svedala Barmac and Nuplex operate in more stable environments. Yet their intelligence functions are no less well developed. Nuplex has a small but active R&D laboratory, and both companies are constantly working with customers to identify better ways of meeting their needs.

The final component of the systemic whole that sustains the system's operational units is identity, the purpose or raison d'être of the system, its soul and its place in the world. Virtually all these companies have a very strong sense of self that channels and directs their activities. Until its recent takeover by Lion Nathan, Montana made much of its standing as a New Zealand wine company. On a number of occasions its owners eschewed attractive offers of buying into Australian wine companies, because, as Peter Anderson points out, the company philosophy has been to

> ... invest in all the capital resources needed to develop the land, and to create wealth for New Zealand. And that is a very strong philosophy in this company ... we feel ourselves very much a New Zealand company.

Strong as these identities may be, they are not inviolable or cast in stone. Some of these companies are willing to create new identities in the face of new business opportunities.

Cognitivism/viable systems: the overall impression

Overall, these companies exhibit most of the theoretical requirements of viability. At the operational level they have evolved mechanisms for understanding and delivering on customer requirements. In the wider system they have developed mechanisms to ensure that there is adequate coordination, control, intelligence, a sense of identity and guiding purpose, and a flow of information that sustains these activities. These companies show that, just as it *is* possible to use a map to plan a route, so it is possible to design an organisational system with specific purposes in mind. Achieving specific goals in a continually changing environment is something that managers must work on — analytically, culturally and structurally. There is evidence to suggest that the firms in this study are doing this.

But, as always, there is another side to this story. For a start, it would be wrong to assume that because there is a good deal of this purposeful thinking, strategic planning and organisational system-building going on, these activities account for a firm's competitive capability and/or its evolutionary trajectory. Because the organisational system is multidimensional and is populated by relatively autonomous human beings, it operates according to its own logic.

The assumption of an overriding identity that is translated into goals raises another issue. Some of these companies started out with a very limited conception of self; certainly there was no clear overall destination in mind.

> . . . the next point looking down the road was the decision as to what . . . we were going to do . . . the business was there and was sort of drifting along . . . (but) we didn't have a company mission or anything like that at that time . . . (Rick Wells)

Even if there is a clear sense of identity, and organisational structures and processes are carefully crafted with this in mind, there may be other reasons why the company has been successful. There was a period, for example, when Gallagher was doing very well in business terms, in spite of having a seriously outmoded and inefficient production system. At Formway a certain amount of internal chaos and *dis*organisation is a key mechanism that supports creativity and innovation.

Some of these companies seem to have followed a somewhat haphazard and indeterminate evolutionary path, rather than any cognitivist road map. Why, for example, did PEC develop a capability in security systems when it started out in mechanical pumps? How did Nuplex convert a capability in resin production into one of waste management, and why did the company acquire a manufacturing facility in Vietnam and not one in Korea or Malaysia? We could ask similar questions about all these companies, and the cognitivist/strategic intent model will not provide an answer.

Another issue has to do with the people who have been involved in these firms. The cognitivist/viable systems model concentrates on the roles, not on the real people who might occupy them, and emphasises rational decision processes, downplaying the importance of intuitive forces and emotion. Rational explanations may be particularly helpful to a manager who needs to be seen as the captain of the ship and/or in control of his/her own destiny. But this does not sit comfortably with what we have been hearing about these New Zealand firms. It is the real people that count, rather than the roles they occupy or the structures and systems surrounding them. Several managers spoke to us about the credence they give to intuition and 'gut feeling' in making decisions. A couple even remarked on how little they *wanted* to be, or actually were, in control of the company.

COGNITION: A CLOSED SYSTEM PERSPECTIVE

Experimental work carried out in neurophysiology (Maturana, 1983; Maturana and Varela, 1987) raises serious doubts about the claim that the human nervous system is open to information from the environment, that it works with representations, and that adaptive behaviour is guided largely by intent. Such work suggests that to the internal components there is no 'outside', only internal correlations of neuronal activity.

Part of this thinking hinges on the idea that complex systems are 'structure determined', i.e. what happens to a system depends on the system. The structure of the system itself determines which external forces can perturb it and what the outcome of that will be.

On the face of it, this portrayal of the nervous system as operationally closed and structure-determined presents a major difficulty. If it is closed and circular, and does not work with representations, then what accounts for its evolutionary development? More important, what accounts for the manifest adaptability of human beings to their environments?

The answer to this question revolves around three key sources of change in living systems:

- the flow of molecules through the system;
- internal dynamics;
- a process of mutual adjustment and co-evolution known as structural coupling.

It is real people who count

Living systems, so the argument goes, acquire their basic class identity — their *organisation* (italicised to distinguish this term from organisation in the sense of company or enterprise) — as a result of the distinctive closed circular manner in which their molecules relate to each other. This involves networks of molecules producing molecules, which then help to produce the same networks that produced them. This closed, circular, self-producing *dynamic* is common to all biological living systems.

While *organisation* remains constant, *structure* (in this case how the identity is realised in particular concrete examples) can change around it. In living systems there is an infinitely large amount of structural variation within and across different biological species and within a single living system through its lifetime.

But there is a constant flow of molecules through the system, i.e. molecules enter the system, participate in the dynamic, then leave or, more commonly, die.

To some extent the structure of the living system reflects the characteristics of the molecules that flow through it.

In organisational terms the obvious parallel to the flow of molecules are the people who enter the company, participate in it and then leave. The basic identity (*organisation*) of the company might remain constant for some time, but how this identity is realised (*structure*) depends very much on who participates in it.

Although it is a bit banal to say that people *really* count, this is a point that management textbooks often miss. Even sophisticated diagnostic models, such as the viable systems model, that attempt to understand the functioning of an organisation with a view to improving it, deal mainly with impersonal and disembodied constructs such as roles and tasks.

And we are not just saying here that real people count: we are drawing attention to *how much* they count. We believe that the personalities, personal qualities, preferences, emotions and values of the key actors involved in these companies are pivotal in understanding both the direction these companies take and their competitive capability.

Emotions are particularly important. Like the gears in a car, emotions determine what people can and will do, and what they will not do, or will do only reluctantly. These emotions are partly personal and partly shared. It is the shared emotional predispositions, learnt as people go about their daily business, that become enshrined in the very fabric of these companies. People then do things in a certain way, but not because of some job description or planning report or direct instruction, but because that is what they have learnt and are predisposed to do.

Chapter 2 describes how, in a number of these companies, second-generation family members drove the internationalisation process. Their priorities and ambitions were substantially different from those of the preceding generation. Tait Electronics provides an example of how the background experiences and prefer- ences of the owner/chief executive impact on company direction. Tait's initial shift into the British market for mobile phones had as much, if not more, to do with Angus Tait's familiarity with British culture than with some detailed analysis of possible markets.

The influence of specific individuals is not restricted to the senior executives and company owners. When new members enter the organisation, company direction and — since these people are often not easily replaced — competitive position can alter dramatically. At PEC, Kevin Low, Tony Dobbs and Rob Wilkinson exerted a major influence on the technical, marketing and strategy formulation sides of the business respectively. And Graham Dawson, in the face of some internal resistance, championed and persisted with what later was to become the hugely successful CARDAX security side of the business. In all the companies studied there are such people who, in one way or another, have left their mark on the business.

In companies such as Svedala Barmac and Montana, the personal commitment of owners and senior executives to create wealth not only for themselves and their employees, but also for their local communities and for the country as a whole, has for many years been enshrined in both their actions and their corporate mission statements. Moreover, key personnel can impact on the overall company ethos and its day-to-day functioning. At Montana, for example, Peter Jackson says that:

> The people who become involved with wine . . . are passionate . . . they are quite unique personalities. If you look at these successful wine companies in New Zealand you will find that they have all been led by people of great passion and vision.

He then goes on to describe how these qualities are reflected in the functioning of the companies. Likewise, when Fred Holland was asked what, if anything, had remained constant during three decades of change at Nuplex, he answered that it was a personally driven but organisation-wide commitment to 'do what is best by the customer; to always think about how we can help and improve our service to the customer'. This customer orientation is part of the structural configuration of the company but it also reflects the personal make-up of Nuplex personnel.

John Williams and Rick Wells also stress the importance of all employees being emotionally committed to the company ethos and mission. As John Williams puts it, this commitment had to be there because: 'If you have to drag people along all the time it is just too hard in an innovative environment . . . [the PEC people] were all different but they had this basic quality.'

He draws attention to a link between his own high level of self-esteem and the creative and innovative ethos that for many years pervaded the company.

> I have very high self-esteem. . . . I do not have to always have my ideas acted on . . . . I love to see someone else select an idea and have it acted on . . . it is great to see people grow . . . it is like having a wok in the middle of the table . . . once people throw their ideas over the edge they had to disown it and look at what was in the wok and build on the very best and not ride their own ideas to boost their own self-esteem.

Williams then goes on to lament the dilution of this organisational characteristic after the business was reorganised into three semi-autonomous business units. The 'lower price' sale of PEC to another company in 1999 as a quid pro quo for the buyer agreeing to retain Williams's ethos and management style bears further witness to his belief in their importance.

Just as variations crop up as new members are included, the same can happen when old ones retire, or when there is a turnover in top management or, as in John Williams's case, when their influence becomes diluted.

Internal dynamics

Internal dynamics can also cause changes in operationally closed biological systems. These can be incremental (in ageing, for example) or discontinuous (as in stage-related change). This idea has become very popular in the organisational and strategic management literature (see, for example, Cameron and Whetton, 1983; Stubbart and Smalley, 1999; Gioia and Chittipedi, 1991), but many of these theories take an unnecessarily deterministic line on corporate evolution. We do not accept that organisational change is pre-programmed and determined by an inner logic. Internal dynamics are clearly important, but they are not the only factor involved.

One thing is clear, however. These companies *have* moved through a number of stages as they have aged and grown. Not everyone to whom we spoke agreed that major transitions such as going global and coping with gushers are necessarily synonymous with progress. Those periods are difficult and painful, and require a major expenditure of energy plus careful management. As Warren Rickard (Tait Electronics) puts it: 'There are always those steps . . . [that you must] agonise over. It doesn't matter what the size of the company is, there always seems to be that big step in front of you. . . .'

There are a number of reasons why these companies have managed to survive and eventually profit from these turbulent periods. Partly it has to do with the ability of their key people, who have had to find ways of mobilising the support of the workforce. Partly it is because, for many of them, constant change has become a way of life. The structures of these companies have an organic or plastic quality that is noticeably different from the rather rigid or ossified quality that often characterises organisations operating in more stable environments.

The development stage of these companies also seems to be important in explaining why they are able to make effective transitions. By international standards most of them are relatively small. And because they are relatively young as well, they have not yet evolved the rigid and highly bureaucratic ways of operating that can bedevil some of their larger competitors. Indeed, companies like PEC and Nuplex have responded to growth by establishing autonomous business units; this strategy reflects their directors' understanding that growth and bureaucratisation can adversely affect a company's overall agility and innovative capacity.

These relatively small companies also have the advantage of avoiding what are often referred to as competency traps. When practices are repeated day after day people become more adept at them and more likely to continue using them. But when circumstances change procedures designed for a particular context can become irrelevant or dysfunctional under changed circumstances; people carry on doing what they do best rather than looking for more effective options. By and large, our companies have neither been around long enough nor stood still long enough to experience this difficulty. Although long-term staff tenure creates the potential for competency traps, mechanisms such as internal transfers, job flexibility and promotion from within mitigate against this. In some cases operating in a large number of different cultural contexts also helps.

Being relatively small has other advantages. Most of these companies have a very strong external focus. Because they lack skills in key areas and cannot do everything on their own they have come to rely on external collaborators. This provides a good balance between 'diving in', i.e. developing your own knowledge capabilities, and 'stepping out', i.e. breaking institutionalised frames and traditional ways of thinking. Almost all these companies engage in stepping out activities of one sort or another.

Finally, being relatively small means some of these companies can avoid getting stuck in past or present identities and evaluating environmental opportunities and threats in these terms. PEC and Formway offer the best examples. They have been able to reinvent themselves a number of times within the bounds of their structural capabilities. Nuplex's recent move into waste management from its traditional base in resin production shows that it too has been capable of developing a new identity out of an existing one.

Structural coupling

Structural coupling and the evolution of competitive capability
The flow of molecules through a living system and its own internal dynamics have a major impact on its structure, but they do not tell the whole story. And nor do they answer the intriguing question of how living systems in general, and human beings in particular, are so manifestly well adapted to their environments. At this point, the third source of change, structural coupling, assumes some importance, since it provides the mechanism that links the inside of the living system with the outside world.

In very simple terms, structural coupling is a congruence or fit between two operationally independent systems: in this case a system and its environment. As long as there are recurrent interactions between the two systems they both change. The system determines which external events can perturb it, and what the outcome of that will be.

Consider, for example, the process through which an ill-fitting soft leather shoe or slipper gradually becomes more comfortable as a result of recurrent interactions with the foot of its owner. The structural changes that take place in the shoe are determined by it, not by the foot. Yet when it comes to the end of its useful life, even a cursory glance at its distorted contours reveals the specific encounters it has had with the foot of its owner over its lifetime. The location of areas of hard skin on the foot allows us to say the same about the foot. Through a process of adaptation, the two systems have changed congruently; each one is subject to its own internal laws or its own structure determinism.

The same applies to companies. They are grounded in local and historic contexts and are shaped by the changing contexts in which they operate. At any point in time, the characteristics of the company mirror its past interactions. Thereafter, it is the company itself that determines what happens to it. In this view, organisational evolution is the result of interaction between external events and the characteristics of the firm.

So what light can these ideas about structure determinism and structural coupling shed on competitive differentiation? In simple terms structural coupling explains how systems of common origin become differentiated as a result of the interplay between the historical conditions under which they live, and their intrinsic structural characteristics. In biology, this might help to explain how different species can emerge from a common ancestral organism. In the case of business enterprises it helps to explain the basis of competitive differentiation.

In the case of biological differentiation Maturana and Varela (1987:108–110) use the analogy of someone flicking down drops of water on the sharp peak of a hill. Repeating this experiment many times reveals that some drops — the larger and heavier ones, for example — form a straight-line channel down the hill. Others meet obstacles that they elude by moving off to the left or right in different ways because of their small structural differences in weight, size, speed of travel and so forth. Slight changes in the wind will also move some of the droplets away from the initial direction. Eventually it will be possible to observe many channels of drift down the hill. These result from the interaction between the structural characteristics of the droplets and the irregularities of the terrain and the wind. Looking from above, it should be possible to see the starting point in the centre and a whole series of crooked lines extending away from the centre in all directions. Some of these lines are curtailed because the emergent structural form of the water droplet is not compatible with the environmental feature that it encounters. In this case adaptation ceases. Other lines continue to move on, branch-like, away from the original starting point to all points of the compass. The location and positioning of these lines, relative to each other, and at a particular moment in time, represent a complex pattern of system differentiation.

What does this analogy reveal about the competitive capability of enterprises? Let us imagine that a company has evolved to a position that is roughly equivalent to the six o'clock position when looking from above. Let us further imagine that the optimum, in competitive capability terms, is ten o'clock. How easy is it to get from six to ten? Obviously this will depend on the particular competitive action or behaviour the company is attempting to mimic, but we can say that the positioning of the company is not arbitrary. It is where it is because of the interplay between its historical interactions and its structural characteristics, and reversing or nullifying these may be very difficult, if not impossible. The same can be said about the companies in this study: they occupy relatively strong competitive positions because of the interplay between their historical interactions and their structural characteristics.

In this study we have merely been able to identify a number of historical events that *might* account for the competitive strength of these firms. We have suggested that tax breaks, export incentives and tariff protection at important periods have been vital to their subsequent global competitiveness. And we have suggested that key individuals and collaborative partners can influence the course taken by particular companies.

The relationship between a company and a collaborative partner or a multi-national parent is particularly interesting. As the two (structurally coupled) systems co-evolve through their interactions, each one will inevitably trigger changes in the other. In the case of the relationship between a multinational subsidiary and its parent (see Chapter 6) the quid pro quo for having access to superior funding is that the subsidiary has less control over its strategic direction (e.g. Svedala Barmac). If its own strategy is not consistent with that of the parent or if it is a relatively small player in the overall owner business (e.g. Nuplex) then adequate funding may be difficult to obtain. In the longer term this may make the subsidiary vulnerable to other owner types operating in the same competitive market.

These firms seem to have learnt that they should choose their collaborative partners carefully. In a number of cases, the companies went on to bigger and better things through leverage off a collaborative arrangement. Conversely, there are other examples where managers have either avoided or terminated a relationship with a collaborator because they have foreseen undesirable long-term effects. Formway, for example, severed its ties with a German partner for exactly this reason.

Finally, there are serendipitous events. A droplet of water meets an obstacle and the course of its movement down the hill is altered. The same can be said of organisational evolution. Take, for example, Nuplex's recent emerging presence in Vietnam. To say, as the cognitivist/viable systems perspective might, that this reflects a strategic move on the part of the company is only partly true. In purchasing its major Australian competitor, Nuplex managed to acquire a production facility in Vietnam. In typical Fred Holland/Nuplex style, the company then looked to gain maximum leverage from this opportunity. Through a similar process, in this case through its membership of FURNZ (the Furniture Manufacturers Association of New Zealand) and a link with Fletcher Challenge, which has a major North American presence, Formway has leveraged entry into that market. Although this sort of development may be compatible with the company's broad strategic direction, it is not the *product* of strategic planning as such.

So much for organisational evolution, but what of strategic management? The following image is quite helpful in conveying a sense of how companies like Formway, Nuplex and PEC have been managed. Imagine that you are able to grasp in two hands a plastic model of the hill already mentioned. The goal is to guide a droplet of water towards a particular target by moving the model to the left or the right, and by tipping it forwards or backwards. In this exercise the water droplet represents the company, the target represents a position of competitive strength in a particular market, and the model of the hill, with its contours and varying textures, represents the business environment. The person holding the model and attempting to control the movement of the droplet is the company owner or chief executive.

Obviously, in predicting the movement of the droplet, it helps to have a clear understanding of its (continually changing) structure, and of the terrain over which it must travel. But because gravity is such a powerful force it may not always be possible to avoid all the obstacles on the way down the hill, or to steer the droplet into channels that can direct or increase its momentum towards the target. Indeed some models, such as those that represent the deregulated New Zealand business environment of the 1990s, may not have any of these channels. Best efforts aside, there will be a good deal of unpredictability about the droplet's progress. Occasionally a droplet will fail to reach the bottom, having dried out or become blocked by difficult terrain. Most reach the bottom, but unless it is a very large and powerful droplet of water (which is very rare in this part of the world), there are several unanticipated changes of direction as it moves down the hill. This means that the original target must be continually re-evaluated in the light of experience and in the light of new targets becoming available.

On seeing opportunities

Opportunities and threats do not, as cognitivist logic has it, exist 'out there'. Instead they exist only if there are processes at work within the company that 'bring them forth'.

> Some people seize opportunities . . . other people do not even notice them . . . when you have 250 people always looking for a new idea . . . now that is a creative force. (John Williams)

> Everyone in this organisation is looking for better ways of serving the customer. (Fred Holland)

> The whole company is geared up to thinking about how we might come up with a better product. (Rick Wells)

From a competitive capability angle this structural openness to 'seeing' things is undoubtedly a step in the right direction, but is it sufficient? According to the logic of structure determinism the world we human beings see inevitably bears the indelible mark of our own structure: what we see depends as much on us as it does on what might be taken to exist 'externally'. Logically, then, to understand the business environment strategists must first understand the factors within the company which are empowering or restricting people's ability to identify opportunities and threats. In other words, looking outside from inside is potentially quite limiting. Fortunately, as we saw earlier, most of these companies engage in extensive external activities and have deliberately set out to court external relationships.

On not 'forcing it' and respecting the coherence of the whole system

External events do not *determine* the substance, direction and/or the timing of organisational change, which means, from a competitive capability and viability angle, that attempting to 'work against' the system can be counter-productive. External events can only trigger possibilities that are already embodied in the structure of the system. As the technology development cases cited in Chapter 3 suggest, it is a case of an external perturbation acting on 'fertile ground'.

Managers must, therefore, understand the structural characteristics of their firms, and resist the temptation to force change on the organisation, even when a particular environmental circumstance might appear to 'demand' a particular response. The managers of some of our companies do understand that change might be necessary, but they do not allow external circumstances to dictate its pace and substance.

> You basically have to have a philosophy that you are following and identify the routes that could bring the philosophy to pass. I am a great believer in that if something is right it will eventually happen . . . as long as you keep moving down those routes you do not have to force it. (Fred Holland)

Warren Rickard, echoing Fred Holland's 'not forcing it' philosophy, admits that it has taken two years to establish the new management team at Tait Electronics. Delighted with this outcome, Rickard remarks that the process is now 'dropping into place' extremely well.

Internationalisation provides further examples. When, for example, export incentives and deregulation of the domestic economy precipitated internationalisation in these firms, it was a case of the former acting on pre-existing capabilities; it was not a case of creating new ones. Criterion, for example, had an already developed export capability that DFC and export incentive funding was able to trigger to great effect. Similarly, as Fred Holland remarks, Nuplex took advantage of tax and export incentives to develop markets in Asia. However:

> . . . unlike [Company X and Company Y], we did not structure our whole company on them . . . we never got carried away. If the thing didn't make good business sense just doing it because of incentives doesn't make sense, [but] a lot of people made that mistake.

For Gallagher and Svedala Barmac deregulation simply *accelerated* the pace of internationalisation. And Formway did not attempt to break into the Australian market until the company was ready, several years after deregulation. Many other New Zealand companies rushed offshore when the domestic market was opened to overseas competition, but Formway waited until the timing was better. At roughly the same time, and for the same reason, PEC's John Williams was limiting his horizons to the Southern Hemisphere rather than making a full onslaught on the global market.

As long as a biological system survives, its structure consists of a coherent set of interrelated characteristics. In business enterprises, however, coherence is more likely to be a source of competitive capability than a basic requirement for survival. Companies with limited operational coherence can survive in competitive environments, but it is difficult to imagine how they can prosper beyond the short term. Remember the Bendon debacle where operational capabilities were unable to match excessive demand generated by a highly successful marketing campaign.

This suggests that managers need to have two kinds of understanding. First, irrespective of whether some new development is triggered externally or internally, they need to know whether it is organisationally feasible. In other words, is this something that the company can and/or should be doing? Second, managers need to be able to evaluate any such development in the context of how it fits into the whole organisational system.

But this fitting the structure of the system idea should not be taken to mean that there is an inevitable conservatism in the way organisations function. In a sense the term structure determinism is rather misleading since it suggests that organisational processes are internally driven. This is partly true, but since survival dictates that the system adapts itself to the environment, managers cannot afford to turn a blind eye to environmental changes. All that structure determinism is really saying is that the precise nature of the internal changes taking place depends upon the structural characteristics of the system.

As long as a biological system survives under new environmental conditions its structure will eventually cohere. For business managers, however, it is desirable that coherences disturbed by a necessary structural change should be re-established sooner rather than later. In our firms coherence has been re-established quickly partly because of the dictates of economic survival. The survival of all these companies has been under threat at least once during these transition periods: clearly, this has provided a strong incentive to quickly make the necessary changes.

But there is more to it than that. These companies may lack the financial backing and cash surpluses of international competitors but their relatively small size, their youth and, especially, the understanding of employees that change is ever-present, gives these companies an agility that some of their competitors lack. When these factors are combined with a leadership that fosters change, envisages future possibilities and invents ways to bring these about, it is clear how these companies have been able to quickly re-establish coherence.

Cognitivist logic suggested that the key to competitive capability is to design an organisation that can navigate the various opportunities and threats in the wider environment. The closed system perspective, however, suggests that competitive capability rests as much upon knowing the organisation: looking from the outside in is as important, if not more important, than looking from the inside out. Understanding the history of the organisation helps managers to decide what developments are and are not possible.

On learning through experience and trial and error, and 'going with the flow'
Since it is important not to impose on a system changes that are alien to its structure, or for which it is not ready, how should managers make these judgements? One pattern we see in these companies is their reliance on experience and intuition in judging what will and will not work. Cognitivism,

with its heavy emphasis on logical and rational 'analyse-diagnose-plan' processes, pays scant regard to the knowledge and understanding that arise from accumulated organisational experience and intuition.

For Rick Wells, 'It doesn't matter what the data says, if we do not have direct experience that something works, or if doesn't feel right, we do not do it.' This is tantamount to saying that managers gain as much knowledge of relevant system structures by interacting with them, as they do through formal inquiry processes.

As Chapter 5 shows, in some of these companies, new ideas about manufacturing processes have become established through a highly pragmatic process of trial and error. Combinations of ideas are stitched together on the basis of 'if it works then we'll use it' rather than on the basis of theoretical consistency. Development through trial and error can also be seen in marketing. Consistent with the structure determinism view, companies cannot dictate how customers will respond to their products. Whereas larger competitors might deal with this situation by commissioning expensive market research, some of the companies in this study have responded by adopting a sow and reap strategy, especially in relation to entering overseas markets (see Chapter 2). Clearly this is a form of operational interaction.

According to the closed system perspective, structural coupling is not only a mechanism for adaptation but also a process of cognition. Imagine, for example, an amoeba surrounding and engulfing a particle of food in its medium. The amoeba does not have a nervous system and its membrane boundary is non-permeable. It does not, therefore, 'take in' and process information about the external world. Neither, as the cognitivist perspective would suggest, does it act with intent.

So how does the amoeba manage to engulf the food? The answer has to do with the highly sophisticated level to which it is structurally coupled to its medium. Chemicals in the medium trigger changes of state and movement in the amoeba so that it eventually surrounds the food. According to this line of thinking, structural coupling is a form of knowing associated not just with the brain or, in organisational terms with strategic action, but with the whole process of individual and organisational living. The mental and strategic processes that take place in human beings, and in organisations, are part of much wider and more fundamental cognitive processes.

This perspective acknowledges the importance of intuition, the 'gut feeling' in organisational decision-making that has already been noted in our firms. It also raises the possibility that spontaneous adaptive micro-processes throughout the whole organisation might be as important, in competitive capability terms, as the rational-analytical activities occurring at management level.

Some of these companies give considerable autonomy to employees in lower echelons. And at more senior levels many of the owners and senior executives to whom we spoke emphasised the importance of hiring people with talent and then, as one manager put it, 'letting them have their head'.

The strategy of *'letting things happen'* because the organisation 'knows' is theoretically sound but only if managers remove elements that clearly do not fit. This has not always happened in our firms. Managers have waited too long to downsize or to withdraw products that failed to capture the imagination of the market. At Svedala Barmac, for example, it took a firm directive from the Swedish owners to convince local managers that they should discontinue a range of obviously unprofitable product lines. As discussed in Chapter 8, problems arose when Tait relied solely on technology and overlooked market signals. Likewise PEC persisted with its Locolog technology (a railways equivalent of the well-known aircraft black box) for too long, believing that the market would eventually cotton on to the potential of the product. It never did.

COMPETITIVE DEVELOPMENTS AS A CONVERGENCE OF FORCES

We have looked at the three main sources of structural change in biological systems as if they were relatively independent of one another but, in practice, the evolving structure of a biological system reflects the combined effect of all three. In this final section we look at some pivotal developments in the history of these firms, to show how particular developments were triggered by external perturbations to structures whose characteristics reflected the combined force of human agency, internal dynamics and past historical circumstances.

The first such example occurred in the 1970s when Tait Electronics launched its range of transistorised mobile radios in the British market. It went on to secure a 20 per cent market share in Britain and subsequently a 5–10 per cent share of the world market.

How did this development come about? First, because of the company's own growth. By the early 1970s Tait had secured 70 per cent of the New Zealand market for transistorised radios. With limited potential for domestic growth the company looked to overseas markets. Second, key people were instrumental. The pivotal figure was Angus Tait, the quintessential entrepreneur. His vigilance in responding to new opportunities and energy in seeking new challenges is legendary. Since he had direct experience of the British market, launching the product line there was a logical choice. The third factor is company history and the resource capabilities acquired over the preceding years; in this case the key factor was knowledge of transistorisation technology and mobile radios in particular. Tait had a product that was competitive in the British market: its production costs were much lower than those in Britain and so it was possible to sell profitably into that market.

Putting all this together we can say that there was a pre-existing structurally embedded predisposition for the company to launch into the British market. What made it happen? In this case export incentives in the 1970s, export development loans from the Development Finance Corporation and export guarantees.

The next example is Formway's introduction of the Zaf range of office chairs, which took place towards the end of the 1980s. In the middle of that decade Formway was ready to embark on a new project, having directed profits from the hugely successful ErgoStation computer desk into redeveloping obsolete plant and production technologies.

It is impossible to separate this development from the personal qualities and ambitions of the key people who were running the company at the time. These qualities included a high level of intellectual capability, a determination to develop a well-designed product with design and aesthetic integrity and a passion for providing top-quality customer service. Rick Wells and his partners saw the development of the Zaf chair as being pivotal in creating a distinctive Formway brand. Earlier product lines had succeeded in business terms but had not created brand awareness. The Zaf initiative built upon organisation-wide capabilities in chair design, research, development and manufacturing, and all these structural characteristics converged during a major local boom for new office buildings. The trigger for the Zaf development was the existence, on the company's doorstep, of a market for an office chair that improved significantly on previous products. Driving this market were project/purchasing managers who saw furniture as an integral component of the corporate brand, and who, in the face of concerns about productivity and repetitive strain injury, placed a premium on ergonomic design.

The third and final example is the process through which PEC developed a new computer-based product, running on a local area network and combining capabilities in close circuit television, intercom and security access control.

In the years immediately before this development, PEC management had decided that the company's long-term future depended upon its becoming a major regional supplier by 1990 and a significant global supplier by the year 2000. In this scenario, developing successful products for these markets would be critical. A key human factor was the willingness of senior managers to allow others, including outsiders, to bring new product ideas into the company. As with the earlier examples, the company's existing capabilities were the third key factor. For PEC these were in the areas of access control and microelectronics generally. What was the trigger? In this case, the trigger was an apparently irrelevant, but highly fortuitous event. Kevin Low, the company technical director, attended a dinner party where he met a university-based science and technology researcher. As a result of the conversation between these two individuals the idea of CARDAX NT was born. This was later adopted by the company as a major product innovation.

CONCLUSION

In looking at the evolution of competitive capability, this chapter has offered some theoretical perspectives rooted in biology and in theories of cognition. It has applied a quite different set of concepts and terminology to issues covered in more detail in earlier chapters. Interestingly, most of its conclusions echo what has already been said.

The main conclusion is that building a company with the capacity to survive, let alone thrive, in the highly competitive and turbulent arena of international commerce is only partly a consequence of strategic intent and the logical and rational mental processes of key people. To some extent it *is* about knowing what you are trying to achieve, knowing the environment in which you are operating and then having the skills and resources to fabricate an organisational 'machine' that can take you where you want to go. This chapter has, however, argued that this perspective, with its strong emphasis on goal-seeking, cannot entirely and adequately explain evolutionary developments. Purposes and goals are convenient organisational tools that people use to explain their experiences, but just because they frequently show up in people's explanations does not mean that they are the main or even a key driver of organisational behaviour. Managers do have the power to trigger organisational change, but we should not overestimate the power of these actions because there are many such triggers. The idea of purpose may be a useful one, but purposes certainly have no place in biology and their relevance in helping us to understand organisations may well be overstated.

Because the dominant model of cognition has these limitations, this chapter has looked to alternative models to provide additional insights and more adequate explanations of how these companies operate.

We have argued that the structure of the organisation is a coherent whole of interdependent parts which is a product of two key elements: design and strategic intent on the part of key people, and forces for change that are present in operationally closed systems.

Finally conventional wisdom has it that knowing and responding to the environment is vital to competitive capability. The alternative model of cognition allows us to contemplate the possibility that knowing the company is as important if not more important than understanding the environment. Paradoxically, it further suggests that a comprehensive understanding of the latter is conditional upon an understanding of the former.

Chapter 10

Overview: The Evolution of Competitive Capability in New Zealand

WHAT ARE THE KEY FEATURES OF OUR WORLD-CLASS COMPANIES?

The companies in this study have succeeded in creating and maintaining a successful competitive position over many years. Their success is strongly linked to a number of characteristics that they all share:

- These companies draw competitive advantage not from a single attribute, but rather from a broad scope of resources and attributes that distinguish them from their competitors, and from less successful companies (Chapter 1).
- Within each company these resources and attributes are in balance, creating a portfolio of capability in which each part is strong enough to support the demands placed on it by the others.
- The individual capabilities come together to deliver an integrated value proposition to all stakeholders, of whom the customer is arguably the most crucial to company success. These companies consider this property of coherence to be their most important competitive advantage.
- These capabilities are projected out into markets well beyond New Zealand. These companies are global or regional leaders in their field.
- Conversely, the scope of product markets is typically narrow and focused: the more global the reach, the tighter the product range.

HOW DO NEW ZEALAND COMPANIES BECOME WORLD-CLASS?

Our key research question was 'How do you grow world-class competitive capability from a New Zealand base?' How have our companies achieved this status? How have they come to be characterised by the features listed above?

Has the process been a sequential one, as some have argued (see Baden-Fuller and Stopford, 1994), in which capabilities have been added like building blocks on a wall? We see no evidence of a universal sequential order. In such a process the properties of balance and coherence would be achieved only towards the end when most of the blocks were in place. Yet the history of these firms shows that balance and coherence have been important properties throughout their development, and that any weakening of these properties has been both a major source of organisational stress and a stimulus to competitive evolution.

Is the process something akin to simple chemical reactions, in which A and B are drawn together to form a chemical bond? Configurations of capability do appear to be drawn together by forces beyond the intent of the company's 'architects', and chemical bonding suggests the property of coherence. But if this is chemistry, it is very complex chemistry that cannot be understood one reaction at a time. In chemistry the formation of, say, H_2O from its component molecules is a universal, unvarying process, but in the case of these companies there are no universal laws or patterns. The combination of capabilities and the way they fit together is distinctive to each firm. Furthermore, the coming together of two capabilities is a product not just of the capabilities themselves, but of a broader set of forces, including:

- other surrounding capabilities, (these in turn produced over long and distinctive histories);
- the company's strategy;
- the aims of the firm's owners and managers; and
- surrounding competitive conditions.

Is the growth of competitive capability a planned and managed process, in which the development path is first designed and then executed? On the one hand there is plenty of cognitive activity in these companies as managers try to foresee and shape the flow of events, and to learn from past experience. But on the other hand the complexity and pace of these processes goes well beyond what can be understood or controlled by human agents. Coherences must be discovered, they cannot be predicted. For example, the manufacturing strategies used to control complexity have been 'discovered' by these firms in reverse order to their inherent logic (see Chapter 4, p.86). In biological systems evolution has no pre-meditated end-point and the direction of biological evolution can be understood only in hindsight. The same is largely true of the evolution of these companies, (although it is much faster than its species counterpart!). Chapter 9 discussed in detail the limits of the rational goal-directed perspective on company evolution.

In our view, the evolution of competitive capability is best seen as a process of growth in a complex system (the firm) in co-evolution with its (complex) environment. Success is neither automatic nor predictable nor smooth. There are no sure-to-rise formulas that anyone can imitate. Instead the rewards go to the organisations that constantly recreate advantage to suit an evolving market-place. This image of ongoing mutual adaptation between organisation and environment was described in Chapter 9 as 'structural coupling' and is akin to the biological processes of organism adaptation to changing environmental conditions.

Does the complexity of these evolutions mean that no general lessons can be extracted from the experience of these firms? We think not. We believe it is possible to identify recurring patterns in the development of these companies, patterns that other New Zealand firms can be expected to experience, in whole or in part.

TWO PATHS TO INTERNATIONAL SUCCESS

Although every company's story is unique, Chapter 2 identified two distinct development paths taken by these firms, each governed by its own distinct logic:

- becoming global leaders;
- becoming regional leaders.

Global leaders have achieved an extensive global reach, invariably as the result of a local innovation with world-market potential. The speed and scale of these transitions have forced companies in this group to focus the scope of their operations. Often indirect methods of market development are used, through networks of long-term co-operative relationships. These more globalised firms concentrate their global manufacturing at home.

Innovation has been an absolute prerequisite to global leadership in these firms (Chapter 3). The essential role played by home-grown innovation in transforming these companies into global leaders is one of the more significant results of our work. A vital part of this transition has been a transformation from 'broad dabblers' into 'focused technology specialists'. Chapter 3 uncovered a number of self-reinforcing processes that drive this crucial change.

Regional leaders achieve leading positions in both New Zealand and Australia with product lines that are broader than those of more focused global firms. They prefer direct representation in these markets, and the establishment of production or assembly operations on both sides of the Tasman.

The pattern of internationalisation displayed in these firms is thus opposite to the theory that has emerged from larger, Northern Hemisphere economies. That theory predicts that more globalised firms will establish their own sales and manufacturing operations offshore, but for these New Zealand firms it is the regional leaders who use these strategies. This is one of the major findings of our study.

THE DISTINCTIVE KIWI CONTEXT

Both the global and the regional development paths are strongly shaped by the *distinctive context* in which they occur, namely the small isolated economy that is New Zealand. The two key differences in context are:

- The scale of expansion from a tiny home base, and the rate of growth it requires (the gusher) make the whole process distinctively risky.
- These firms bring very limited resources to bear on the huge task of going global in a short period of time.

The Kiwi Response
To overcome these distinctive limits of scale, space and time, Kiwi modes and methods of internationalisation are also quite distinctive (Chapter 2). They include:

- *The sow and reap strategy*, in which the company uses inexpensive methods to test its appeal in several markets and products simultaneously, and then focuses its efforts on the most promising opportunities.

- *The focus and grow strategy*, which follows the sow and reap phase; when a promising product or market is identified, the company focuses its limited resources into the new venture. Focus can happen in three ways: on a particular product line, on a market segment or on a position in the value chain.

- *The use of networks and partners*. Relationships are a key strategy used to overcome the limits of the firm's resources. Networks of close business relations are used for gaining market information and distributing products (Chapter 2), and for the supply of components and materials (Chapter 4). Partners also provide a channel for gaining technology (Chapter 3).

- *High-mix/low-volume manufacturing*, which delivers the product variety required for global markets by greatly reducing the cycle time of manufacturing processes (Chapter 4), enabled in turn by high-performance workplace relations (Chapter 5).
- *Consolidation of manufacturing in New Zealand.* Whereas the common overseas pattern is for a global company to distribute its manufacturing to various countries, our global leaders retain manufacturing in New Zealand in order to consolidate economies of scale in what are still quite small businesses in global terms.

These distinctive approaches to internationalisation have allowed our exemplar companies to overcome limitations of :

- size (going from the small New Zealand market to the huge global market);
- time (the gusher);
- knowledge (networks and partners bring knowledge of overseas markets and technology).

Relationship management

The networks and partners that are one of the distinctive features of Kiwi patterns of internationalisation deserve special attention. Our study has found that high-quality relationships are one of the keys to success for these companies. These relationships encompass:

- Domestic business networks, through which our exemplar companies learnt the skills of collaboration before extending offshore (Chapter 2).
- Networks of distributors in overseas markets, from which the companies gain vital local information and access to markets (Chapter 2).
- Partnerships, which give the company access to overseas technology and know-how (Chapter 3).
- High-quality workplace relationships (Chapter 5).
- The quality of relations between the leader and the workforce. Leaders of these exemplar companies are typically strong 'people people', who gain great satisfaction from sharing the success of the enterprise with

those around them. They demonstrate such attributes as innovation, a willingness to grow, listening skills, energy and resilience. These leaders are the source of the behavioural norms that support high-quality, long-term relationships, both within the organisation and beyond. They are the ultimate source of a widespread network of social cohesion through which the firm's valuable strategic coherences are built (Chapter 6).

The value of national culture

A distinctively Kiwi approach to achieving international advantage is also a product of our distinctive national culture, as discussed in Chapter 7. This culture is a resource on which our companies have drawn to create success: they not only reflect national culture but also contribute to it. Aspects of national culture that have been important in this way include:

- Ingenuity (doing more with less), a trait born of isolation, but one that the forces of globalisation may be weakening.
- A positive, confident outlook and being prepared to 'have a go'.
- 'All-rounderness', with a breadth of experience unusual in larger and more specialised economies.
- An openness to communication across all strata of society, which enhances rich networks of relationships and the learning that flows through them.

These traits provide no automatic path to international advantage: they must be converted into organisational capabilities that produce distinctive value offshore. Nonetheless, these firms and their leaders are distinguished by their commitment to New Zealand and their belief in the value of its culture.

CONTINUOUS CHANGE AND THE PROPERTY OF COHERENCE — THE AGILE ORGANISATION

We have described the evolution of these companies as a process of continuous adaptation to a changing environment. Central to this process is the property of *coherence*, an attribute highly valued for its competitive power — constantly pursued, yet shifting and elusive.

Changing conditions call for change in a firm's strategy and capabilities. When this happens, the balance of the firm's complex configuration of inter-dependent capabilities is disturbed and thus coherence is weakened. Companies and leaders work strenuously to re-establish coherence during these intense periods of change. The faster a firm can do so, the better. In other words the organisation needs to be *agile*.

It is the search for a new coherence, the need to find a new balance, that leads these firms to change patterns of operation, to modify existing capabilities and to develop new ones. It is the periodic change and recreation of coherence that acts as the organisation's guide and teacher. In the language of biological systems, structural coupling is itself a form of knowing, and one that marshals the entire organisation's wisdom (Chapter 9).

The complexity of these adaptations is typified by the development of manufacturing capabilities as set out in Chapter 4. The rapid growth in demand for product (the gusher), together with the increase in product-variants required to meet the needs of global markets, overwhelmed manufacturing systems designed for a different world. When firms tried to deliver the high-mix, low-volume product flows required by their new situation, the result was typically lowered delivery performance, large increases in inventory, a shop floor bogged down by WIP and information overload. In this situation the companies had to develop a wide range of operational capabilities simultaneously in order to restore balance as quickly as possible.

The result was nothing short of a revolution in the manufacturing processes in these firms, involving process control, materials management, engineering, quality systems, workforce improvement and participation. At the heart of these initiatives were drives towards:

- Greater flexibility to accommodate a variety of product flows in smaller lots, thus doing away with the need to hold large inventories of WIP and finished goods.
- Greatly reduced cycle times within manufacturing, and lead times for customer orders, to improve customer service and responsiveness from a low-inventory environment.

The detailed examination of these developments in Chapter 4 revealed that these firms did not adhere slavishly to any overseas model of operations development, but took an eclectic approach and combined those ideas, from various prescriptions, that worked for them.

Agility
Vital to the development of these new manufacturing capabilities has been the pursuit of high-quality workplace relations, which in particular contribute to organisational *agility* (Chapter 5). An agile organisation needs employees who can rapidly assess the need for change, and quickly alter resource deployment.

Spontaneous collaboration, initiative and rapid learning are also key character-istics. Although these companies display a range of HR policies and practices, and each company's evolutionary story is unique, they commonly demonstrate several of the key features that promote agility:

- A strong commitment to cross-functional multiskilled teams, operating with considerable autonomy and decision-making discretion.
- A commitment to training programmes that combine the continuous development of a broad range of skills with the articulation of the organisation's core values. This approach required the development of cultures of mutual benefit and long-term commitment, supported by reward systems that linked remuneration to the performance of the team or enterprise.

The leaders of these firms typically demonstrate high levels of energy, an eagerness to accept repeated challenges of personal growth (Chapter 6), and high levels of emotional commitment and self-confidence (Chapter 9).

The development of new manufacturing systems and workplace practices, described in Chapters 4 and 5, shows how complex is the task of recreating coherence for novel and unfamiliar conditions. As Chapter 4 explained, the evolution of these changes followed a path of learning through experience that successively uncovered new levels of capability development: the process was one of discovery rather than intent.

The key role played by coherence in guiding the evolution of these firms explains why these firms show such coherence and balance in their portfolios of capability (Chapter 1). Their success has always required coherence, both inside and outside the firm, and the pursuit of coherence has been their guide through the untracked transitions that have taken them from tiny start-ups to global or regional leadership.

The third distinguishing feature of these portfolios noted in Chapter 1, their broad scope, is the result of leverage.

LEVERAGE

Leverage is the use of one successful experience or attribute to achieve a new level of success, often in a different area. As with a physical lever, the effort associated with the first experience or attribute has a magnified effect in facilitating the next. Leverage is associated with learning: a *learning organisation* is one that can apply the lessons learnt from one experience to the next development phase.

Technological leverage
Chapter 3 described how these companies have leveraged off the learning associated with each vintage of product and with each generation of customer. This learning is vital to subsequent innovation. Interestingly some companies report having needed their international networks to learn how good their products were!

Geographical leverage
When these firms expand their markets within a region they use the business network knowledge and experience acquired within one country to expand into neighbouring countries (Chapter 2). Tait's internationalisation process illustrates this well. To enter the Chinese market Tait used its dealer network in Hong Kong. To enter the South American market it used its dealer networks in Miami together with contacts from South America established at an international trade fair. To enter other countries in Southern Africa it used its distributor in South Africa. Success for Tait with distributors in one market has meant expansion into the whole region.

Financial leverage
Another common pattern is to use the financial success of one phase of development to fund the next phase. At Formway Furniture, for example, the hugely successful ErgoStation Workstation funded the company's next phase of development, the Zaf chair. Profits from this phase were then fed into the development of systems furniture.

Resource leverage
New capabilities in these firms are invariably built upon resources and competencies built up through prior experience. For example:

- The geographic scope of marketing capabilities is extended by leveraging off a prior advantage in product innovation (Chapters 2 and 3).
- Global market scope both demands and allows the development of high-mix, low-volume manufacturing capabilities characterised by their distinctive flexibility and agility (Chapters 4 and 5).
- High-quality production and high-quality workplace relations create and sustain valuable reputations for the firm's products and services.

It follows that a world-class portfolio of competitive capabilities takes time to emerge. For the global leaders in our study the development period is measured in decades rather than years.[1]

It also follows that the evolutionary paths followed by these firms are given distinctive direction by the capabilities that they gradually assemble. Companies starting out in the same industry (such as Criterion and Formway) quickly diverge from each other as one generation of distinctive capabilities becomes the base from which to leverage still more distinctive capabilities in future. Chapter 9 has characterised this process as drops of water running down the side of a mountain, each taking its own path through the complex landforms, even when they all begin at the same starting point of the mountain's peak.

EVOLUTIONARY INFLUENCES OUTSIDE THE FIRM

The evolution of competitive capability in these firms is best seen as a process of co-evolution between the firm and its environment. We have already noted how distinctive attributes of the New Zealand context have influenced these evolutions. We also made particular investigations into the influences of the firms' owners, and of government.

Owners

These companies cover four broad categories of owner-type: public stock corporation (PSC), owner-managed enterprise (OME), multinational subsidiary (MNS) and cooperative-owned enterprise (COE) (Chapter 6). Each owner type has distinctive strengths that shape the evolution of capabilities towards those in which the owner can make a distinctive contribution. The distinctive strength of both the MNS and the PSC is the contribution that professional management makes to organisational learning, and to the pursuit of a broad, balanced and coherent portfolio of capabilities. For the OME, the distinctive strength is the creation and sustenance of long-term relationships of reciprocal dependency and benefit. The distinctive strength of the COE is the creation of very close relationships with one supplier group.

These firms have also offset the weaknesses inherent in each owner type by borrowing attributes of other owner types. OMEs have imported management systems, often embodied in experienced managers, to offset the OME's reliance on the single owner-manager. MNSs do better when given the autonomy to develop their strategy and capabilities in ways that OMEs take for granted. COE boards work to offset the inherently imbalanced goals of supplier-dominated governance.

Government

The relationship between the policy environment created by government and the growth of world-class competitive companies is complex and not easily prescribed. Indeed, the experience of these firms suggests that it does not matter what government does: they have constructed competitive advantage from the former regime of government intervention and 'rugged landscapes' and again from the dismantling of that regime (Chapter 8).

Nonetheless, this study has highlighted a number of issues that merit attention in any process of policy development:

- The desirability of supporting flexibility in workplace relationships;
- The adequacy of New Zealand's tiny venture capital markets to support the very high-risk innovations, and the going global transitions, which have been central to the evolution of competitive capability in these firms;
- The mixed bag of costs and benefits held out by foreign ownership;
- The adequacy of current conditions for fostering the early growth and development of nascent enterprises, by contrast to the former environment of rugged landscapes. These provided many sheltered niches, many artificially created by border protection, which fostered competencies in small-scale/high-variety businesses, close customer contact and a breadth of capability, which these firms later turned to advantage offshore.

Triggers to change

The recent history of manufacturing in New Zealand is characterised by successive challenges. In the 1970s Britain entered the EEC and this spelt the end of preferential access for New Zealand products in to the British market. For many manufacturers, the resulting foreign exchange crisis triggered the process of internationalisation (Chapter 2). In the 1980s deregulation of the economy exposed the cost disadvantages of local producers and this challenged manufacturers to make major changes to their operating capabilities (Chapter 4). Our companies have succeeded where others have failed in rising to these challenges.

A CONCLUSION

We took on this study because we felt that New Zealand needed to better understand what is involved in growing world-class competitors from a local base. We believe that our study has improved that understanding with:

- Detailed histories of a number of the country's most successful enterprises (see appendix).
- Descriptions of the bases on which these firms have established

competitive advantage in markets around the world, most particularly the uncommon scope, balance and coherence of their capability portfolios; and distinctive attributes of New Zealand's culture.

- The identification of two distinct development paths — to global or regional leadership — each with its own distinct business logic.
- An appreciation of the key role played by local innovation in launching every exemplar of global leadership in this study.
- Descriptions of the strategies that have been used to achieve these remarkable results from a tiny home base: the strategies of sow and reap and focus and grow; of networking relationships with business partners at home and offshore; of high-mix/low-volume production; and of high-performance workplace relations.
- An appreciation of the unusual scale, speed and risk of the transitions that periodically transform these firms: the gusher and going global.
- A theory of the process that guides the evolution of these firms through these unforseeable paths: the theory of evolving coherences.

Above all, our work suggests that the evolution of competitive capability in New Zealand firms is a story distinctive to ourselves, or at least to small isolated economies. Both the competitive advantages assembled by these firms, and the evolution of these capabilities, have been powerfully shaped by their New Zealand context and history. These firms are in no sense small-scale copies of overseas success formulas. This study can therefore claim to offer a better guide to the development of world-class businesses in New Zealand than models based on overseas experience, from economies with quite different attributes and histories.

The challenge is to foster more companies that can achieve what these companies have achieved. How can this be done? The country's experience has taught us that picking winners and planned development are not the answer. Our own study has shown just how difficult it is to predict which businesses will achieve international success from a New Zealand base. Who would have thought, for example, that an international leader in rock-crushing machinery would emerge from Matamata?

These companies have shown themselves to be adept at creating new competitive capabilities, both during and after the former regime of government intervention. This suggests that the most important drivers for the creation of capabilities lie within the firm:

- The agility and persistence required to adapt quickly during the radical transformations involved in leaving behind one set of coherences and creating another;

- The energy to seek out such transformations, and to pursue the growth potential inherent in the business;
- A willingness to let go of the past, as for example in the focus and grow strategy, but also in all episodes of capability development;
- But also an ability to leverage off past experience and capabilities so that the firm is constantly adding to, and building up, its past strengths;
- Managing the risks of these transitions: by not forcing the pace, but rather riding sympathetic forces of change with a loose hand on the tiller;
- By not overstretching the balance and coherence of an established portfolio of capabilities; and by fostering an acceptance of change and risk-taking within the firm through a long-term commitment to employees.

The firms in our study have demonstrated a capacity to grow through a number of these radical reconfigurations. They have succeeded in part because of their mastery of these dynamic practices; but also precisely because they have undergone several of these transitions, and have kept themselves supple and open to change.

Despite the ability of these firms to reconstitute themselves several times over, neither they nor we would claim that their past success will necessarily extend into the future. We can learn much from the way in which these exemplary firms have evolved, but the positions of success they have reached are constantly under threat and maintaining them requires constant effort and adaptation.

Looking at New Zealand today, compared with the world these firms grew up in, three changes strike us as particularly important.

First, the transformation of business structures and relationships brought about by the explosion in communications technologies and capacity. Recent conferences on these emerging trends have pointed to the 'deconstruction' that is resulting from businesses and consumers finding faster, cheaper, broader and more competitive ways of doing business. How will all of this affect the processes that have, over many years, created broad-based, balanced and coherent portfolios of advantage in our firms? Will the high-quality, long-term personal relationships and reputations that underpin the distinctive advantages of these firms lose their value in a world where (to stretch a point) everyone knows everyone and everything? Will the value created by these firms be achieved more effectively by replacing organisational transactions with transactions that take place through markets? These are questions we intend to pursue in our ongoing work with New Zealand firms that have grown up in the Internet age.

Second, the regime of economic management in New Zealand has changed radically since the era of protection that fostered the early growth of many of these companies. With our economy now more open to the forces of globalisation, it is a moot point whether there is now the same potential to develop global advantages from a distinctively New Zealand background. On the one hand, the opportunities for global advantage are more apparent in an economy where domestic prices approximate global values. On the other, global homogenisation of New Zealand's commercial, cultural, social and governmental practice would erode the distinctive attributes on which competitive advantage can be built. Our ongoing work with companies that have grown up since the reforms of the mid-1980s aims to discover just how many of the lessons of success from an earlier generation still apply today.

Third, the pursuit of global advantage is increasingly being established on the basis of proprietary knowledge. We are also working with some local examples of science-based enterprise to understand more about the creation of knowledge-intensive, world-leading businesses from our tiny base of intellectual capital. More generally, we are also exploring the contribution of distinctive knowledge to competitive success.

Like the companies we have studied, we must expect that the world moves on, and that our understanding of the paths to competitive advantage should change also. The question of how to grow world-class enterprises from a New Zealand base should not be allowed to go away.

But these firms gain advantage by continuing to find new ways to create value. We would expect that, although they might be used rather differently in future, the processes we have uncovered will continue to be part of the competitive success of firms in New Zealand. Indeed, the dozens of seminars we have run up and down the country in the opening year of the new millennium suggest that our ideas have considerable relevance and value for today's managers.

One of our conclusions, in particular, seems likely to remain valid for any future world. Because sustainable competitive advantage is derived from distinctively Kiwi attributes and experiences, New Zealand firms will always find these advantageous when New Zealand conditions require New Zealand solutions. Slavish copying of other countries' success formulas is not the answer.

New Zealand will prosper to the extent that it takes its own realities seriously, respects the models of success that it does produce and works hard to understand and promulgate them. The search for global advantage may best be served, at all levels of the community, by avoiding the uncritical adoption of all things foreign, and by celebrating, and turning to advantage, what is distinctively New Zealand.

Appendix

Brief Company Histories

THE CRITERION GROUP

Criterion today — a new business model

From humble beginnings in the family garage in the mid-1960s, Wally and Brian Smaill have built Criterion Furniture into Australasia's largest manufacturer and marketer of ready-to-assemble (RTA) furniture, with significant markets in the United States, Singapore, Hong Kong, Guam and the Philippines, in addition to its home markets in Australia and New Zealand.

Over the first 20 years of its existence, the company's development was sustained and even dramatic. At one time Criterion held up to a quarter of the giant American market for its leading product line. But the late 1980s produced the Asian financial crisis, a radical shift in the American market and equally radical changes to economic management policies in its New Zealand home base. The impact of these changes on the company was sudden and severe. In recent years it has had to reinvent a strategy around a new business model.

The new strategic design was based on the following principles:

1. A refocus on the Australian market. Criterion has maintained a presence in the American market but Australia is now Criterion's dominant offshore market.
2. Focus on consumer and office furniture products with Criterion's own brand name.
3. An extension of product lines into home and commercial furniture.

Competitive strategy

Operationally, Criterion produces precision-engineered furniture for high-volume, low-cost manufacture. The machines used must be able to produce a wide range of products and finishes, and production systems are designed to achieve optimal flow of materials. In total, there are 200 base products, which support 850 products in different colours and finishes, involving 2600 components.

RTA furniture facilitates a broad market scope by designing and fabricating furniture units that can be shipped in flat packs of components, and are easy to assemble by the end customer: whether it is a retailer, distributor, OEM (original equipment manufacturer)[1] or final consumer.

Criterion exports over 70 per cent of its production, and has the capacity to manufacture over half a million units of furniture per year. Turnover is over $50 million.

Criterion's competitive strategy is based on superior designs, technology, quality and scale.

To support its competitive differentiation, Criterion believes its distinctive competencies are in RTA systems design and manufacture, mass production technology, design innovation, financial control systems, planning and distribution systems, a motivated and committed workforce, reducing production lead times, and marketing and branding.

The view ahead

As it looks ahead, Criterion is focusing on the following five strategic issues, or themes, as the basis for its future success:
1. Further reductions in lead times.
2. Differentiation of the product portfolio to enhance added value.
3. Improvements in product quality, both in products and processes.
4. Increasing the capabilities of Criterion's team members.
5. Enhancing the firm's ability to measure its performance, in all aspects of business.

History

From garage to factory 1964–1975

Wally and Brian Smaill started the business by making cabinets for audio speakers in 1964. They had little knowledge of cabinet making. It was their quest for better tooling, bigger machines and automation that drove their development. Wally and Brian were constantly looking for an easier way to complete a task; this resulted in improved processes and increased efficiency.

In 1971, with financial help from their step-brother, the Smaills bought a 223-square-metre factory and this grew to 1160 square metres in the first five years. As the scale of operations grew Criterion added specialised features to their products by designing their own tooling and buying specialised machines.

Surfing the Pacific 1976–1989

By the mid-1970s Criterion was a significant player in the New Zealand market. As part of a deliberate strategy to prepare for exporting, the company had invested in dowel-jointing machinery, allowing cabinets to be shipped in flat packs.

In 1976 Criterion left its first factory and purpose-built a new one as a platform for export growth. The new equipment, together with the building, involved an investment of over $1 million. The company received export suspensory loans from the government-owned Development Finance Corporation (DFC) to cover half the cost. At the time, the loan was more than the company's annual turnover. In the new plant, higher levels of precision were achieved and economies of scale were increased. Criterion sold its RTA packs directly to electronics firms in Australia. Business in Australia was good, and Criterion grew at 60–70 per cent a year.

In 1979 Criterion made its first move into the American market, using testimonials from Australian firms to build credibility. Criterion's speaker cabinets were not competitive against larger-volume American manufacturers so they focused on making cabinets for one-brand full stereo systems. The new concept was slow to take off but by the late 1980s Criterion was exporting 95 per cent of its production.

Their ease of assembly made them popular with consumer electronics marketers, and the quality of the product impressed consumers. An American testing agency rated Criterion's cabinets first, third and fourth in a test of eight cabinet systems on the American market. Success in the United States resulted in Criterion growing tenfold over the 1980s.

Growth on this scale was not without its challenges. In one year, Criterion air-freighted 880,000 kilos of flat packs to the United States to meet its delivery commitment, the equivalent of eight 747 cargo loads.

The wave breaks

Towards the end of the 1980s the wave broke. The election of the Labour government in 1984 resulted in removal of the export incentives that had helped to fuel Criterion's growth. The Smaills had anticipated their wave of success breaking and even expected it to come sooner. From 1988 to 1990 the huge United States bonanza effectively evaporated as the market for one-brand audio systems matured with the introduction of mini-systems.

FORMWAY FURNITURE LTD

Formway today

Formway is a privately owned company that was acquired in 1981 by Rick Wells and Allan Brown. It has its headquarters in Wellington with three operating subsidiaries covering Australia, New Zealand and the Formway design studio.

Formway is vertically integrated: office furniture solutions are designed, manufactured, distributed and retailed. Formway has worked closely with collaborators on marketing and design concepts. The company has developed close relationships with customers and architects, and this facilitates customer participation in the design process, as well as increasing demand through product customisation.

The foundations for Formway's success are innovation (intellectual capital), design (a reputation for quality of design and products), prompt delivery and product quality.

In 1996 Formway's share of the New Zealand chair market was estimated at 18 per cent, but less than 2 per cent of the Australian market. Over the 1990s, the company has extended its product scope into systems furniture and its vertical integration into retail operations. More recently, Formway has been looking to expand by developing market opportunities in the United States and Europe for both its seating and systems furniture products.

History

Formway was established in 1956. When Rick Wells and Allan Brown acquired the company, it was a small business with a lot of ideas, but no depth in management, no marketing and no quality checks. One of the first things the new owners did was to introduce quality checks and improve product quality.

Initially the company specialised in chairs. Although there was no distribution structure, the company quickly set up a network of distributors in New Zealand. Formway also relied on sales to government departments, two substantial buyers in the early years being the Post Office and the Bank of New Zealand. Buyers played a significant role in providing input and setting the standards for Formway.

The widespread introduction of personal computers and word processing equipment in the early 1980s created a strong market demand for height-adjustable seating and workstations, as well as increasing concern over what was then called repetitive strain injury (RSI).

In response to this demand Formway launched the ErgoStation adjustable computer workstation. This was hugely successful: sales doubled each year between 1984 and 1986. The company managed the dislocative effects and delays of rapid growth by being honest with customers about the status of production. Also the company had an excellent relationship with its bankers. Another policy that helped Formway during this time was to price according to what the market would bear.

The success and profitability of the ErgoStation provided the platform for the company's next phase of development. In 1989, after a three-year development period, with a strong cash flow and a larger and more sophisticated manufacturing operation, the Zaf chair was launched.

The great success of the Zaf range was built on a reputation for product quality and design. As with the ErgoStation, Formway kept buyers and influencers closely involved in the design. In design work, Formway consults with its 'specifier community': architects, interior designers and health and safety professionals.

Part of the Zaf project involved the development of an extensive network of suppliers. Today, this includes nearly 250 suppliers from all over New Zealand. Formway conducts quality reviews annually and has long-term contracts with reliable suppliers.

Formway has sought to maximise its own contribution to the knowledge content of its designs by bringing in-house more complex value-adding stages such as polyurethane moulding, 3D plywood manufacture and powder coating.

The success of the Zaf chair produced great years for Formway in 1989 and 1990. Following careful research, the company entered the Australian market in 1990. The trans-Tasman expansion was driven mainly by the company's desire for growth and its fear of standing still. The step was also perceived as part of Formway's mission to achieve internationally competitive quality products. Furthermore, the New Zealand market alone could not sustain the costs of product development.

The company set up an assembly base in Sydney to overcome shipping constraints and to speed up delivery. It also developed a distribution network in Australia, initially using independent agents in the major centres. The main challenge when working with distributors was to transfer product knowledge. Conferences held in New Zealand brought distributors together to introduce them to Formway and its products.

The property crash of the late 1980s hit sales hard. In 1991 one-third of the companies in the office furniture industry went bust or shut up shop. Formway had to take the difficult decision to shed staff and downsize. The company survived because it had designed a new economical chair called Key, aimed at a lower price point in the market, and also because of its early entry into Australia.

As part of its recovery strategy Formway expanded its product range with a move into systems furniture. Focusing on the demand for flexibility in organizations, Formway's Inc Worksystem was released in 1996. An organic version of the Inc line, the new Free systems range was launched in 1998.

Driven mainly by the company's belief that it can enhance customer value through direct representation, Formway adopted a strategy of forward integration into retail. This involved replacing agents with the company's own showrooms and sales staff. Once again, this was to enhance the ability to create value from the core knowledge content of its products.

Over the last two years the company has established offshore licence partners for some of its most advanced products. The partners have been granted manufacture and distribution rights for specific territories, primarily in North America and Europe. Under these agreements Formway also supplies components and expertise.

Today Formway employs 240 staff over seven locations and has an annual turnover approaching $50 million.

GALLAGHER GROUP

Gallagher Group today

The Gallagher Group was founded in 1938 by Bill Gallagher senior, father of the present managing director. He was a dairy farmer by occupation and an inventor by heart. It is a privately owned company that specialised initially in agricultural machinery.

Today Gallagher is regarded as an international leader in its field, and the world's largest manufacturer of electric fences. It also specialises in gates, perimeter and door access, and security control. The company is involved in engineering, plastics and a tool-making operation. Agricultural and wildlife fencing now represents 80 per cent of Gallagher's business, security fencing 10 per cent, and plastics the remainder.

The Group markets its products to over 130 countries, has distribution agencies in just less than 100, and has become a small company with a 'global reach'. This network has a combined turnover of about NZ$120m per annum.

Gallagher seeks to secure distribution worldwide so that combined sales into a range of markets will build critical volumes to provide economies of scale in production. Distribution channels into Europe, Australia and the UK have been established since the 1970s; South America, USA and Asia have been developed more recently.

The company has progressively reinforced its technological leadership with other forms of competitive appeal. In the company's view, Gallagher competes on speed to market, low variable cost, multiple features, quality and a full product range.

History

The early business was founded on a broad range of agricultural equipment including gas producers and trailer-mounted top dressing equipment. The range also included battery-powered electric fences.

After the Second World War Bill Gallagher senior opened a small factory. A very good 'people person', Bill Senior established a culture of teamwork among his workforce, who were his friends as well as his employees. His policy was to share the company's successes through generous year-end staff bonuses.

From the Korean War wool-price boom onwards, New Zealand's prosperity leapt ahead throughout the 1950s and 1960s, transforming an impoverished depression-hit economy into one of the most wealthy countries in the world. Gallagher's agricultural machinery business was lifted up on this wave of prosperity.

By the 1960s, Bill senior's interest in the business weakened and he turned to the construction of two large cruising vessels. His sons John and Bill Junior joined the business in the early 1960s and had a strong influence on future policy.

The economic climate of the day favoured New Zealand industry: internal demand was high; and regulations provided protection against overseas goods being imported into New Zealand.

In the early 1960s the Ruakura Research Centre, home of government-funded agricultural research, developed the basic technology for a mains-powered electric fence. The new technology was taken up by a number of Gallagher's competitors. After an eight-year period of development, Gallagher produced a commercially viable electric fence energiser in 1969.

By this time Bill Gallagher junior had taken over the running of the business from his father. In the mid-1970s a Labour government introduced incentives for exporting. Among these were loans issued from government-owned Development Finance Corporation and tied to growth in a company's exports. Bill Gallagher had already established an Australian distribution network and decided to use the company's new electric fencing systems to launch a European operation. In a few intense years in the late 1970s, Bill Gallagher established a network of dealers across Europe, and battled his way through the maze of European national regulations on the use of electrified fencing.

The electric fence business grew very rapidly and Gallagher exited general agricultural machinery to focus on fencing. In 1982, Gallagher expanded into the plastic componentry used in fencing systems by acquiring Specialised Plastics Ltd and toolmakers Sunplus Engineering Limited. In 1987 the company bought Sunshine Plastics as well.

In 1984 a reforming Labour government phased out export incentives and Gallagher's domestic machinery sales halved due to a recession. Gallagher's offshore markets were sound businesses but the disruption of cash flows challenged the firm's financial balance. Gallagher launched a major initiative aimed at improving the cost structure of the company. Employment was cut from approximately 200 to 150, mostly in the mechanical engineering side of the business. Significant gains in inventory management and work flow were made with the introduction of an MRPII system. The company also renewed its efforts in the technology of electric fencing to produce Smart Power energisers, which have been the company's leading fencing system in the 1990s.

In the late 1980s Gallagher's South African operation also came up with a new application for the company's technology — security fencing systems. Instead of keeping animals in, these were designed to keep human intruders out. Gallagher has since developed markets for its security systems in 13 countries around the world.

In the late 1990s, Gallagher also extended its offerings in the security market through the acquisition of Cardax (International) Ltd. This added door access control to the Group's product offerings, as well as providing synergies with manufacturing and distribution, and experience in software development.

KIWI DAIRIES

Kiwi Dairies today

The dairy industry has been a cornerstone of New Zealand's economic and cultural history. Today, Kiwi Co-operative Dairies Ltd (Kiwi Dairies) contributes significantly to the local economy both as an employer and as a creator of wealth and livelihood for shareholders. As an exporter of dairy products through the New Zealand Dairy Board, it accounts for 6 per cent of New Zealand's total export earnings.

Kiwi Dairies is the result of many mergers between dairy companies, initially within Taranaki, and then into the lower half of the North Island, and beyond.

In the 1960s there were 42 co-operative dairy companies in the Taranaki district; by 1998 there was only one — Kiwi Dairies.

Kiwi Dairies was formed in 1963 as the result of an amalgamation of the Joll and Kaupokonui Co-operative Dairy Companies. It is entirely owned as a cooperative by the 4000 dairy farmers who supply it with milk. Kiwi Dairies now operates the largest dairy factory in the world on a single site at Hawera. It is the second largest dairy processor in New Zealand and controls all the milk supply in the lower half of the North Island, representing 37 per cent of New Zealand's milk supply.

Kiwi Dairies has 6000 shareholders and 4000 employees. With an annual turnover of $2 billion, it ranks as one of New Zealand's top twelve companies. Ninety-five per cent of the company's production is exported.

Kiwi Dairies' main competitor is Waikato-based New Zealand Dairy Group, the country's largest dairy producer. The companies compete in the local dairy market but more than 90 per cent of their output is marketed offshore jointly through the New Zealand Dairy Board.

Sources of advantage and competitive strategies

Kiwi Dairies' sources of advantage include:

1. Economies of scale. The company's chief competency is efficiency through size, and associated economies of scale in volume manufacturing. This has conferred a cost leadership position.
2. Technology and network. Size and capital base have provided sufficient investment for the company to be at the cutting edge of industry technology. Technology has been used to increase production capacity while allowing operational flexibility for innovation in product design.
3. By merger and amalgamation Kiwi Dairies has built up a network of milk transportation and processing covering the whole of the lower half of the North Island. Duplication of this network by a potential competitor would entail a formidable investment.
4. Economies of experience and learning. Kiwi Dairies has a wealth of knowledge and skill accrued through time and experience. Economies of experience, for instance in mergers, have been gained through the repetition of processes over time. Stakeholders have long associations with the farming/dairy industry.
5. Commitment and leadership. Many of the key people involved in the organisation are passionate about farming and dairying. The quality of past leadership and visionary decision-making, for example the pursuit of economies of scale through consolidation onto a single site, has been sustained over 40 years.

Kiwi Dairies' competitive strategies include:

1. Cost leadership. This is Kiwi Dairies' most significant competitive strategy. It is achieved through size and critical mass, with associated economies of scale and excellence in operations. Each significant merger has enhanced the company's ability to increase capital investment and to finance further growth, as well as to increase output, maximising returns to shareholders.

2. Quality. A reputation for quality is an important competitive strategy. All production departments and product stores are certified to ISO International Quality standards. The company has also achieved certification for the ISO International Quality Standard for Environmental Quality and Performance.

3. R&D. High investment in research and development, both in products and processes, is essential in maintaining leadership in operational excellence. In-house research and development is provided through Kiwi Dairies subsidiary, Kiwitech.

4. Technological development makes use of company and overseas knowledge and experience. For instance, the design and construction of the Powder 5 plant incorporated company experience in the operation of Powder 3 and Powder 4 plants as well as purchased technology from the international Dutch company, Stork Friesland.

5. In-house innovations enable Kiwi Dairies to be world leaders in many technologies. For instance, Flavourtech is a leading-edge flavour improvement technology.

6. Acquisition of domestic retailer brands. The recent merger with Tui has substantially increased Kiwi Dairies' ability to compete in the local market by acquiring Mainland and its high-value brands, e.g. Mainland, Ferndale and Valumetric. In December 1998 Kiwi Dairies' subsidiary Mainland announced its purchase of Brierley Investments' stake in Food Solutions. Kiwi Dairies is now one of the two biggest food companies in New Zealand.

History

Kiwi Dairies' strategy over the past 20 years has been clear and uncomplicated. An emphasis on aggressive growth and expansion has only recently been combined with an emphasis on product diversification and the building of other competencies.

Growth by merger and acquisition 1963–1998
Kiwi Dairies has steadily pursued a strategy of growth through merger since the

1960s. By the early 1980s mergers had left four dairy companies in Taranaki. In 1982 Kiwi Dairies and Taranaki Dairy Company merged. In 1992 Kiwi Dairies amalgamated with the remaining dairy company in Taranaki, resulting in ownership of all the milk in the Taranaki region.

A significant change in workplace relationships occurred in the early 1990s, coinciding with Craig Norgate's appointment as CEO. Until that time, the management style had been somewhat bureaucratic, with an emphasis on hierarchy and a view of the business as a commodity processor. Norgate challenged and shifted these views towards a more empowered workplace, the logic being that motivated staff produce satisfied customers, at a profit.

In 1996 Kiwi merged with Tui Milk Products, the first merger outside of the Taranaki region, to consolidate milk processing across the lower North Island. Subsequent mergers and investments in Timaru, Hawke's Bay and the South Island further increased Kiwi Dairies' interests outside the Taranaki region.

The strategy of consolidation onto a single site at Hawera was facilitated by deregulation of the transport industry in the 1980s. Kiwi Dairies also uses a rail link to move milk to Hawera from Hawke's Bay on the other side of the island.

MONTANA WINES LTD

At its birth in the 1930s Montana was nothing more than a tiny family vineyard founded upon a half-acre of dreams on a ridge in the Waitakere Ranges, west of Auckland. Today Montana Wines Ltd is New Zealand's leading winemaker in both the domestic and export markets, and has established internationally acclaimed brands such as Montana Estates, Montana Reserve and Church Road, to name just a few.

It has also forged distribution agreements with a number of other leading New Zealand wine producers such as C. J. Pask, Babich, Lawson's Dry Hills, Te Motu Vineyards and Wither Hills, for example. Montana also has the exclusive New Zealand distribution rights for several renowned international wine brands.

A frequent pioneer in New Zealand's wine industry, Montana's vines reach across the country's three major grape-growing regions: Marlborough, Gisborne and Hawke's Bay.

The company holds approximately 57 per cent of New Zealand's domestic market share by volume and 50 per cent of New Zealand's total export wine volume, shipping about 9 million litres annually to around 30 international destinations.

Montana's export drive focuses mainly on Britain (its largest export market), the United States (where its wines are marketed under the name Brancott Vineyards) and Australia. Considerable offshore growth is forecast: the company expects exports to double over the next five years.

A world-class wine producer, Montana has won numerous prestigious international awards for its wines, including the White Wine of the Year award at the London International Wine Challenge competitions in 1997 and 1999. At the huge InterVin International Wine Competition 2000, which was judged concurrently in New York and Toronto and attracted more than 2000 entries from 25 countries, Montana was one of only five wineries to win at least five gold medals and collect the coveted Andrew Sharp Award of Excellence.

Much of Montana's expansion has occurred during the past ten years under the tutelage of Peter Hubscher, its managing director since 1991. Hubscher, who began his career at Montana as a winemaker, was Deloitte Touche Tohmatsu New Zealand Executive of the Year in 1999.

Although Montana continues to produce wines for all segments of the domestic market, since the late 1980s it has concentrated on expanding its share of the premium wine market, choosing to channel investment funds into the high-quality wines favoured by today's increasingly sophisticated wine consumers, rather than focus on low-end commodity products. Nowadays, thanks to careful vineyard site selection procedures and advanced vineyard management techniques, the company harvests about 65 per cent of the grapes used in its premium wines from its own vineyards. By contrast, most of its lower-priced wines, such as cask products, are made from local contract growers' grapes or are blended from bulk imported wine.

Montana is a large employer, with around 800 permanent staff, including 40 positions in Australia, plus a handful in Britain and the United States, the latter operating through Seagram Chateau and Estate Wine Company distributors. At vintage time, the payroll increases considerably as hundreds more temporary workers are hired to help in the vineyards and wineries.

Yet although Montana Wines dominates the local wine scene, in the international scale of things it is not a large player — only about one-fifth of the size of the Australian giant, Southcorp.

The company credits much of its success to having built a progressive and inclusive workplace culture. Teamwork is regarded as paramount. Staff turnover is generally low; loyalty and commitment are high. Key organisational capabilities include strong leadership, a balanced work and family culture, a commitment to long-term relationships with customers and suppliers, plus a five-year business planning period that reflects the long lead times associated with wine production. The company boasts strict quality standards at all levels. In 1992 Montana became the first Australasian winery to obtain ISO9002 accreditation, the international standard for quality management and customer service.

The company's corporate office is located in Glen Innes, Auckland, and houses a large bottling facility, winery and warehousing complex. Auckland-based sales staff are situated a short distance away in Pakuranga, and regional sales offices are dotted around the country.

History

When Ivan Yukich began selling wine produced from his half-acre Titirangi vineyard in the 1930s, beer was New Zealand's preferred alcoholic drink and demand for wine ran at little more than a trickle. A Croatian immigrant, Yukich named his vineyard Montana, meaning mountain.

But Ivan, and later his sons Frank and Mate, were convinced of New Zealand's winemaking potential. Armed with this conviction they expanded their winemaking business, little by little. By 1964 Montana's vineyard area totalled 50 acres and produced 50,000 gallons of wine a year.

Their expansion programme continued to gather momentum throughout the 1960s and 1970s, setting the pace in New Zealand's then fledgling wine industry. Mate and Frank continued to believe that New Zealanders would gradually outgrow their taste for sherry and develop a penchant for table wine.

The company opened wine retail stores and, to boost its distribution and investment capabilities, teamed up with wholesale liquor merchant Campbell and Ehrenfried and financier Rolf Porter.

The company's growth was nudged along by the increasing liberalisation of liquor licensing in New Zealand during the 1960s. Palates were shifting too, albeit very slowly, towards better quality wines, just as the Yukich family predicted, although in those days the company still put sales volumes ahead of quality.

In the 1970s Montana produced very successful brands of the sparkling 'pop' wines that were popular at the time: Cold Duck, Montana Pearl and Poulet Poulet.

To support its growth, Montana sought out new grape resources and set its sights on Gisborne. Here it established supply contracts with local growers and, in so doing, spearheaded Gisborne's development as a major grape-growing region. But land prices in Gisborne soon increased, forcing Montana to look further afield for the additional fruit it needed to meet the emerging demand for non-sparkling table wine.

This time the company turned its attentions to Marlborough, then sheep and cattle farming territory where the land was cheap, but blessed with the low rainfall, high sunshine hours and free-draining soils on which grapevines thrive.

Although no one had tried growing grapes commercially in the region before, in 1973 Montana bought large tracts of land on the Wairau River flats and planted its first grapes there in 1975. It was a move that would reshape the wine industry. Today, Marlborough is the country's premier wine region and has become synonymous with sauvignon blanc, the country's signature wine.

Nineteen seventy-three proved a pivotal year for Montana for another reason too. Joseph E. Seagram, the multinational distilling and winemaking company, obtained a 40 per cent share of Montana, bringing a wealth of viticultural and oenological expertise as well as capital investment and valuable introductions to overseas markets.

From the mid-1980s onwards, the removal of import licensing and the phasing out of import tariffs encouraged increased importation of wine from overseas. These developments, coupled with the realisation that no future remained for the production of low-priced, commodity wines in New Zealand, encouraged Montana to redouble its efforts to quickly produce world-class wines and base the company's future growth on exporting. As the variety and quality of wines available in New Zealand climbed, consumers became increasingly discriminating, a trend Montana had itself encouraged by running wine appreciation courses for retailers and consumers.

As part of this quality strategy Montana formed partnerships with two major wine houses in Europe: first with Deutz Grand Champagne in 1987 to extend its range and quality of méthode traditionnelle or sparkling wine; and later, in 1990, with Cordier to help the company improve its red winemaking techniques. Both relationships undoubtedly helped Montana's winemaking expertise take quantum leaps.

By 1993, Montana's estimated worth was between $191 and $210 million and the company was regarded as the jewel in the crown of its owners, Corporate Investments. A few years later, in 1999, Corporate Investments changed its name to Montana Group. The following year, it sold off a number of interests, such as trucking, to concentrate on further investment in Montana Wines, culminating in the purchase of the company's biggest local rival, Corbans Wines, in November 2000.

NUPLEX INDUSTRIES LTD

In March 1998, Nuplex Industries, New Zealand's largest chemical company, took over Australian Chemical Holdings (ACH) to become the largest chemical company in Australasia. The acquisition capped nearly 50 years of steady development for a company with one of the longest histories of listing on the New Zealand Stock Exchange. Since its inception in 1952, the company's capital has grown from £500 to $110 million. Between 1981 and 1998, Nuplex's turnover increased thirteen-fold from $25 million to $320 million.

Today

Nuplex boasts a vast product range, which numbers in the thousands. The firm has three divisions, resins, construction products and special waste treatment, of which resins is the largest. Each division operates as a separate profit centre, and each has a general manager reporting to the CEO. The resins division manufactures resins and polymers for the paint, printing ink, adhesives and fibreglass-reinforced plastics industries. The construction products division applies resins from the resins division to flooring, coatings, waterproofing, roofing and adhesive products. The special waste division collects, processes, recycles and disposes of waste, with the objective of recovering the maximum value from the waste stream.

A hint of Nuplex's competitive strategy is found in the statement 'we are determined to be the best'. The company strives to achieve this through 'excellent customer service, a willingness to customise products, a good return on investment and a broad view of the total industry'. Nuplex prides itself on its ability to take a long-term view, and recognise upcoming threats and opportunities. According to current chairman Fred Holland, Nuplex's researchers are working to meet the demand for environmentally friendly products. 'We are rapidly moving our technology into these areas to keep ahead of the demands leading into the next century.' In Nuplex, one out of every ten staff members are research and development chemists, and 5 per cent of turnover goes into research and development.

Rationalisation of the New Zealand resins industry over the 1980s saw the industry reduce from ten to four companies. Economies of scale and strict environmental controls preclude the entry of new domestic-based competition. Although globalisation has allowed overseas competitors to enter the New Zealand market, they typically lack the necessary local distribution network and ability to adapt their products to the local market.

1952–1967 Floor Tiles and Parquet Ltd

The origins of Nuplex go back to a company founded by Bill Campbell in 1952, which laid floor tiles and parquet. During the 1950s Bill Campbell imported and installed seamless resin-based flooring, which could be poured on like cement. His flooring wore better and cracked less than cement. Early sales were to hospitals and schools. While importing the resin-based flooring products to New Zealand, Bill Campbell sought technology links in Britain, Germany and the United States. In 1962, Revertex, a British company that supplied floor resins to Campbell, established a joint venture with Floor Tiles and Parquet (named Revertex NZ Ltd) to make resins in New Zealand and thus avoid import tariffs. Special skills were required to install the product correctly, so Revertex NZ set up a licensed distributor network that is still in place for Nuplex today. Floor Tiles and Parquet's move into manufacturing was driven by the constraints imposed by import licensing, which did not allow Bill Campbell to import a satisfactory amount of the resin-based product. The company has had only two CEOs since its inception: Bill Campbell until 1981, when Fred Holland succeeded him. Bill Campbell stayed on as chairman until 1998.

1967–1980 Revertex Industries (NZ) Ltd

In 1967, Floor Tiles and Parquet merged with Revertex NZ to form Revertex Industries NZ. New Zealand's market was so small that the company had to seek additional products to capture economies of scope and scale. New lines of business were opened in adhesives, printing ink, surface coatings and paint. Revertex acquired licences from overseas for the manufacture and distribution of resins in New Zealand. This broad range of licences differentiated the company from many of its competitors, who were committed to a single supplier. The company's licensing relationships have grown into a network of technology partnering in which Nuplex is now very much an equal partner. By the late 1990s approximately 50 per cent of total sales were based on Nuplex's own technology.

Revertex began to build competencies in several different product technologies and part of the company's philosophy has been to look for new products for established markets and new markets for established products. As Fred Holland states, 'We will make anything that is required for the markets we service, and we will try and sell anything which can be made in the units we've got.' This breadth of experience in multiple technologies and markets is now a point of strength for Nuplex against much larger, and more focused, global competitors.

Foreign control

The 1980s were a period of domination by majority offshore shareholders, initially United States-based Monsanto, through its Australian subsidiary, and then from 1988 Kerry Packer's Consolidated Press Holdings. During this time the company realised both the advantages and limitations of foreign control. Overseas ownership limited the company's export and investment strategies.

On the positive side, it gained early exposure to concepts of safety, health and environmental protection, and to rigorous planning and budgeting disciplines. Furthermore, Fred Holland believes that the discipline of keeping demanding offshore owners happy was good experience for the company's eventual emancipation as a widely held New Zealand stock. During this period there was a strong bond between management and employees.

In 1983 the Closer Economic Relations (CER) agreement freed up trade with Australia. A fire in the Penrose resin plant and laboratory in 1984 slowed the company's growth for three years but allowed for the building of a superior plant with the latest technology and sophisticated safety and design features.

Realising that import protection would not last forever, and that industry rationalisation was inevitable, Revertex devoted the 1980s to leading the rationalisation process. It acquired underperforming companies and consolidated their production, distribution and infrastructure. The volume of throughput increased and the business became more cost-effective through economies of scale. Rationalisation of the resins industry began earlier and proceeded faster in New Zealand than in Australia. By leading industry rationalisation in New Zealand, Revertex had built a distinctive expertise in acquisitions and takeovers, which it sought to apply in Australia. Such ambitions were frustrated, however, until Revertex ceased to be under the control of an overseas firm.

1990s Nuplex Industries Ltd

Consolidated Press Holdings sold their 73 per cent holding in Revertex in 1990 and the company was renamed Nuplex Industries. As Fred Holland says, 'We could now do what was right for this company, rather than what was right for an American company or an Australian company.' The 1990s have seen Nuplex extending its position of leadership to both sides of the Tasman by acquiring and rationalising other companies, involving both expansion within the resins industry and diversification into the waste management industry. In 1998 Nuplex acquired Australian Chemical Holdings, an underperforming resins manufacturer twice Nuplex's size, and thus became the largest resins manufacturer in Australasia. Nuplex also diversified into special waste treatment with the acquisition of New Zealand-based United Environmental in 1995, and the opening of a solvent recycling operation in Australia in 1997. These businesses contributed between a quarter and a third of Nuplex's profits in the late 1990s, although their contribution has lessened somewhat since then.

South East Asia is a new focus for Nuplex's growth. Part of the ACH acquisition was the only resin plant in Vietnam, which has significantly increased Nuplex's profile in the region. The company has successfully followed a niche strategy by providing specialist products and services to the upper end of the

South East Asian market. Nuplex's relatively small size enables it to tailor products to meet small scale, specific customer needs, avoiding the 'take it or leave it' approach of the larger European and American firms. As Fred Holland says, 'Our success offshore shows we can do well with a very small share in large overseas markets.' In 2000, Fred Holland relinquished the role of CEO, retaining the position of chairman.

PEC (NEW ZEALAND) LTD

Until June 1999 PEC was a privately owned company based in Marton. In that year it was taken over by the Gallagher Group on the retirement of PEC's long-time owner and chief executive, John Williams. As of 1998, PEC produced three main product types: retail point of sale systems for service stations, security access systems and electronic petrol pumps. Exports represented 80 per cent of the company's business and had increased 625 per cent in the previous four years. PEC has sold around 3000 retail point-of-sale (POS) systems for service stations in Southern Hemisphere countries, where it has almost 100 per cent of top-end POS business from Shell and Caltex. It is one of the leading suppliers of electronic petrol pumps in the New Zealand market. The company's security-access and monitoring systems have been sold internationally to countries including Britain, Australia, Hungary and certain South East Asian countries.

Today

As of 1998, PEC was organised into five divisions: three product divisions, a manufacturing division and a hardware division. Each product division has its own marketing team. PEC has 250 staff members in New Zealand and around 40 based permanently overseas. The company's strategy is to attract, develop and retain high-quality staff members. PEC's culture is to be tolerant of risk, and the company does not leave innovation to the research team alone. According to John Williams, the company's structure facilitates 'the upward transfer of innovative suggestions and flow of information in both directions'.

PEC also focuses on building and maintaining close relationships with its customers, ensuring its services always meet, and regularly exceed, expectations. The company has a world-wide distribution network of approximately 40 distributors. PEC's account managers and technical staff visit customers and distributors on a regular basis. Strong customer relations with the two global oil companies, Shell and Caltex, have been particularly important to the company's success.

History

Created by John Williams's father, Reg, PEC was established in 1939 to manufacture munitions. After the war, the company produced mechanical and hydraulic machinery for the local oil industry. By 1955 the company was manufacturing petrol pumps. By 1960 PEC had become the major supplier of petrol pumps in New Zealand.

In 1965 John Williams took over management of the company from his father. Within a couple of years he was convinced that electronics was a technology PEC could not be without. By 1969 PEC had produced a coin-operated pump using the new technology, and by 1972 had introduced the M System, the first self-serve pump in the Southern Hemisphere. PEC followed this with the world's first microprocessor-controlled self-serve console in 1977, and petrol pumps.

These products gained leading market shares in New Zealand and were also the platform for PEC's launch into the Australian market for petrol pumps, leveraging off the company's relationships with New Zealand subsidiaries of the same international oil majors, especially Caltex and Shell. Elegant and functional designs added to the pumps' appeal.

John Williams recruited a visionary technologist, Kevin Low, to PEC. His great insight into the potential of microprocessors guided the company into the development of automated retail systems for service stations. In the mid-1980s PEC introduced the EFPEC, the first integrated point-of-sale (POS) service station system in the world. In 1987, PEC beat IBM (Australia) and other international competitors to supply 400 EFPECs to the Caltex chain of service stations in Australia. Furthermore, the company's 8850 POS system was a particular success and came to represent half of total PEC sales by the mid-1990s.

Kevin Low also encouraged PEC to extend into security control systems with its CARDAX system. CARDAX has earned a reputation both internationally and domestically and has attracted significant business outside New Zealand, including the London Underground, major universities and telecom organisations in many markets.

Rapid growth during the 1980s led John Williams to outsource much of PEC's manufacturing processes in an attempt to limit staff numbers to about 100 because he did not want to lose the company's innovative culture as the company grew.

Williams is an ardent believer in the innovative abilities of New Zealanders, and in the high standards of business performance demanded by New Zealand

(and Australian) consumers. He sees these qualities producing the most competitive and challenging markets in the world.

John Williams was struck by John Naisbitt's *Megatrends* and was well aware of the trend from national to global. As a private company, which had funded its growth from retained profits alone, he did not feel that PEC was able to become a fully global company straight from its success in Australasia. In the early 1990s John Williams, and the PEC management team, decided to market PEC's new products — 8850 for service station retail and CARDAX III for security — to multiregional world markets. These were the Southern Hemisphere for 8850 and selected regional markets for CARDAX. This expansion was again funded from the company's own resources.

PEC's entry into new markets in the early 1990s increased the diversity of customer requirements, and prompted a change of strategy for the company. It recruited more staff for its marketing team to meet the customisation needs of individual oil industry affiliates. Furthermore, PEC increased its staff numbers in software development. Overall, the company changed from being solely technology-driven to also being market-driven.

By 1995 the retail 8550 POS system became PEC's core product, and accounted for more than 50 per cent of sales. The security-access and alarm monitoring systems gradually increased share in the business, while the traditional petrol pump sales decreased as a percentage of PEC's total sales.

Since 1995 PEC has re-emphasised the importance of product innovation, representing a shift from the previous five years when efforts were directed towards customising the existing system. In 1998–1999 PEC sought equity investment from within New Zealand to fund its expansion from a successful regional supplier in the world, to being a truly global supplier in conjunction with strategic partners Unisys, for service station retail, and Johnson Controls and others for CARDAX. When these equity partnerships failed to materialise, the company was bought by the Gallagher Group.

SCOTT TECHNOLOGY LTD

Scott Technology Ltd is a medium-sized New Zealand-based engineering firm that designs, builds and installs hi-tech modular production systems for the world's multinational domestic appliance manufacturers. Its engineering expertise, can-do attitude, and philosophy of being the leader, not the follower has enabled the company to dominate the American market in its chosen niche, and boast sales well in excess of $100 million since first entering the market.

History

Initially known as J. & A. P. Scott, the company started in the automotive industry selling spare car parts in Dunedin and Invercargill. During the Second World War the New Zealand government added a new dimension to the company as a metrology lab — a keeper of weights and measures. The company then became gauge and toolmakers for the munitions industry, including the manufacture of mortar shells. This was the company's initial boost into technology.

During the buoyant years after the war, Scott manufactured washing machines and dryers for the local market. This post-war era was marked by tremendous demand and a policy regime of protection from imports. The experience J. & A. P. Scott gained in the domestic appliance industry would be of great value later in its development. In 1965 Graham Batts, now Scott's joint managing director, won an industrial scholarship to study hydraulics and pneumatics in Britain.

In 1966 Scott started building 'clever' production machinery based on this new-found knowledge. Scott made speciality machines for many applications, which ranged from machine design and manufacturing businesses to its core automotive and toolmaking interests. But the company was poorly managed and in 1968 Graham Marsh, a local Dunedin businessman who was part owner of an automotive business, took control, bringing with him much needed management and finance skills. Graham Marsh restructured J. & A. P. Scott, closing the toolmaking division and merging the automotive division with his other automotive interest.

In 1969 Graham Batts was appointed managing director, and Scott Technology began to narrow its focus to the design and manufacture of production machinery for the domestic appliance industry, with Fisher and Paykel as a major customer. The company's design capability, precision engineering and intellectual capital provided the advantages that would continue for the next 30 years.

J. & A. P. Scott became a New Zealand pioneer in the use of pneumatic controlled and PLC (programme logic controlled) technology. The traditional production system used in the manufacture of domestic appliances was slow, costly, large, noisy, labour-intensive and required constant maintenance. The revolutionary Scott PLC machines required far less labour, were relatively small, quiet and more reliable owing to design simplicity. They were also quicker, and able to produce a range of products and sizes.

In 1978 Kelvinator in Australia, who had seen Scott production lines at Fisher and Paykel, ordered a production line for refrigerators. This was Scott's first export order and was highly successful.

Following on from success in Australia, enquiries came from the American parents of Australian subsidiaries that had been equipped with Scott lines. In 1984 Graham Batts went to the United States to explore these opportunities further. The Kiwi engineer's flexibility impressed potential customers. After his first visit Batts promised to work up a proposal on his return to New Zealand, but on his way to the airport realised that this was Scott's big chance. So he rented a motel room for the weekend and made free-hand sketches that were delivered to the client on Monday morning and won Scott the deal.

While previously the company's largest system had been for $300,000, this new contract was worth $6.5 million. The big increase in scale caused Scott many headaches and the system was ultimately delivered a year late. Although the delay could have been disastrous for Scott's reputation, the plant worked so well that it has become a model for similar plants throughout the United States. Scott quickly built up a large order book from American customers on the strength of this first installation. By 1987, the now Scott Technology Ltd employed 90 staff in Dunedin and Christchurch and almost 100 per cent of its sales were from abroad. When deregulation occurred in the mid-1980s, it had little impact on the company.

In the late 1980s, however, Sweden's Electrolux bought Frigidaire (United States) and pulled the plug on a lot of the company's spending. Scott unfortunately sold a high proportion of their manufactured items to Frigidaire, and sales disappeared overnight. This, along with the stockmarket crash of 1987 and a slow American economy, meant Scott had a few lean years and recorded its first loss in four decades. Graham Batts then moved to the United States for three years to stimulate demand, and quickly learnt that it was more effective to sell directly to a multinational's headquarters rather than individual factories. Peter Whitehead took the role of CEO back in New Zealand, and the two-leader arrangement has worked well since.

In early 1989, in a technology transfer partnership, Scott Technology became 50 per cent owned by the MetCoil Systems Corp in the United States. Initially those involved were very positive about the partnership's benefits of enhanced technology and finance, but unfortunately the two cultures were very different and the New Zealanders were not impressed with their partner's engineering competence. The relationship was terminated in 1993.

The period since 1989 has been a highly successful one for the company, with almost record sales in each successive year. Tougher environmental legislation in the United States in the early 1990s forced many American plants to upgrade machinery or rebuild, which provided more demand for Scott Technology's products. The company's export success was recognised in 1991 by the Prime Minister's Export Award. Scott's machine-making business increasingly expanded beyond the American market through its relationships with three major multinationals: Electrolux, Whirlpool and GE.

In 1997 Scott Technology was spun off from Graham Marsh's other interests (the Donaghy's Group) and achieved its own listing on the New Zealand Stock Exchange. Since being floated, the company has continued expansion into new markets such as India, South America and China. Scott Technology's continued American success is best illustrated by the fact that 80 per cent of all range hoods in the United States are manufactured on Scott's systems. To accommodate the continued rise in demand for its systems, the company has expanded its production capacity and staffing levels since its flotation. The company seldom advertises and does not want agents, but instead elicits sales by reputation and by contact at the senior level.

SVEDELA BARMAC LTD

Svedala Barmac exports quarrying equipment throughout the world. From its unlikely base in Matamata, the company manufactures and markets New Zealand-developed Barmac rock-crushing machines for the international mining and cement industries. The company exports over 90 per cent of production and won the prestigious Exporter of the Year award in 1997. Svedala Barmac's overseas sales account for 10 per cent of New Zealand's heavy machinery exports.

Today

The company's Barmac crusher was developed in the 1970s by Bryan Bartley and Jim McDonald using stone to crush stone, rather than the conventional steel jaws or hammers. The technology is effective only for the last stages of rock crushing, in which stones of 50-millimetre diameter are reduced to gravel and sand, but it is this final stage that often determines the quality of the final product. The revolutionary vertical shaft impact (VSI) design has great advantages in cost and durability, provided it is correctly installed.

The company bases its competitive advantage on a high degree of standardisation of the Barmac machine with customisation to suit local quarrying conditions. The quality of service and support for installation is a key advantage. Svedala Barmac's objective is to visit twice a year every site where its product is installed, but with 2500 machines installed this task is becoming impractical. It usually takes Barmac service people two years to become fully proficient with the Barmac process. This represents a significant cost to Svedala Barmac but a substantial benefit for its customers.

The Barmac is sold in about 60 countries in every major region of the globe In addition to providing excellent service support, Svedala Barmac's marketing strategy is to overcome the geographical and organisational distance between the company and its customers.

Svedala Barmac invests around 4 per cent of its annual turnover into research and development, where the emphasis is on continuous improvement rather than fundamental change. The company does not expect innovation to come solely from its R&D team, as suggestions often originate in the quarry. Svedala Barmac has a very flat, team-based structure: the supervisor of each team reports directly to the CEO Andi Lusty, who receives about ten such reports.

History

Having developed the Barmac, McDonald and Bartley licensed it during the 1970s to a total of twelve licensees who would be responsible for manufacture, marketing, sales and maintenance. Three of these subcontracted manufacturing to P. L. Tidmarsh Ltd, later renamed Tidco, a Matamata-based engineering firm owned and run by Paul Tidmarsh. Tidmarsh and his company built a reputation for quality and a strong work ethic, presenting Barmac as a premium product.

In 1980 Tidmarsh acquired what was to be the final licence issued by Barmac Associates, to develop the North American market, bringing in Andi Lusty as a minority shareholder in the American venture. Two other licences for the American market were issued on the same day, and Tidco's American venture grew quickly against that competition. Andi Lusty built a network of local dealers and distributors to quickly increase Tidco's capacity to sell and service the Barmac machine in the United States. Dealers were required to pay for machines for stock, which provided Tidco with the cash flow for growth, and ensured the dealers' commitment to produce sales. Andi Lusty preferred not to give over full responsibility for sales and marketing to the dealers.

Over the late 1980s Tidco gradually bought out other Barmac licensees. Today there is only one independent Barmac licensee, based in Japan.

A worldwide recession resulted in a sharp fall in sales in 1989, exacerbated by earlier unsuccessful attempts at diversification. This led to a search for a major investor for the business. Svedala Industri of Sweden had tried unsuccessfully to develop a machine to compete directly with Barmac and was the logical candidate. As a result Svedala bought Tidco in 1990, and Andi Lusty remained as managing director while Paul Tidmarsh left the business a year later.

Svedala's global strategy has been to rationalise its global product lines and keep subsidiaries focused on their core business, in Barmac's case manufacturing and selling the Barmac machine. The company has benefited from access to Svedala's global distribution network of Svedala houses.

Overall, access to the Svedala distribution network and capital has produced a strong decade of growth for the Barmac business. In the early 1990s, Svedala Industri invested considerable capital in the company, which raised productivity, lowered production costs and improved quality, timing and morale. The lower production costs enabled Svedala Barmac to enter new markets. In 1995, Svedala Industri acquired Barmac Associates, the company that held the Barmac patents. Thus Svedala now controls the future development of the product. In 1997, the company won both the Regional Exporter of the Year Award and the New Zealand Exporter of the Year Award, which increased the profile of Barmac both inside the Svedala Group and within New Zealand.

TAIT ELECTRONICS LTD

Tait Electronics is the creation of its visionary leader, Sir Angus Tait, who has inspired the company's success in a career spanning most of New Zealand's post-war history. Today Tait Electronics exports 90 per cent of its sales to over 80 countries. The Christchurch-based company employs around 1000 people and has an annual turnover of over $150 million. Tait invests 10–15 per cent of sales in R&D and believes this is the lifeline of its long-term sustainability and growth. With nearly 200 design and software engineers, the company's R&D capability is the largest in Australasia. Angus Tait believes that the company's private ownership has been important in sustaining this level of reinvestment. At 80, Sir Angus remains the executive chairman and the public face of the company, but day-to-day management of the company has passed to a chief executive, Warren Rickard.

Today

Tait Electronics produces mobile radios, which are useful wherever dispersed teams of people work on a common task. Mobile radio offers a complete communications network on its own, and as such continues to have special attractions in applications where channel integrity and security are important, such as fire services and police.

Tait Electronics recognises its competitive advantage to be cost effectiveness and a continuous investment in technology. With production now highly auto-mated, the key cost item is the cost-effectiveness of the company's 200 design engineers. Here Tait has an advantage over its global competitors: for quality of life reasons, engineers will work in Christchurch for much less than in Germany or France.

Tait Electronics also draws competitive advantage from the cluster of companies and infrastructure that has developed in Christchurch, involving both industry and university ties. The supporting industrial infrastructure includes metal and plastics firms that make enclosures and chassis, printed circuit board makers and wiring manufacturers. Also, each year Tait takes 20–30 graduates from Canterbury University for the company's design team. Angus Tait is also strongly committed to Canterbury and takes pride in the growth of regional electronics firms that his company has helped to foster. In 1999 Angus Tait was knighted in recognition of his outstanding accomplishments, and his contributions to New Zealand industry.

The company has subsidiaries in 11 countries, and dealer networks in another 70. Subsidiaries or joint ventures are used to get accurate information about the market and control the marketing and distribution of its products.

Although, with incursion from cellular technology, the mobile radio market is getting smaller, Tait is getting a larger slice of that market as firms are forced from the industry. One decisive factor in Tait's success has been to not compete directly with mass-produced radios. Tait implemented niche marketing early and looked to produce products where 'design qualities are more crucial than labour content'. Tait designers try to build generic products that will meet the technical specifications in a number of markets; designing a product to a higher specification may add to the cost, but will mean it can be sold in more markets. Tailoring is done through the Custom Solutions Group. The ability to tailor the product for the customer is difficult for larger companies to match. Motorola is the largest competitor with approximately 60 per cent of the world mobile radio market. Tait has a 2–3 per cent share of the world market.

History

Returning from wartime work on radar in Britain, Angus Tait established his first business (A. M. Tait Ltd) in 1950, to make and sell mobile radios. Tait's mobile radios were the first to be made in New Zealand, and the pent-up demand meant that business was good. The company grew quickly and employed around 100 people. Looking back, Tait describes this early business as opportunistic, disorganised and run on 'blind optimism'. He was convinced that technology would solve all problems. A recession in 1967 exposed the shaky financial basis of the business and it went into receivership. The experience was painful, but Angus Tait learnt that where he lacked competence or interest he should hire people to complement his own efforts.

In 1969 Tait started all over again, taking with him some key people from his first business. The new company's first product was a citizen band (CB) radio. Compared with the mobile radio, the CB radio was something of a toy. It produced less than a quarter of the power output, had much shorter range and was less reliable than the mobile radio. But Tait's production of the CB radio provided a lifeline for the company by generating the cash to keep it alive. Furthermore, the experience enabled Tait to develop the VHF mobile radio, which it was the first to release in New Zealand in 1973.

The New Zealand mobile radio industry grew rapidly, encouraged by the development of a national network of transmitting stations installed by the New Zealand Post Office. Tait designs quickly grew to dominate the local market and in 1976 the company moved into the British market, first through a local distributor, and then through its own sales office. The logistics of supplying the new market from 20,000 kilometres away were daunting. Fortunately for the company, it received financial help from the Export Guarantee Office and the Development Finance Corporation. The company's value-for-money designs were very successful in Britain, where it quickly attained a substantial market share. To this day Tait remains one of the principal players in mobile radio in Britain, and in Europe.

Liberalisation of the domestic market in the years following 1984 was a blow to the entire electronics sector, Tait included. In 1986 Tait Electronics committed to achieving world-class manufacturing capability through automation. Although this stretched the company financially, the labour time required per radio ultimately fell from six hours to twelve minutes. As Angus Tait recalls, 'We developed very strong fingers — because we were hanging from the cliff face by our fingernails.'

During the 1990s, the company played an active role in the development of the MPT1327 European standard for mobile radio, which has since become the de facto global standard. Tait produced the first radio to meet the MPT1327 standard, and the T2000 has been the basis for the company's continued global success. Hundreds of these systems have been installed around the world, including full national systems.

Rather than sell the business, Angus Tait recently transferred his majority shareholding in the company to a charitable trust, with education as the beneficiary. His commitment to the community is demonstrated in his statement 'What is the advantage of a bag of gold over a structure that provides careers for lots of people and puts products into the world that are well respected?'

Notes

1 Foundations of Competitive Advantage

1. See Brian Arthur, 1996.
2. See, for example, Black and Boal, 1994.
3. The distinction is suggested by Grant (1991) and widely followed. Competencies carries the same meaning of an ability to apply resources to a purpose. Unfortunately, the terms resources, capabilities and competencies have meanings that can overlap, equate or even reverse, depending on the author. The confusion of language is evidence of the newness of RBV theory.
4. See Amit and Schoemaker, 1993.
5. This section draws on histories of these companies written for this study by Dianne Lee (Gallagher Group), Sherif Millad (Formway Furniture) and Ken McCarthy and Douglas Mabey (Nuplex Industries).
6. This section draws on a history of Svedala Barmac co-authored for this study by Ken McCarthy.
7. There are always some surprises. Lusty reports that at a recent service school a customer had admitted to running the machine backwards: 'It fell in half!'
8. This section draws on a history of Montana Wines written for this study by Pauline Copland.
9. This section draws on a history of Tait Electronics written for this study by Ken McCarthy.
10. Trunked radio systems use computers to allocate traffic to available capacity and eliminate waiting for a specific channel to come free.
11. This section draws on a history of Formway Furniture written for this study by Sherif Millad.
12. For many of these companies (e.g.

Nuplex and Montana), the network of these relationships is global and keeps managers forewarned of emerging industry trends.
13. This section draws on a history of Nuplex Industries written for this study by Ken McCarthy and Douglas Mabey.
14. This section draws on histories of these companies written for this study by Jayne Krisjanous (Kiwi Dairies) and Colin Campbell-Hunt (Criterion Group).
15. This section draws on a history of Svedala Barmac co-authored for this study by Ken McCarthy.
16. See Barney (1986) for a discussion of organisation culture as a source of competitive advantage.
17. See *A Season of Excellence?*, Campbell-Hunt and Corbett, 1996.
18. *Ibid.*, p.48.
19. Knuckey, Leung-Wai and Meskill, 1999, p.27.
20. See footnote 3.
21. Ng, 1999.
22. It is a question being asked by researchers globally (Miller, 1996). As yet, there are no answers.

2 Internationalisation

1. A similar finding was made in Portugal which, like New Zealand, is a small country and also feels isolated from its major markets, as it is on the periphery of Europe (Fontes and Coombs, 1997). In Portugal technology-based firms were confronted with constraints regarding local supply and demand of technology. They used their business networks and relationships to access advanced market knowledge and technology in order to overcome these constraints and help them internationalise.

2. Bendon Industries participated in an earlier study of competitive capability. See G. Ng, MMS Thesis, Victoria University of Wellington, 1999.

3 Innovation and Technology Strategy

1. The same point has been made in a recent paper by Sorenson (2000).
2. Kevin Low later joined PEC as its technical leader.
3. The lack of local partners initiating global networks has also been noted for small countries, e.g. Portugal, see Fontes and Coombs (1997).
4. The term is borrowed from the evolutionary biologist, Stuart Kaufmann. See Levinthal, 1995. Landscapes are discussed further in Chapter 8.
5. Not all the firms necessarily took the leap, or did so in a smaller scale than they might have done, as they felt they were constrained by resources.

6 Leaders and Owners

1. Students of leadership in business will note that the question being asked here is novel. Where the leadership literature has examined leaders' influence on immediate performance, through factors such as employee motivation, this question looks at their contribution to the long-term resource-based sources of advantage in the firm, and their role in the evolutionary processes that create them, as uncovered in this study. Although personal traits have proved to be insufficient predictors of immediate performance, there is no reason to assume a similar result here. Leaders do differ from other people in their traits (see Kirkpatrick and Locke, 1991, for a review), and it is reasonable to ask what traits have contributed to the accumulation of a firm's capability over time.
2. You may recall Formway's 'speed down the corridor' test from Chapter 1.
3. The attributes emerging from this study have only one point in common with those of interest to current leadership

theory: energy. The remainder have emerged as a result of the novelty of this enquiry, and relate to the leader's capacity for long-term change and commitment.
4. It is a symptom of New Zealand's small size that subsidiary relationships among our firms are all with offshore owners.
5. The extent to which this happens varies among MNCs. Goshal and Bartlett (1995) describe what they regard as exemplary degrees of autonomy left to subsidiaries by MNCs such as ABB. But they make clear that such companies are the exception. Eisenhardt and Galunic (2000) also argue for the benefits of autonomy in business units.
6. There is evidence too of national differences in MNS financing strategies, stemming from different institutional structures in the parent's home economy. See Thomas and Waring, 1999.
7. That restrictions to MNS autonomy should limit evolution of the firm's capabilities is also suggested in a recent study by Birkinshaw, Hood and Jonsson (1998).
8. These distinctive attributes of the family-owned firm are attracting increasing attention, e.g. their ability to take longer-term horizons (James, 1999) and to invest relationships with distinctively high levels of trust and integrity (Fiegner, Brown, Prince and File, 1996; Ram and Holiday, 1993).
9. See Greiner, 1972.
10. EVA, Economic Value Added, assesses the extent to which the business has added or attracted value from the shareholder. At Gallagher, a very sophisticated EVA-based system has been installed to guide a range of decisions from executive compensation to product pricing.
11. With the downsizing of many corporate offices in New Zealand, as a consequence of globalisation and changes of ownership, people like Formway's Rick Wells wonder where experienced managers are going to come from in future.
12. These were first codified 150 years ago by the Rochdale pioneer society, and have been updated by the International

Cooperative Alliance in 1937, 1966 and 1995.

13. Peterson and Anderson (1996) offer a valuable review of the strategies thought to be distinctive to COEs. They find that support for long-term, close supplier relationships is frequently cited as a benefit by COE managers, along with a conservative investment strategy.

7 Managing with a Piece of No. 8 Wire

1. In talking about 'Kiwi' and 'New Zealand' national identity I acknowledge that those terms are not the ones that everyone living in Aotearoa/New Zealand identifies with. In particular, many Maori do not identify with the term 'Kiwi'. As is discussed later in the chapter, Kiwi identity is not inclusive, but represents a certain dominant version of national reality.

2. This concept of national culture is linked to the ways that organisational culture is discussed in terms of 'narrative' (Barry and Elmes, 1997; Czarniawska, 1997; Law, 1994) and 'sensemaking' (Weick, 1995), and to current debates about whether or how organisational culture can be 'socially engineered' by senior managers (Martin and Frost, 1998).

8 The Role of Government

1. Our ongoing work will take up some of these questions. In the next phase of our project we will be studying companies that have grown up since the reforms. As part of this work, we will also take a particular interest in IT-driven and science-based businesses.

2. A thorough history of the DFC would be a valuable contribution to our understanding of this period and the lessons it has for us today. Our limited investigation suggested that, in its earlier years, the DFC played the useful role of

funding export-led proposals and imposing valued financial disciplines on the recipients. Those are the contributions remembered by the firms in our study. At the time of financial market deregulation, it seems that the DFC acquired wider ambitions which it was unable to realise and which destroyed it. The later history of the DFC may be an example of an organisation failing to retain the balance and coherence that are such features of our businesses.

3. We hope our ongoing work will address this question.

4. See Levinthal (1995) for the application of the 'rugged landscape' metaphor to market conditions.

5. Sorenson (2000) makes essentially the same point: that product variety and searching are particularly important when market potential for a firm is uncertain.

6. Once again, this is a question we hope to shed light on in our ongoing studies.

7. Tait Electronics' stimulus to the Christchurch cluster of electronics industries is an exception.

10 Overview

1. It has been put to us that the world moves at a much faster pace now than it did in the latter part of the 20th century when these companies were growing up. Our ongoing work aims to discover whether the evolution of competitive capability has indeed speeded up in a deregulated, cyber-linked world.

Appendix

1. Original equipment manufacturers make a product for another company to be sold entirely under that company's brand. The identity of the original manufacturer is hidden from the consumer.

Bibliography

Amit, R. and P. J. H. Schoemaker (1993). 'Strategic Assets and Organisational Rent', *Strategic Management Journal*, 14, 33-46.

Anderson, B. (1991). *Imagined Communities: Reflections on the origin and spread of nationalism*, rev. and extended ed., London, Verso.

Arthur, W. B. (1996). 'Increasing Returns and the New World of Business', *Harvard Business Review*, July-August, 199-209.

Baden-Fuller, C. and Stopford, J. M. (1994). *Rejuvenating the Mature Business*, Boston, Harvard Business School Press.

Barney, J. (1986). 'Organisation Culture: Can it be a Source of Sustained Competitive Advantage?', *Academy of Management Review*, 11, 656-665.

Barney, J.(1997). *Gaining and Sustaining Competitive Advantage*, Addison Wesley.

Barry, D. and M. Elwes (1997). 'Strategy retold: Towards a narrative view of strategic discourse', *Academy of Management Review*, 22, 429-52.

Beer, S. (1972). *Brain of the Firm*, London, Allen Lane.

Beer, S. (1979). *Heart of Enterprise*, Chichester, Wiley.

Beer, S. (1985). *Diagnosing the System for Organization*, Chichester, Wiley.

Bettis, R. A. and C. K. Prahalad (1995). 'The Dominant Logic: Retrospective and Extension', *Strategic Management Journal*, 16, 5-14.

Bhabha, H. (ed.) (1990). *Nation and Narration*, London, Routledge.

Birchfield, R. (2000, April). 'Innovation', *Management*, 62-63.

Birkinshaw, J., N. Hood and S. Jonsson (1998). 'Building Firm-specific Advantages in Multi-national Corporations: The Role of Subsidiary Initiative', *Strategic Management Journal*, 19, 221-241.

Black, J. A. and K. B. Boal (1994). 'Strategic Resources: Traits, configurations and paths to sustainable advantage', *Strategic Management Journal*, 15, Summer, 131-148.

Bradford, M. (1997, 8 August). 'Call it Kiwi ingenuity or reform, just do it better', *National Business Review*, 18.

Brocklesby, J., J. Davies et al. (1995). 'Demystifying the Viable Systems Model as a Tool in Organisational Analysis', *Asia Pacific Journal of Operational Research*, 12(1), 65-86.

Cameron, K. and D. Whetton (1983). 'Perceptions of Organisational Effectiveness over Organisational Life Cycles', *Administrative Science Quarterly*, 26(4), 525-545.

Campbell-Hunt, C. and L. M. Corbett (1996). *A Season of Excellence?*, Wellington, New Zealand Institute for Economic Research.

Capra, F. (1996). *The Web of Life: A new synthesis of mind and matter*, London, Flamingo.

Chase, R. B., N. J. Aquilano. and F. R. Jacobs (1998). *Production and Operations Management — Manufacturing and Services*, 8th ed., New York, Irwin McGraw-Hill.

Clark, H. (2000, 18 May). 'Government announces major investment in arts, culture and heritage', ministerial announcement, Wellington.

Cohen, W. and D. Levinthal(1990). 'Absorptive Capacity: A new perspective on learning and innovation', *Administration Science Quarterly*, 35, 128-152.

Corbett, L. M. (1996). *New Zealand Manufacturing: Strategies and Performance 1996*, Summary Report of the 1996 New Zealand Manufacturing Futures Survey, Graduate School of Business and Government Management, Victoria University of Wellington, Wellington.

Corbett, L. M. (1998). *New Zealand Manufacturing: 1998 Strategies and Performance*, Graduate School of Business and Government Management, Victoria University of Wellington, Wellington.

Creative New Zealand (1998). *The Cultural Field in Foresight: Submission to the Foresight Project*, Cultural Foresight Group, CNZ.

Creative New Zealand (1999). *Seizing the Future — Cultural Value in the Knowledge Economy*, Cultural Foresight Seminar 3, Turnbull House, Wellington, 9 March 1999, Cultural Foresight Group, CNZ

Crossan, M. M., H. W. Lane and R. E. White (1999). 'An Organisational Learning Framework: From intuition to institution', *Academy of Management Review*, 24, 522-537.

Czarniawska, B. (1997). *Narrating the Organization: Dramas of Institutional Identity*, London, University of Chicago Press.

Dean, J. W. Jr and D. E. Bowen (1994). 'Management theory and total quality: Improving research and practice through theory development', *Academy of Management Review*, 19, 3, 392-418.

Dyer, L. and R. A. Shafer (1999). 'From Human Resource Strategy to Organizational Effectiveness: Lessons from Research on Organizational Agility', in Gerald F. Ferris, Patrick M. Wright, Lee D. Dyer, John W. Boudreau, George T. Milkovich (eds), *Strategic Human Resources Management in the Twenty-First Century*, Supplement 4, London, Jai Press Inc.

Eisenhardt, K. M. (1989). 'Building Theories from Case Study Research', *Academy of Management Review*, 14, 532-550.

Eisenhardt, M. and D. C. Galunic (2000). 'Coevolving: At last a way to make synergies work', *Harvard Business Review*, January-February, 91-101.

Espejo, R., W. Schuhmann, M. Schwaninger, U. Bilello (1996). *Organisational Transformation and Learning*, Chichester, Wiley.

Ferdows, K. and A. De Meyer (1990). 'Lasting Improvements in Manufacturing Performance: In search of a new theory', *Journal of Operations Management*, 9, 2, 168-184.

Fiegner, M. K., B. M. Brown, R. A. Prince and K. M. File (1996). 'Passing on Strategic Vision', *Journal of Small Business Management*, 34(3), 15-26.

Fleras, A. and P. Spoonley (1999). *Recalling Aotearoa: Indigenous politics and ethnic relations in New Zealand*, Auckland, Oxford University Press.

Fletcher, H. (1999). 'How can New Zealand win the globalisation game?', *Auckland Business Review*, 1 (1), 75-81.

Flynn, B. B., R. G. Schroeder and E. J. Flynn (1999). 'World-class manufacturing: An investigation of Hayes and Wheelwright's foundation', *Journal of Operations Management*, 17, 3, 249-269.

Friedman, A. (1977). *Industry and Labour*, London, Macmillan.

Frizelle, G. (1998). *The Management of Complexity in Manufacturing*, London, Business Intelligence Limited.

Frizelle, G. and E. Woodcock (1995). 'Measuring complexity as an aid to developing operational strategy', *International Journal of Operations and Production Management*, 15, 5, 26-41.

Fombrun, C. J. (1996). *Reputation: Realizing value from the corporate image*, Boston, Harvard Business School Press.

Fontes, M. and R. Coombs (1997). 'The Coincidence of Technology and Market Objectives in the Internationalisation of New Technology-Based Firms', *International Small Business Journal*, 15 (4), 14-35.

Ford, D. (1988). *Develop Your Technology Strategy*, Long Range Planning, 21, 85-95.

Ford, D., L-E. Gadde, H. Hakansson, A. Lundgren, I. Snehota, P. Turnbull and D. Wilson (1998). *Managing Business Relationships*, Chichester, Wiley.

Ford, D. and R. Thomas (1997). 'Technology Strategy in Networks', *International Journal of Technology Management*, 14, 596-612.

Frank, R. H. (1988). *Passions Within Reason: The strategic role of the emotions*, New York, Norton.

Fukuyama, F. (1992). *The End of History and the Last Man*, New York, Avon.

Fuller, R. B. (1985). *Synergetics 2*, New York, Macmillan.

Gioia, D. A. and K. Chittipeddi (1991). 'Sensemaking and Sensegiving in Strategic Change Initiation', *Strategic Management Journal*, 12, 433-448.

Goodman, R. S. and E. J. Kruger (1988). 'Data Dredging or Legitimate Research Method? Historiography and its potential for management research', *Academy of Management Review*, 13, 315-325.

Goshal, S. and C. A. Bartlett (1995). 'Changing the Role of Top Management: Beyond Structure to Process', *Harvard Business Review*, January-February, 86-96.

Grant, R. M. (1991). 'The Resource-based Theory of Competitive Advantage: Implications for strategy formulation', *California Management Review*, 3, 114-135.

Greiner, L. E. (1972). 'Evolution and Revolution as Organisations Grow', *Harvard Business Review*, July-August, 37-46.

Grice, S. and P. Fleming (1999). 'Opening Our Global (Eyes): The (dis)appearing politics narrating globalisation', in N. Monin, J. Monin and R. Walker (eds), *Narratives of Business and Society: Differing New Zealand Voices*, Auckland, Longman, 321-334.

Hakansson, H. and I. Snehota. (1995). *Developing Relationships in Business Networks*, London, Routledge.

Harley, R. and M. Volkerling (1999). 'Cultural Capital?' in N. Monin, J. Monin and R. Walker (eds), *Narratives of Business and Society: Differing New Zealand voices*, Auckland, Longman, 301-311.

Hayes, R. H. and G. P. Pisano (1994). 'Beyond World-class: The new manufacturing strategy', *Harvard Business Review*, 72, 1, 77-84.

Hayes, R. H. and S. C. Wheelwright (1984). *Restoring Our Competitive Edge: Competing through manufacturing*, New York, Wiley.

Hayes, R. H., S. C. Wheelwright and K. B. Clark (1988). *Dynamic Manufacturing: Creating the learning organization*, New York, Free Press.

Heeringa, V. (2000, May). 'Built to Last, Big Time', *Unlimited*, 5.

Hill, S. (1995). 'Globalization or Indigenization: New alignments between knowledge and culture', *Knowledge and Policy: The International Journal of Knowledge Transfer and Utilization*, 8 (2), 88-112.

Hill, T. (1985). *Manufacturing Strategy*, London, Macmillan.

Hooper, K. (1999, 27 October). 'No salvation in fictitious Kiwi ingenuity', *Independent*, 14.

Hopkins, J. and J. Riley (1999). *Inventions from the Shed*, Auckland, HarperCollins.

Hubbard, A. (2000, 2 January). 'New dawn, new identity', *Sunday Star Times*, A1.

Hunter, A. (1999, October). 'Brand Maori takes off', *NZ Business*, 32-35.

Inder, R. (1996, 12 April). 'Singapore buys Kiwi ingenuity', *National Business Review*, 43.

Inkson, K., D. Thomas and S. Barry (1999). 'Overseas Experience: Increasing individual and national competitiveness', *Auckland Business Review*, 1 (1), 52-61.

Jacques, E. (1990). 'In Praise of Hierarchy', *Harvard Business Review*, 127-133, January-February.

James, C. (1993, July). 'Who owns New Zealand?', *Management*, 36.

James, H. S. Jr (1999). 'Owner as Manager, Extended Horizons and the Family Firm', *International Journal of Economics and Business*, 6(1), 41-55.

Johanson, J. and J-E. Vahlne (1977). 'The Internationalisation Process of the Firm', *Journal of International Business Studies*, Vol. 8, (Spring/Summer), 23-32.

Jones, B. (1990). *Sleepers, Wake!: Technology and the future of work*, Melbourne, Oxford University Press.

Jones, B. (1991). *Australia as an Information Society: Grasping New paradigms*, Report of the House of Representatives Standing Committee for Long Term Strategies, Canberra, Australian Government Publishing Service.

Jones, B. (1999, 6 December). Speech to the Annual Conference of the Australia and New Zealand Academy of Management, 6 December. [Written paper not available].

Kay, J. (1993). *Foundations of Corporate Success*, Oxford University Press.

Kelsey, J. (1996, 21 March). 'Globalisation, Nationalism, Sovereignty and Citizenship', paper given at the first seminar in the series 'Communications Technologies — What are their Social and Cultural Implications for New Zealand?', http://www.vuw.ac.nz/humanz/seminar/seminarkelsey.html

Kelsey, J. (1999). *Reclaiming the Future: New Zealand and the global economy*, Wellington, Bridget Williams Books.

Kennedy, J. F. (1961, 20 January). Inaugural Address, Washington, DC, http://www.cs.umb.edu/jfklibrary/

Khurana, A. (1999). 'Managing Complex Production Processes', *Sloan Management Review*, 40, 2, 85-97.

Kirkpatrick, S. A. and E. A. Locke (1991). 'Leadership: Do traits matter?', *Academy of Management Executive*, 5(2), 48-60.

Knights, D. and G. Morgan (1991). 'Corporate Strategy, Organizations, and Subjectivity: A critique', *Organization Studies*, 12 (2), 251-273.

Knuckey, S., J. Leung-Wai and M. Meskill (1999). *Gearing Up: A study of best manufacturing practice in New Zealand*, Wellington, Ministry of Commerce.

Krogh, G. V. and J. Roos (1995). *Organizational Epistemology*, London, Macmillan Press.

Krogh, G. V., J. Roos and D. Kleine (1998). *Knowing in Firms: Understanding, managing and measuring knowledge*, London, Sage.

Law, J. (1994). 'Organization, Narrative and Strategy', in J. Hassard and M. Parker (eds), *Towards a New Theory of Organizations*, London, Routledge, 248-268.

Law, R., H. Campbell and J. Dolan (eds) (1999). *Masculinities in Aotearoa/New Zealand*, Palmerston North, Dunmore Press.

Levinthal, D. A. (1995). 'Strategic Management and the Exploration of Diversity', in C. A. Montgomery, *Resource-based and Evolutionary Theories of the Firm*, Kluwer.

Lorenzoni, G and A. Lipparini (1999). 'The Leveraging of Interfirm Relationships as a Distinctive Organisational Capability: A longitudinal study', *Strategic Management Journal*, 20, 317-338.

Luke, T. W. (1996, 21 March). 'Nationality and Sovereignty in the New World Order', a paper given at the first seminar in the series 'Communications Technologies —What are their Social and Cultural Implications for New Zealand?', http://www.vuw.ac.nz/humanz/seminar/seminarluke.html

McEvily, B. and A. Zaheer (1999). 'Bridging Ties: A source of firm heterogeneity in competitive capabilities', *Strategic Management Journal*, 20, 1133-1156.

McGrath, R. G., I. C. MacMillan and S. Venkataraman (1995). 'Defining and Developing Competence: A strategic process paradigm', *Strategic Management Journal*, 16, 505-512.

Madhok, A. (1997). 'Cost, Value and Foreign Market Entry Mode: The transaction and the firm', *Strategic Management Journal*, 18, 39-61.

Martin, J. and P. Frost. (1998). 'The Organizational Culture War Games: A struggle for intellectual dominance' in S. Clegg, C. Hardy and W. Nord (eds), *Handbook of Organization Studies*, London, Sage, 599-621.

Maturana, H. (1983). 'What is it to See?', *Arch. Biol. Med. Exp.*, 16, 255-269.

Maturana, H. (1988). 'Reality: The search for objectivity or the quest for a compelling argument', *Irish Journal of Psychology*, 9, 25-82.

Maturana, H. (1990). 'Science and Daily Life: The ontology of scientific explanations', in W. Krohn, G. Kuppers and H. Nowotny, *Self-organization: Portrait of a scientific revolution*, Dordrecht, Kluwer, 12-35.

Maturana, H. and F. Varela (1987). *The Tree of Knowledge — The biological roots of human understanding*, Boston, Shambhala.

Meyer, A. D., A. S. Tsui and C. R. Hinings (1993). 'Configurational Approaches to Organisational Analysis', *Academy of Management Journal*, 36, 1175-1195.

Miller, D. (1996). 'Configurations Revisited', *Strategic Management Journal*, 17, 505-512.

Miller, D. (1993) 'The Architecture of Simplicity', *Academy of Management Journal*, 18(1), 116-138.

Miller, J. G. and A. V. Roth (1994). 'A Taxonomy of Manufacturing Strategies', *Management Science*, 40, 3, 285-304.

Minister for Information Technology's Advisory Group (1999). 'The Knowledge Economy: A submission to the New Zealand government, Wellington, Minister for Information Technology's Advisory Group, http://www.knowledge.gen.nz

Nahapiet, J. and S. Ghoshal (1998). 'Social Capital, Intellectual Capital and the Organisational Advantage', *Academy of Management Review*, 23, 242-266.

Naisbitt, J. (1982). *Megatrends: Ten new directions transforming our lives*, New York, Warner Books.

Nakane, J. (1986). *Manufacturing Futures Survey in Japan: a comparative survey 1983–1986*, Tokyo, Waseda University.

Nelson, R. R. and S. G. Winter (1982). *An Evolutionary Theory of Economic Change*, Cambridge MA, Harvard University Press.

New Zealand Dictionary Centre (1991). Victoria University of Wellington, August/September, 101.

New Zealand Government Enterprise and Innovation Team (1999). *Bright Future: Five steps ahead*, http://www.stepsahead.org.nz/

New Zealand Treasury (1990). 1990 Briefing papers, Wellington, Treasury.

Ng, G. (1999). 'The Evolution of Competitive Advantage Within New Zealand Organisations', Master of Management Studies Thesis, Victoria University of Wellington.

Nonaka, I. and H. Takeuchi (1995), *The Knowledge Creating Company*, Oxford University Press.

Ohmae, K. (1991). *The Borderless World: Power and strategy in the interlinked Economy*, New York, Harpers.

Orsman, H. W. (1997). *The Dictionary of New Zealand English: A dictionary of New Zealandisms on historical principles*, Auckland, Oxford University Press.

Peterson, H. C. and B. L. Anderson (1996). 'Cooperative Strategy: Theory and Practice', *Agribusiness*, 12(4), 371-383.

Pfeffer, J. (1994). *Competitive Advantage through People*, Boston, Harvard Business School Press.

Polyani, M. (1967). *The Tacit Dimension*, London, Routledge and Kegan Paul.

Porter, M. (1998a). *The Competitive Advantage of Nations*, republished with a new introduction, New York, Free Press.

Porter, M. (1998b). Address, Wellington Town Hall, http://www.clusternavigators.com/porter_paper.htm

Porter, M.E. (1996). 'What is Strategy?', *Harvard Business Review*, November-December, 61-78.

Porter, M. E. (1998). 'Clusters and the New Economics of Competition', *Harvard Business Review*, November-December, 77-90.

Prahalad, C. K. and G. Hamel (1990). 'The Core Competence of the Corporation', *Harvard Business Review*, May-June.

Ram, M. and R. Holliday (1993). 'Relative Merits: Family Culture and Kinship in Small Firms', *Sociology*, 27(4), 629-648.

Roberts, K. (1998, 28 August). 'New Zealand on the Edge', address to the New Zealand Tourism Industry Association Conference, Auckland.

Schilling, M. A. (1998). 'Technological Lockout: An integrative model of the economic and strategic factors driving technology success and failure', *Academy of Management Review*, 23(2), 267-284.

Senge, P. M. (1990). *The Fifth Discipline: The art and practice of the learning organisation*, New York, Doubleday.

Skinner, W. (1969). 'Manufacturing: missing link in corporate strategy', *Harvard Business Review*, May-June, 136-145.

Simon, H. (1996). *Hidden Champions*, Boston, Harvard Business School Press.

Slack, N., S. Chambers, C. Harland, A. Harrison and R. Johnston (1995). Operations Management, London, Pitman Publishing.

Sorenson, O. (2000). 'Letting the Market Work for You: An evolutionary perspective on product strategy', *Strategic Management Journal*, 21, 577-592.

Sparrow, J. (1998). *Knowledge in Organizations*, London, Sage.

Springall, L. (2000, 3 May). 'Are New Zealand's skills going down the gurgler?', *Independent*, 14.

Stubbart, C. I. and R. D. Smalley (1999). 'The Deceptive Allure of Stage Models of Strategic Processes', *Journal of Management Inquiry*, 8(3), 273-285.

Tapsell, S. (1997). 'Is Maori management different?', *Management*, 47.

Teece, D. and G. Pisano (1994). 'The Dynamic Capability of Firms: an Introduction', *Industrial and Corporate Change*, 3, 537-556.

Thomas. L. G. and G. Waring (1999). 'Competing Capitalisms: Capital investment in American, German and Japanese firms', *Strategic Management Journal*, 20, 729-748.

Upton, D. M. (1995). What really makes factories flexible?', *Harvard Business Review*, 73, 4, 74-84.

Varela, F., E. Thompson, et al. (1991). *The Embodied Mind — Cognitive science and human experience*, Cambridge, MA, MIT Press.

Voss, C. A. (1995). 'Alternative Paradigms for Manufacturing Strategy', *International Journal of Operations and Production Management*, 15, 4, 5-16.

Walker, G., B. Kogut and W. Shan (1997). 'Social Capital, Structural Holes and the Formation of an Industry Network', *Organization Science*, 8(2), 109-125.

Weick, K. (1995). *Sensemaking in Organizations*, Thousand Oaks, CA, Sage.

Wetherell, M. and J. Potter (1992). *Mapping the Language of Racism: Discourse and the legitimation of exploitation*, New York, Harvesters/Wheatsheaf.

Wheelwright, S. C. (1981). 'Japan — where operations are really strategic', *Harvard Business Review*, 59, 4, 67-75.

Williams, K., C. Haslam, S. Johal and J. Williams (1994). *Cars: Analysis, history, cases*, Providence RI, Berghahn.

Index

34, 36, 38-40, 46, 48, 49, 50, 51, 53, 59, 61-64, 67, 70-73, 77, 78, 83, 84, 86, 87, 89-91, 93, 142, 145, 154, 165, 171, 172, 182, 188-90, 192, 196, 199-201, 204, 206, 207, 209-11, 215, 220-3
quick response manufacturing 81, 84, 85

R&D 37, 49, 50, 57, 58, 78, 84, 90, 96, 108, 118, 119, 127, 151,167, 207, 221, 222
recruitment 92, 165, 166
regional leaders 36, 38, 39, 46, 87, 184, 186, 187
relationships 5-8, 10-13, 22, 23, 25-27, 31, 33, 34, 39-41, 46, 50-52, 56, 58, 91-94, 101, 102, 104, 107, 115, 116, 118, 123, 127-9, 131, 132, 134, 140, 141, 143, 158, 164, 177, 186, 187-9, 193-6, 201, 208, 210, 211, 213, 215, 216, 220, 225-7, 229-31
reliability 12, 25, 61-63, 86, 89
reputation 6-8, 10, 15, 16-19, 24, 26, 30, 32-34, 36, 39, 60, 66, 69, 89, 102, 103, 109, 127, 130, 136, 141, 158, 192, 196, 201, 202, 207, 216, 219-21, 229
resource-based view 5, 65, 158
reward systems 61, 66, 76, 191
robotics 60, 74, 76
Ruakura Research Centre 204

short run (production) 72, 73, 85, 130
skill development 97
social capital 19, 232, 233
sow & reap 35, 36, 38, 46, 154, 180, 187, 195
standard(s) 15, 18, 23, 33, 40, 44, 47, 53, 55, 57, 58, 62, 67, 72, 136, 167, 172, 201, 207, 210, 216
structural coupling 169, 173, 174, 180, 190
subsidies 150, 157
succession planning 91, 92
suppliers 6, 12, 20, 31, 33, 40, 41, 52, 53, 57, 58, 71, 83-85, 118, 123, 128, 130, 134, 143, 202, 210, 215

tall poppy syndrome 135
teams 1-3, 9, 13, 14, 18, 20, 25, 66, 68, 75, 76, 83,

88-92, 96, 98-101, 103, 165, 166, 178, 191, 199, 204, 209, 210, 215, 217, 221-3, 232
technology 2, 6, 8, 11-13, 17-19, 21, 22, 31, 32, 35-37, 43, 45-58, 61, 63-67, 73, 74, 78, 79, 81, 91, 96, 100-103, 105, 108, 109, 112, 115, 116, 118, 119, 122-4, 126, 130, 134, 137, 138, 140, 141, 144, 150, 151, 153, 154, 162-4, 166, 177, 181, 182, 186, 188, 199, 200, 205-207, 212-14, 216-20, 222, 223, 225, 229, 230, 232
technology strategy 12, 45-47, 49, 51, 53, 55, 57, 162, 229
TQM (Total Quality Management) 63, 82
trade fairs 43, 192
trade unions 68, 83, 90
training 13, 24, 25, 34, 66-68, 74, 84, 88, 94-97, 100, 101, 129, 136, 191
transition 38, 46, 48, 50, 57, 102, 105, 120, 121, 126, 152, 153, 155, 156, 158, 172, 179, 186, 191, 194-6
trial & error 179, 180
trust 6, 7, 11, 34, 68, 94, 98, 107, 115, 117, 224, 226

value chain 15, 37, 66, 187
vertical integration 61, 201
viability 160, 161, 167, 177
viable systems 162, 166-8, 170, 176, 228
vision 24, 51, 64, 95, 100, 129, 139, 146, 147, 171, 206, 216, 222, 229
VRIO (Value/Rare/Imitate/Organisation: criteria for sustainable advantage) 5, 6
VSM (Viable Systems Model) 162

WIP (Work in Progress Inventory) 70, 75, 76, 81, 84, 190
work design 61, 66, 68, 73, 81, 82-84, 93, 96, 99, 100, 106, 131, 88-91, 100, 101
workforce 14, 24-26, 34, 143, 150, 172, 188, 190, 199, 204
workplace reform 90-91
world-class manufacturers 65-72, 84, 85